A Chorus of Prophetic Voices

For Paul,
companion longer than life

A Chorus of Prophetic Voices

Introducing the Prophetic
Literature of Ancient Israel

Mark McEntire

WJK WESTMINSTER
JOHN KNOX PRESS
LOUISVILLE · KENTUCKY

© 2015 Mark McEntire

First edition
Published by Westminster John Knox Press
Louisville, Kentucky

15 16 17 18 19 20 21 22 23 24 — 10 9 8 7 6 5 4 3 2 1

Unless otherwise indicated, Scripture quotations are from the New Revised Standard Version of the Bible, copyright © 1989 by the Division of Christian Education of the National Council of the Churches of Christ in the U.S.A., and used by permission— some places adapted by the use of "YHWH" for "the LORD." Quotations marked AT are the author's translation.

Book design by Sharon Adams
Cover design by Lisa Buckley Design

Library of Congress Cataloging-in-Publication Data
McEntire, Mark Harold, 1960–
 A chorus of prophetic voices : introducing the prophetic literature of ancient Israel / Mark McEntire. — First edition.
  pages cm
 ISBN 978-0-664-23998-5 (alk. paper)
 1. Bible. Prophets—Criticism, interpretation, etc. I. Title.
 BS1505.52.M43 2015
 224'.061—dc23

                                                                      2014049529

♾ The paper used in this publication meets the minimum requirements of the American National Standard for Information Sciences—Permanence of Paper for Printed Library Materials, ANSI Z39.48-1992.

Most Westminster John Knox Press books are available at special quantity discounts when purchased in bulk by corporations, organizations, and special-interest groups. For more information, please e-mail SpecialSales@wjkbooks.com.

Contents (Condensed)

Contents (Full)

Tables

Discussion Boxes

Preface

Several excellent introductions to the prophetic literature of Israel are currently available, so it is fair to ask why one more is necessary. *A Chorus of Prophetic Voices* attempts to distinguish itself by giving careful attention to four aspects of the prophetic literature that are crucial to understanding it.

1. *Moment.* The origins of the prophetic literature lie in a traumatizing set of events in the story of ancient Israel. Over a period of about three centuries, the tiny nations called Israel and Judah were crushed by the ambitions and movements of empires to their east and west. Even when they were able to make an attempt at recovery, it was a halting process, still subject to imperial power. The challenge of how to think about their identity in relation to their God under these circumstances was the force that drove the development of these traditions.

2. *Character.* The prophets who generated these traditions are present in the scrolls as literary characters, but in very different ways. Isaiah is a cool, detached royal adviser who vanishes from major portions of the book. Jeremiah is an agonizing figure, whose life is intertwined with the book named for him in the most intimate ways. Ezekiel is a strange visionary and street performer who rarely interacts with any other human being. Christian tradition has typically treated the twelve smaller books from Hosea to Malachi as individual pieces, but this book will examine them collectively as components of a prophetic scroll called the Book of the Twelve. The twelve characters who combine to make the Book of the Twelve are often entirely invisible, yet include Hosea, whose family is an embodiment of Israel's relationship to YHWH; and Jonah, whose strange exploits make him a favorite of children's stories.

3. *Voice.* The final literary shapes of the four great prophetic scrolls produce a voice for each that is distinct from the prophetic character for which it is named. These are all composite texts that grew and developed as artistic works of literature far beyond the lives of those individuals. Learning to attend to these literary voices will involve examination of each entire scroll from start to finish.

4. *Canon.* At some point these four traditions began interacting with each other, and eventually they became part of the canonical collection of prophetic literature. The scrolls are often speaking about the same events and asking similar questions, so it is also necessary to hear them together, as a chorus of four distinct voices.

Neglect of any of these four aspects will produce an incomplete picture of this part of the Bible. The primary strength of introductions produced in the second half of the twentieth century, with history as their driving force, was the way they attended to the first two aspects, *moment* and *character*. As the focus of Old Testament studies shifted over the last two decades to literary issues and a concentration on the final form of the text, the aspect of *voice* became the primary target of introductions to the prophetic literature. A new focal point led to productive new ways of asking what large, complex works of literature like the books of Isaiah and Jeremiah are about. The cost of the determination to give attention to the unique literary voice of each prophetic scroll, however, was to frequently isolate each voice from the others, so that *canon* received inadequate attention. *A Chorus of Prophetic Voices* offers a remedy for that isolation. The book requires a unique design to help readers encounter the prophetic scrolls as distinct voices, but performing together. Such a task requires careful movement back and forth among the various scrolls, learning to hear each one individually, then hearing each scroll along with the others.

Each of the four prophetic scrolls receives a careful introduction as a unified work of literature that speaks in a characteristic way. These discussions will be in chapters 2 (Isaiah), 3 (the Twelve), 5 (Jeremiah), and 6 (Ezekiel). A significant element in each case will be an examination of how the prophet(s) performs as a literary character in the finished book. Along with presentations of Isaiah and the Book of the Twelve as finished scrolls, chapters 2 and 3 will also examine how these bodies of tradition respond to the Assyrian crisis of the eighth century in ancient Israel. Readers will then be able to consider together parts of Isaiah, Hosea, Amos, and Micah, which address similar issues at the same point in the story of Israel.

The Babylonian crisis in ancient Israel receives attention in all four of the great prophetic scrolls. After a reminder of the nature of the scroll of Isaiah, developed in chapter 2, chapter 4 presents this scroll's response to the

Babylonian threat, invasion, destruction, and captivity. The opening of the discussion of the Babylonian period provides the occasion to bring the voices of Jeremiah and Ezekiel, both of which begin in the Babylonian period, into the discussion. Chapters 5 and 6 develop full portraits of these two scrolls, including the role of the prophets they are named for as *characters* within them. Chapters 5 and 6 combine Jeremiah and Ezekiel's responses to the Babylonian crisis with Isaiah's response. The discussion of the Babylonian period will end by bringing the voice of the Book of the Twelve into the conversation. Chapter 7 will remind the reader of the distinct nature of this scroll, then examine the components specific to this part of Israel's story. By the end of chapter 7, all four scrolls will have spoken about the pivotal events of the early sixth century BCE.

After introducing all four of the prophetic scrolls, *A Chorus of Prophetic Voices* enters the discussion of the prophetic response to the Judean restoration, so each chapter from 8 to 11 will open by retuning the ear of the reader to these four *voices*, then examining each scroll in turn as it addresses the struggle of Judah's restoration in the Persian period. Each of these chapters will close with an attempt to understand how the forces involved in the rebuilding task shaped the final form of each particular scroll.

Chapter 12 completes the book's effort to present these four scrolls as works finished in the aftermath of the destruction of Israel, scrolls that employ prophetic *characters* and the words they uttered during the crises that led up to the destruction. Such a conclusion pushes back against the dominant, entrenched assumption, particularly within Christian reading contexts, that the prophetic tradition reached its pinnacle in preexilic Israel, then declined into nonexistence during the Second Temple period. The perspective of the prophetic literature presented here leads to a contrary conclusion. The prophetic literature is the climax of a process that produced these four scrolls for Israel, a people living in a context of dispersion and imperial domination. Prophecy did not cease or disappear, but it became textualized and thereby served as a portable and adaptable resource that provided both challenge and comfort in any context, even our own.

Acknowledgments

I wrote the bulk of this book during a sabbatical leave in the fall of 2013, so I need to thank Belmont University for granting the leave and my colleagues in the College of Theology and Christian Ministry for taking up the extra workload in my absence. For many years I have taught a course on the prophetic literature at Belmont for which this book is designed as a textbook. Thank you to all my students through the years, particularly the group in the spring 2014 semester who used a draft form of the book and provided helpful feedback. I completed most of the work in the Divinity Library at Vanderbilt University, so I wish to thank the staff of both the library and the Divinity School for the assistance those resources provided. Finally, the editorial staff at Westminster John Knox Press has been kind and generous in their assistance throughout the process, and I am grateful to all of them, particularly Bob Ratcliff.

1

Defining Prophetic Literature

Introducing the prophetic literature of the Old Testament should be a daunting task because it is a daunting collection. Its size, variety, and complexity have challenged every interpreter who has sought to make a coherent statement about this set of ancient scrolls that includes Isaiah, Jeremiah, Ezekiel, and the Book of the Twelve. The century of the historical-critical method's dominance provided a fertile environment for introductions to the prophetic literature that attached the prophetic characters and various portions of their books to specific periods in Israel's history. The great accomplishment of these efforts was the grounding of the Israelite prophets in the earthly world of politics, economics, war, and suffering. Materializing the prophets was an effective antidote to the church's long-held tendency to spiritualize the words of the prophets and read them as a disparate collection of esoteric predictions of the distant future. To understand how this introduction operates and why it is organized in a particular way, it is necessary to review the story of the writing of introductions to the prophetic literature at the time of this focus on history, and follow the story to the present moment in the context of biblical studies.

APPROACHES TO INTRODUCING
THE PROPHETIC LITERATURE

Two classic formulations of the historical approach serve to illustrate both its strengths and limitations. In 1967 the portions of Gerhard von Rad's *Old Testament Theology* that addressed the Israelite prophets, primarily those in part 2 of volume 2, were excerpted and developed into an introduction to the prophetic literature.[1] The English translation of this work was published under the title *The Message of the Prophets* and became a standard textbook on the subject for about a quarter century. After treating some introductory issues, the first prophet that von Rad's work directly discussed was Amos, because he seems to have been the earliest, chronologically. The power of von Rad's method is still evident in this discussion as it places this ambiguous prophetic figure within a moment of the development of Israel's traditions when they needed radical critique, and the voice of Amos explodes in this context.[2] Von Rad moved on to treat the other prophets that he placed in the same historical period—Hosea, Isaiah, and Micah. Another example of the historical/chronological approach is the first volume of Abraham Joshua Heschel's classic work *The Prophets: An Introduction*, which begins with an introductory discussion of the nature of prophets and follows with individual chapters on Amos, Hosea, Isaiah 1–39, and Micah, before moving on to Jeremiah.[3] Heschel did not treat all of the prophetic literature in this volume, but the parts he did examine are organized according to a historical scheme similar to the one used by von Rad.

Both of the major limitations of this approach to the prophetic literature arise from a division of the texts that departs from the form in which they are currently found in the canons of Judaism and Christianity. First, von Rad and Heschel separated a "book" like Amos from its place within the Book of the Twelve, between Joel and Obadiah, and they divided Isaiah into the three portions that had become standard by that time, stemming from the classic work of scholars like Bernhard Duhm and Karl Elliger.[4] Hence the literary character of the final forms of the scrolls, and the relationship between the final forms and the individual texts of which they are composed, received little attention, if any. Both introductions had great difficulty in formulating any response to a question like "What is the book of Isaiah about?" The second limitation of a historical/chronological approach is the elevation of the prophetic figures themselves as the originators of the traditions, at the expense of those who composed the final forms, which were often works of artistic genius. Studies like von Rad's followed the efforts of form criticism to get back to the original settings of the small units of prophetic speech, which were always understood to be the oral utterances of the named prophets. The placing of the prophets along a strict historical trajectory that ended in their supposed disappearance inevitably created a sense of decline in the quality of their collective work. In the historical-critical era the idea of decline was part of the scheme of Julius Wellhausen and other prominent scholars who saw a general decline in ancient Israelite religion, from the pristine morality of the eighth-century prophets to the stunted legalism of Second Temple Judaism. When they ignored the nature of the great prophetic scrolls as finished literary works, they missed the process of development of a great literary-theological tradition and saw only decline.[5]

At times von Rad tried to push back against the portrait of decline in his discussion of the prophets of the Persian period, but seemed to give up the point even as he started:

> There can, of course, be no question of comparing messages of such matchless depth and range as those of Jeremiah, Ezekiel, and Deutero-Isaiah, each of whom represents a whole world of prophecy and theology, with those of Trito-Isaiah, Joel, Haggai, Zechariah, and Malachi. None the less we ought to be more chary of such summary judgments as "men of the Silver Age."[6]

By contrast, an approach that begins with the final forms of the scrolls as literary works, recognizing that the last stage of their production is the one most responsible for how we view the whole, is more likely to see the prophetic tradition moving on an upward trajectory throughout these centuries, reaching the pinnacle of its power and creativity in the Persian period. Those whom the form critics judged to be of lesser ability were actually the ones who provided the view of their predecessors that makes them appear to be so powerful and profound. What von Rad identified so well as a "world of prophecy and theology" was the literary accomplishment of the end of the process.

A crucial shift in the reading of the prophetic literature took place in 1978, when Walter Brueggemann published *The Prophetic Imagination*. This groundbreaking book did not fit the format of an introduction to the prophetic literature, but it provided a new hermeneutical lens through which to read this literature. Brueggemann only began to apply this lens to a few prophetic texts in the book, but he and others have continued to use the approach much more broadly since then. In Brueggemann's words, "The task of prophetic ministry is to nurture, nourish, and evoke a consciousness and perception alternative to the consciousness and perception of the dominant culture around us."[7] His understanding contends that the prophets were not just part of their own historical worlds, but also participated in an imaginative world that their own work helped to construct within the literature that presented them as characters.

Nevertheless, Brueggemann's work should not be mistaken for an older view that the prophets were lone, detached, religious geniuses. Such an assumption had been present in the work of Walter Eichrodt, who understood the prophets as persons who were "freed from all ties of class or professional self-consciousness" and "capable of moving through life in majestic solitude."[8] The imaginative work of the prophets in Brueggemann's understanding was deeply communal. This is why his continuing work throughout the remainder of the twentieth century could exist alongside and in important communication with the burgeoning sociological approaches championed by Norman Gottwald and Robert Wilson, which looked more broadly at human cultures and asked questions about the roles that prophets play within communities.[9]

Edgar Conrad's *Reading Isaiah*, published in 1991, provides a superb example of how the ground was shifting beneath the study of the prophetic literature at the end of the twentieth century. Conrad's work was a bold attempt to read the final form of the massive collection called Isaiah as a coherent literary work. He identified and called into question the assumptions behind historical-critical interpretive strategies, most significantly their tendency to place greater importance on materials that could be connected more directly to the great figures for whom the books were named, who had often been viewed through a "Romantic" lens.[10] Instead, Conrad's approach focused on the effects of reading Isaiah in finished form,[11] but this is by no means an ahistorical reading of the text. *Reading Isaiah* very much depends on understanding the interactions between Israel and the other nations of that time, particularly Assyria and Babylon. The primary limitation of this work, however, is its examination of the book of Isaiah in relative isolation from the other components of the prophetic literature, particularly the Book of the Twelve, which address the same span of Israel's story.

Another important step in this direction took place in 2002, when David L. Petersen published *The Prophetic Literature: An Introduction*. To my knowledge, this was the first full, book-length introduction to the prophets that devoted a separate chapter to each scroll. Petersen's introductory chapter gives some attention to common features of the prophetic scrolls, and there are occasional references to how they might speak together, but for the most part the proclamation of each book is treated independently.[12] In Petersen's presentation the prophetic literature consists of four highly developed scrolls, each with its own powerful, literary voice, but they rarely get the opportunity to interact. Nevertheless, for an introductory textbook, this work brought the results of two decades of scholarship that had been shifting the emphasis away from a primarily historical approach that tended to fragment the prophetic scrolls, and toward one that could engage large, finished literary complexes.

Christopher Seitz's 2007 work *Prophecy and Hermeneutics: Toward a New Introduction to the Prophets* seems to have been, in part, an attempt to address this transition. But the book's preoccupation with defining a type of interpretation it calls "figural," and with connecting the prophetic literature in a very specific and immediate way to the New Testament, often gets in the way of understanding this literature on its own terms.[13] Nevertheless, Seitz identified the most significant problem for the production of new introductions to the prophetic literature. The field was moving beyond the dichotomous choices of either a *synchronic* or *diachronic* presentation.[14] These two words are often used to describe two broad categories of approaches to biblical texts, depending on whether they examine how the biblical text developed through time (diachronic) or what they looked like at one particular time, the end of their development (synchronic). Future work would demand attention to both the complex compositional process of the prophetic scrolls that was taking place as the events they addressed were happening, and the overtly literary nature of the final forms as we now find them. My response to this problem has given rise to the unusual organization of this book, as explained in the preface (above) and the section "The Plan of the Book," at the end of this chapter.

Another important innovation in introducing the prophetic literature appeared in 2010 with *You Are My People: An Introduction to Prophetic Literature*, by Louis Stulman and Hyun Chul Paul Kim. Along with a treatment focused on the final forms of the prophetic scrolls, Stulman and Kim chose a specific hermeneutical lens through which to look at all of the prophetic literature, calling the entire corpus "meaning-making literature for communities under siege."[15] This particular reading focus depends on an understanding of the final forms as works of literature because, as written artifacts, their meanings had changed drastically from the meaning of the oral presentations by the prophetic figures of the past, speeches still embedded within them:

> Prophecy as oral communication is raw, iconoclastic, immediate, and exacting. It seeks to bring about fundamental changes in social arrangements, often before the collapse of long-standing and cherished structures—political, religious, economic, and symbolic. Prophecy as written communication attends to survivors. It takes shape during and after the frightful events; all the while it engages in artful reinterpretation and reenactment.[16]

A hermeneutical shift like this one allowed Stulman and Kim to hear and present the voices of the prophetic books, rather than trying to use the prophetic books to travel back and hear the voice of the "authentic" prophets. The scrolls contain oracles that predict future disaster, but the final forms are not predictions of disaster. Rather, they are responses to the disasters after they have happened, as the survivors struggled to find ways to reassemble and continue their lives as individuals and communities.

Reading in this way also began to lead Stulman and Kim away from the emphasis on the prophetic characters as unique and startling figures (without denying that these qualities did indeed define them). Instead, their focus on literary works drew attention to common patterns in the prophetic scrolls and how they might be speaking together, an idea that appears most clearly in their discussion of "Ezekiel within the prophetic corpus." While much of the discussion in this section of their book focuses on the strangeness of the Ezekiel character and his differences from prophetic characters like Isaiah and Jeremiah, the examination of the macrostructure of the book of Ezekiel led Stulman and Kim back to the conclusion that Ezekiel "follow[s] the prophetic proclivity to punctuate disaster with salvation and judgment with hope. This structure supports the contention that the prophetic corpus in its present form is far from a montage of discrete voices."[17] The common shape of the prophetic scrolls will be illustrated in more detail below, but at this stage it is important to emphasize, with Stulman and Kim, that while these traditions have very different starting points, and earlier approaches to the prophetic literature did excellent work in demonstrating those, they had a common end point and participated in a common task. "Akin to Isaiah, Jeremiah, and the Twelve, Ezekiel is beset by an empire's designs toward world domination. It deals with the harsh realities of hegemony and the resulting collapse of long-standing national arrangements. . . . In this manner Ezekiel joins the prophetic chorus as disaster literature and survival literature."[18]

Conrad has recently developed a rationale and methodological approach for specific "intertextual" readings of some pairs or small groups of prophetic books. For example, only Amos and Jeremiah begin with superscriptions using the phrase "The words of Jeremiah/Amos," and are the two prophetic books that most clearly "announce the end of a nation."[19] Conrad argues that the superscriptions are compositional cues to a "model reader," directing linked readings of the prophetic books in their canonical form.[20] Isaiah, Obadiah, and Nahum are the three books described as "a vision" in their opening superscription, which directs readers to consider these books in light of each other.[21] While Conrad's sense of intertextual readings based on cues in the superscriptions that open the books is very specific, such an approach can easily participate in a larger sense of reading the prophetic scrolls together.

The trajectory above traces significant shifts in the study of the prophetic literature over the past century. It began with a focus on the prophets as historical figures proclaiming a moral decline in ancient Israelite society. The rending of the prophetic literature to produce historical data for a reconstruction of ancient Israelite religion gave way to an emphasis on the scrolls as unified works of literature that constructed imaginative worlds of their own, in which readers could explore their experience. The recent advent of trauma studies has reemphasized the historical events to which the prophetic literature responds, yet it has raised new questions about the effects of those events on the audiences of the texts. Because these posttrauma audiences could have been listening to some combination of the four prophetic scrolls, it has become necessary to learn to listen to them together, even as we distinguish their individual voices.

This introduction to the prophetic literature will explore the idea of the prophetic scrolls within the canon functioning together as a chorus more thoroughly than other introductory textbooks have.[22] While the scrolls begin at different times and in different places, they all end in a similar place—trying to make sense of life in the aftermath of national defeat and disaster and at the beginning of a difficult recovery. In order to listen to the prophetic literature in this way, it is necessary to develop some background for reading these scrolls. While this is primarily a literary enterprise, it cannot ignore Israel's history. The prophetic literature, taken together in its finished form, becomes a way of looking at the story of Israel's past in order to provide the resources to live in its own present, so the historical framework in which the words and voices of these scrolls operate must be sketched as clearly as possible. The prophetic figures whose names are on the book are far removed from the production of the scrolls historically, but they still play a vital role as characters within the scrolls, so the way that prophetic characters are developed in biblical literature needs significant attention. Finally, this introductory chapter will present a more complete understanding of the way prophetic scrolls are shaped and placed within the various canonical traditions that now hold them. Attention to the Bible as a collection of literature makes phenomena like the precise order of the books within the canonical collection a more significant issue, so we will proceed there next.

THE LITERARY AND CANONICAL SHAPE OF THE ISRAELITE PROPHETIC LITERATURE

The prophetic literature comes to us in four large collections. In the Jewish canonical tradition the scrolls appear in the order Isaiah, Jeremiah, Ezekiel, and the Twelve and are known as the Latter Prophets, which balance the four scrolls of the Former Prophets known as Joshua, Judges, Samuel, and Kings. Almost all English versions of the Old Testament follow this same order. The scrolls of Isaiah and the Twelve may have the greatest affinity. Each covers approximately the same three-century period of Israel's story, and the prophetic figures themselves are elusive and often absent from the text. Isaiah 1:1 and Hosea 1:1, the first verses in each of these scrolls, both contain a list of Judean kings from the mid to late eighth century BCE, and both end in the era of the rebuilt temple and ongoing restoration of Judah. The Greek Old Testament (as seen in the earliest complete Christian Bible, dated from the fourth and fifth centuries CE), places the Book of the Twelve first, so that it sits side by side with Isaiah. The two middle scrolls in the Jewish canon, Jeremiah and Ezekiel, focus on the last years of the Judean monarchy and the destruction of Jerusalem in the early sixth century BCE. Each of these four scrolls is a distinctive literary work in and of itself, different from the others. Each speaks with its own voice, but in the canon they are often speaking together—in groups of two, three, or four—about the same set of events in Israel's story. This situation presents the great challenge of listening to each of those voices separately, taking account of the full continuity of their message, and listening to them together as they speak together, sometimes in harmony and sometimes in conflict with each other, a challenge which this book attempts to engage.

An important feature that all four of the prophetic scrolls share is a general sense of movement from negative to positive. This can be demonstrated by observing the kinds of literature found within them. The bulk of the prophetic literature consists of literary units called *oracles*. As the basic units of prophetic speech, they can be poetry or prose and vary significantly in length. Oracles are usually classified into two basic groups: oracles of judgment and oracles of salvation. As a general rule, judgment oracles are more common in the first half of each of the scrolls, while salvation oracles are more numerous in the second half. The scrolls of Isaiah, Jeremiah, and Ezekiel all exhibit a fairly dramatic turning point, where this change in tone is quite noticeable. In Isaiah, this shift begins in chapter 40 and coincides with the move from addressing the Assyrian era to addressing the Babylonian era. In Jeremiah and Ezekiel, the turning point is different because both books are speaking primarily to the Babylonian crisis on both sides of the pivot. The full force of divine punishment still lies ahead when the book of Jeremiah reaches the section in chapters 30–33, often called the Book of Consolation. At this point the judgment of God is inevitable, and looking beyond it to restoration is the only point of hope. The book of Ezekiel makes a dramatic turn at the beginning of chapter 36. Ezekiel is a book shaped by four stunning visions. The two that lie before this turning point involve God's departure from the temple in Jerusalem as its destruction looms, and the two that come after the catastrophe point toward the revival of the people of Israel and the rebuilding of the temple.

There are multiple shifts in the book of Ezekiel, but it still presents a single, grand sense of movement from punishment to redemption. The turning point in the Book of the Twelve looks different because it involves some of the smaller books in their entirety. The little books called Habakkuk, Zephaniah, and Haggai move through declarations of protest about the extent of divine punishment in the Babylonian period to the beginnings of new life embodied in the rebuilding of the temple. This turning point for the whole of the Book of the Twelve is accompanied by a similar sense of movement within some of its larger components, like Amos and Micah. All four prophetic scrolls are obviously composite documents, developed over long periods of time by multiple hands. Each has its own tradition, generated by the experience of the prophets, and carried on and developed long after their deaths; yet when they reached their final written stages, they possessed many common features.

Ways of thinking about the literature of the Old Testament have always changed with the shifts in technology that determine the means of their physical production, and this would have included the change from the scroll to the codex. This physical way of storing written information in stacked, bound pages, rather than pages sewed together end to end and rolled, developed during the first and second centuries CE. Israel obviously thought about these four scrolls together as the Latter Prophets at an earlier stage, but until the second century of the Common Era, they were separate physical objects that did not need to be put in a specific order. The advent of the codex and stacked pages, which allowed the entire Jewish canon or Christian Bible to be put into one physical manuscript, required a fixed order. Jewish tradition places these four scrolls in the second section of the canon known as the *Nebi'im*, composing its second half and balancing the four scrolls of the Former Prophets: Joshua, Judges, Samuel, and Kings. The earliest physical demonstration of the internal order of these prophetic books is in the Ben Asher Codices of the tenth and eleventh centuries (commonly designated as Aleppo and Leningrad), which follows the standard order of Isaiah, Jeremiah, Ezekiel, and the Twelve. Two of these four scrolls, Jeremiah and the Twelve, show some variation in their own internal ordering of material when compared to the Greek manuscript tradition.[23]

The Greek canonical tradition is best represented physically by fourth- and fifth-century codices like Sinaiticus, Vaticanus, and Alexandrinus. All of these manuscripts of the prophetic literature are in Christian Bibles, written in Greek. Their placement of the Book of the Twelve first may best be explained by an increased concern for chronology. These manuscripts also place Amos immediately after Hosea, so that the earliest two prophets come first, but other factors such as the geographic identity of these prophets may also have been at work in these decisions. The subject of order within the Book of the Twelve will be addressed in more detail in chapter 3 of this book. The canonical order of the books in the Jewish tradition, and subsequently in almost all English versions of the Old Testament, will have the most influence on how this book proceeds, but an awareness of historical and chronological issues is important at all times while reading this literature.

THE HISTORICAL FRAMEWORK
PRESUMED BY THE PROPHETS

Historical readings of the prophetic literature can collapse under the weight of reconstructions that are too complex and precise, but a broad view of Israel's story may be drawn with reasonable certainty, and points within that story may be identified as parts of a plot to which the prophets and the prophetic scrolls speak. The story is presented in the Old Testament in the narrative books called Samuel, Kings, Chronicles, and Ezra–Nehemiah, which include prophetic characters like Samuel, Nathan, and Gad. Prophets appear early in the story of the Israelite monarchy and are close to the royal court, often acting as advisers to the kings. After the division of the kingdoms in 1 Kings 12, characters like Elijah and Elisha soon appear in the northern kingdom, Israel, but they often operate in opposition to royal power.[24] Eventually the names of a few prophetic figures in the prophetic literature appear in the narrative books of the Old Testament, such as Isaiah (2 Kings 19), Jeremiah (2 Chr. 36), and Haggai and Zechariah (Ezra 5), so there are significant connections between these two collections. The most overt connections are the inclusion of much of 2 Kings 18–20 in Isaiah 36–39 and most of 2 Kings 25 in Jeremiah 52.

The book of Isaiah and the Book of the Twelve both start at the same place in Israel's story, with a superscription naming a sequence of Judean kings who reigned from the mid to late eighth century BCE. The only difference is that Hosea 1:1 names one king from the northern state of Israel during that period. Based upon information from the Bible and sources outside the Bible, this era can be identified: the Assyrian Empire was expanding from Mesopotamia toward Egypt, placing pressure on the smaller nations that lay between the two empires. The period of crisis caused by Assyrian encroachment forms the primary context for much of the first half of the book of Isaiah and much of the Book of the Twelve, from Hosea through Micah. Table 1.1 (below) presents the most significant events from this period of crisis, which serve as a necessary backdrop for reading these parts of the prophetic literature. The earlier portions of the literature were subject to later stages of development that make it difficult to establish the date when any particular passage was written, but this does not prevent the attachment of texts to a particular part of the Bible's narrative plot. A text like the book of Joel presents unique challenges because of its notorious lack of specific historical references, but the placement of Joel between the books called Hosea and Amos steers the reader toward an eighth-century context. The most specific information about the political and military situation in this period comes from the prophetic oracle uttered by Isaiah to King Ahaz of Judah in Isaiah 7:4–9; scattered notes and narratives in 2 Kings 15–20; parallel passages with some adjustments in 2 Chronicles 28–32; and Isaiah 36–39. The basic outline of this information is consistent with the records found in the available Assyrian documents of the period, even if some of the internal details differ.

Table 1.1 Major Events of the Assyrian Crisis

BCE	Major Event
785	Beginning of reign of Uzziah/Azariah over Judah
745	Beginning of reign of Tiglath-Pileser III over Assyria
742	Beginning of reign of Jotham over Judah
737	Beginning of reign of Pekah over Israel
735	Beginning of reign of Ahaz over Judah
735	Approximate date of events known as the Syro-Ephraimitic War
732	Beginning of reign of Hoshea over Israel
727	Beginning of reign of Shalmaneser V over Assyria
722	Beginning of reign of Sargon II over Assyria
722	Fall of Samaria (Israel/the northern kingdom) to the Assyrian army
715	Beginning of reign of Hezekiah over Judah
705	Beginning of reign of Sennacherib over Assyria
701	Sennacherib's invasion of Judah

One point of great historical difficulty is the acknowledgment in 2 Kings 18:13 and Isaiah 36:1–2 that Sennacherib invaded Judah, and in 2 Kings 18:14–16 that Hezekiah paid tribute to the Assyrian king to save Jerusalem from destruction, alongside the conflicting claim in 2 Kings 19:35 and Isaiah 37:36 that the entire Assyrian army died in one night, preventing such an invasion.

There would seem to be a gap of several decades before the next occasion came along that generated prophetic material that made it into Israel's Scriptures. Early in the second half of the seventh century, the Neo-Babylonian Empire began to put pressure on the Assyrians. Its subsequent overthrow of Nineveh in 612 BCE is the subject of the portion of the Book of the Twelve called Nahum. It was not long before the Babylonians developed plans for expansion and began to move toward Egypt, with the remaining nation of Judah in their path. While 2 Kings 20 and Isaiah 39 both present an odd scene in which envoys from Babylon bring a gift to Hezekiah after his illness and are provided with a tour of Jerusalem, the real entrance of the Babylonians into the story of Judah came in 605 BCE, when Nebuchadnezzar, the king of Babylon, defeated Pharaoh Neco of Egypt and took control of the Levant.

The Babylonian incursion initiated a period of two decades of various degrees of political control over Judah. There were at least three deportations of Judean citizens during this period, the last of which coincided with the destruction of Jerusalem and brought the Davidic monarchy to an end. Table 1.2 presents a chronology of this rapid succession of events.

Table 1.2 Major Events of the Babylonian Crisis

BCE	Major Event
612	Fall of Nineveh to the Babylonians
609	Death of King Josiah of Judah
609	Brief reign of Jehoahaz, a son of Josiah
609	Beginning of reign of Jehoiakim, another son of Josiah
605	Accession to the throne of King Nebuchadnezzar of Babylon
598	Beginning of reign of Jehoiachin of Judah
597	First deportation of Israelites to Babylon
597	Beginning of reign of Zedekiah of Judah
586	Destruction of Jerusalem and second deportation
539	Overthrow of Babylon by Cyrus of Persia
538	Edict of Cyrus releasing the exiled Israelites from captivity

The picture of this period presented in the Old Testament, like the Assyrian period, is consistent in its broad contours with the records from Babylonian sources. The vital pieces of information most difficult to determine are the numbers or percentage of Judah's inhabitants who were taken into captivity in Babylon. Some texts in the Old Testament, such as 2 Chronicles 36:20, sound as if vast numbers, even a majority, of the survivors were exiled to Babylon. There is some evidence of overstatement, however, indicating that the majority of Judeans remained in a fairly intact land of Judah.[25] It is more certain that *exile* became the dominant theological motif for the period, regardless of the number of people the Babylonians actually deported.

The defeat of the Neo-Babylonian Empire by Cyrus of Persia marked a formal end to the period of Babylonian captivity, and the decree of Cyrus made it possible for those who had been exiled to return to Judah, but this proved to be no simple task. Six or seven decades after deportation, most Judeans who were in Babylon would have been born there, and many of them chose to stay. Those who returned apparently did so with some degree of Persian sponsorship and provision of resources, but there were many challenges involved in rebuilding Jerusalem and recombining with the community that had remained in Judah. The story of the "restoration" of Judah appears only in the book called Ezra–Nehemiah, a work at least as interested in providing theological interpretation of events as in providing historical reporting. The late sixth and most of the fifth centuries can be legitimately called another crisis in Israel's story, and it gave rise to its own prophets, such as Haggai, Zechariah, Malachi, and the persons who continued to revise the books of Isaiah, Jeremiah, and Ezekiel. Table 1.3 lists some of the significant events of the Restoration crisis.

Table 1.3 Major Events of the Restoration Crisis

BCE	Major Event
538	Decree of Cyrus allowing Jewish exiles to return to Jerusalem
538–520	First return, with Jeshua and Zerubbabel; rebuilding the Jerusalem temple
530	Death of Cyrus
522	Beginning of reign of Darius I over Persia
465	Beginning of reign of Artaxerxes I over Persia
458	Possible date for return of the Ezra group to Jerusalem
446	Likely date for Nehemiah's return; starting reconstruction of Jerusalem's wall

Judah would continue to exist as a province of the Persian Empire until the Greek Empire under Alexander gained control of the area in 332 BCE. The Persian period, and perhaps the early decades of the Greek Period, are generally accepted as the time during which all of the prophetic literature was put into its final form, which means that all of the prophetic scrolls respond to the Restoration crisis, including the failure of the monarchy to reestablish itself and the struggle to develop and regulate a system of worship in the Second Temple.

THE PROPHETS AS FIGURES IN ANCIENT ISRAEL

The place of the prophets in ancient Israelite society is a subject about which we have little direct information. Indirect data can be assembled from at least four important sources: (1) Inferences drawn from the prophetic literature itself; (2) the portrayal of prophetic characters in the other literature of the Old Testament, primarily the Deuteronomistic History (the books of Joshua through 2 Kings) and Chronicles; (3) information about the prophetic behavior in the writings of other cultures in the ancient Near East; and (4) observations about the prophetic roles in modern societies.

The prophetic scrolls do not self-consciously take up the task of defining the role of a prophet in the social world of ancient Israel, but sometimes they offer information that can be used to reconstruct reasonable portraits.

There are serious limitations to this approach, however, because the work of the prophets has been textualized in the final forms of the scrolls: their actions and their speech have been shaped and placed within a written text for literary purposes. Most of the time, prophetic oracles or even stories about the prophets do not offer a full setting or provide a description of an audience or the response of that audience. The words of the prophets lack a social context because in textualized form the reader becomes the audience. The trial of Jeremiah in Jeremiah 26 and the Haggai's interaction with the priests in Haggai 2 are exceptions to the rule; yet even these events have been shaped as literature in order to present the work of the prophet to a later, reading audience, not primarily to tell us how a prophet fit into his own social context.

Table 1.4 Five Prophets of Prophetic Literature
Elsewhere in the Old Testament

Prophet	Where Mentioned
Isaiah	2 Kings 19–20 (mentioned by name 13 times)
	2 Chronicles 26:22; 32:20, 32
Jeremiah	2 Chronicles 35:25; 36:12, 21–22
Jonah	2 Kings 14:25
Haggai	Ezra 5:1; 6:14
Zechariah	Ezra 5:1; 6:14

The fifteen prophets whose names function as labels heading each part of the prophetic literature appear sparsely in the other parts of the Old Testament, as illustrated in table 1.4, but a second indirect source of information about the role of prophets in Israelite society is the portrayal of other prophets in the books known as the Former Prophets and the book of Chronicles.[26] These characters vary tremendously in the depths of their portrayals and the roles they play within the events the text presents. Samuel, for example, is sometimes portrayed as a person of significant political power. He helps select Saul and David as kings of Israel and anoints them, and he advises and critiques Saul in the conduct of his reign. On some occasions, Samuel communicates the divine will to the leaders and the general Israelite population. Nevertheless, part of Samuel's function in the story of Israel, as the text of 1 Samuel presents it, is to relinquish the political power that prophets held by inaugurating the monarchy. Samuel's emotional reaction to Saul's failure in 1 Samuel 15:34–16:1 is difficult to interpret, but part of his grief seems to be over his own loss of significance; he clearly expresses his personal loss of power earlier, in 8:6. Samuel originally operates as priest, prophet, and judge, but by the time he dies, these three roles have been divided among separate people or groups of people within the rapidly developing national institutions of Israel. After Samuel's death, characters like Nathan and Gad appear sporadically in texts that portray them as royal advisers who have access to the king and some influence over him.

The most highly developed character portrayed purely as a prophet in the Deuteronomistic History is Elijah, who takes the role of prophet entirely outside of the sphere of the royal court. Elijah is an oppositional figure to King Ahab and his wife Jezebel, who try to kill the prophet. One very important feature of the Elijah tradition, aside from the fact that it is a set of narratives of significant length that makes him a sustained presence, is that the reader is brought into the relationship between the prophet and YHWH. Thus 1 Kings 21:17–19 presents Elijah's reception of the divine message from God and in a smooth moment of transition moves on to Elijah's transmission of this message to the king.[27] Elijah's role as a mediator of divine presence is emerging more clearly at this point, and this trend will continue in the prophetic scrolls. Brueggemann has identified prophets as one of the five major mediators of divine presence in Israelite tradition, and Elijah most clearly fits his definition of their role: "These uncredentialed, authoritative speakers do not utter universal truths, but speak concretely to a particular time, place, and circumstance. . . . Specifically, the emergence of prophetic mediation in Israel characteristically happened in the presence of and in response to royal power."[28] Characters like Hosea, Amos, Jeremiah, and Ezekiel would follow in the tradition of Elijah and operate outside, and sometimes in opposition to, the structures of political power in Israel, but Isaiah and Haggai would continue to have some formal relation to the political structure.

The third and fourth indirect sources of information about prophetic roles in ancient Israel are the focus of the work of Robert Wilson, who pioneered the use of sociological methods to understand prophets and the prophetic literature in the Old Testament. Wilson used information from ancient cultures around Israel, where there were also figures known as prophets, and observations of contemporary human communities in which prophetic figures are significant. The cultures around Israel, in Egypt and Mesopotamia and other areas in between, exhibit the presence of prophets; a particularly important example of this evidence is the collection of ancient inscriptions from Mesopotamia known as the Mari tablets. Some of these inscriptions, from the early second millennium BCE, illustrate the work of prophets in that time and place, in ways that can shed light on the work of Israelite prophets, both in terms of similarities and differences.[29] These letters from prophets are addressed to the king at Mari at that time, Zimri-Lim, often making predictions about the future, reminding him of past predictions that proved true, and urging support of the institutions housing the prophets. The use of language is reminiscent of the Old Testament prophets in these letters, especially the introductory formula, "Thus says [a deity] . . ." The letters also identify a trance as a means of receiving a message, and the use of a prophet's hair or garment to certify a prophetic message.[30] The role of some type of physical manifestation among prophets in the Old Testament is uncertain. First Samuel 10:9–13 reports ecstatic experience or a "prophetic frenzy" that accompanies the act of prophesying, and some interpreters have understood the characteristic language that precedes the visions of Ezekiel, "The hand of the Lord was on him . . ." (1:3), as a signal of a trancelike state. The use of garments and hair as authentication may remind readers of Ahijah's use of his cloak to give a prophetic message to Jeroboam in 1 Kings 11:29–31, Elisha's claiming of Elijah's mantle in 2 Kings 2:13, Jeremiah's strange use of an undergarment in 13:1–11, or Ezekiel cutting off all of his hair in 5:1–4. From a modern perspective, the behavior of the Israelite prophets can look quite strange, but it may not have been so unusual in the cultures of the ancient Near East.

In light of the sociological background he developed, Wilson found two sets of prophetic traditions in the Old Testament, one of which he called Ephraimite and the other Judean, primarily because of what he saw as their northern and southern origins in ancient Israel. Wilson developed this distinction largely on his identification of characteristic Ephraimite and Judean strands of literature, which now looks overconfident.[31] The lasting impact of Wilson's work was his identification of two social locations of the prophet's intermediary role: the center and the periphery. Central intermediaries typically have some established position in society and are able to play a political role, while peripheral intermediaries are persons without power, who proclaim a need for social change. According to Wilson, the line between the two locations is not always firm, and they can coexist, as they sometimes do within the biblical tradition.[32] One place where Wilson's work needs further development is its application to textualized prophets. He still saw prophecy in ancient Israel as a phenomenon that declined and ceased, because there is no evidence of actual persons continuing to play such a role in Israelite society.[33] A primary assertion of this study is that the work of prophecy continued in textualized prophets, whose influence can be seen in the growing significance of literature.

At about the same time as Wilson, Norman Gottwald was also pioneering the use of sociological approaches to interpreting the Old Testament. The prophetic literature was not Gottwald's most intense or direct area of interest, but it still became a subject of his work. He also saw a dichotomy within the phenomenon of prophecy in ancient Israel, but distinguished between "radical prophecy" and "cult prophecy." Gottwald understood the origins of prophecy to lie in the administrative apparatus of the temple, or of other institutions of worship, but saw in some prophets—like Micah, Amos, and Jeremiah—a movement away from those origins. In his words, "In moving out of the sanctuaries and into the streets, radical prophets were contributing to a counterculture which claimed to be the proper embodiment of Israelite faithfulness to [Yahweh]."[34] There is some tendency in Gottwald's work to romanticize the radical prophets, and some allowance needs to be made for the move back toward what might look like cult prophecy in the postexilic period, when all of Israel was in a relatively powerless and countercultural position in relation to the Persian Empire, but his categories also point in helpful directions.

Discussion Box 1.1 The Experience of Exile

One way in which sociological approaches have been applied to the Bible, including the prophetic literature, is an attempt to understand how exile affects a society. The assumption behind this approach is that if we observe the contemporary displaced communities to which we have direct access, then some of what we learn may be applied to ancient exiled communities, like the people of Judah, to whom we only have indirect access through the literature they left behind. An important example of this is Daniel Smith-Christopher's use of the work of the anthropologist James Scott to examine patterns of resistance to political domination in biblical texts. Scott's great insight was that subordinated people communicate differently in public than they do in private, but a "coded version" or "hidden transcript" of their private communication is still present in their public communication.[35] For Smith-Christopher, this insight is a tool for developing a "theology of exile" based on the hidden transcripts embedded within the public communications of the postexilic citizens of Judah and the Jews of the Diaspora, which became parts of the Old Testament.[36] The challenge is that the private communications of these ancient people are not available to us and must be inferred, and this is where Scott's model, developed from observations of living exiled communities in Asia, is a helpful analog.

The categories of central/peripheral and cult/radical intermediaries may be roughly translated to "establishment" and "antiestablishment" prophets, the categories that this study will typically use. The prophetic figures represented by the characters in the prophetic literature exhibit characteristics of both of these kinds of prophetic activity, and questions concerning their power and status within their society can be an important part of understanding their proclamations. To hear these appropriately, we need to turn to the prophets as they are portrayed as literary characters.

THE PROPHETS AS CHARACTERS IN THE PROPHETIC LITERATURE

An earlier section of this chapter has already demonstrated some of the difficulty readers and interpreters of the Bible have in keeping the prophets as characters separate and distinct from the books that have their names on them. The designation of characters as prophets in earlier parts of the Old Testament—including Abraham, Moses, Deborah, Samuel, Nathan, Gad, Ahijah, Elijah, and Elisha—seems to have an uncertain meaning at first, but toward the end of this list these characters begin to resemble more closely the prophets who have books named for them. Even these figures, however, do not have a consistent connection to their respective bodies of literature. Isaiah, for example, appears sporadically in the book named for him. He is named in chapters 1, 2, 7, 13, 20, and 37–39, and he seems to speak as "I" (first-person singular) to the reader in chapters 6 and 8, but he disappears from view entirely after chapter 39. Isaiah 6 contains the prophet's famous call narrative, which presents a mystery of its own by appearing so far into the book. If Isaiah 6 is the prophet's initial experience that clarified his vocation, then what is Isaiah 1–5? What may be stated most clearly is that the life of the person named Isaiah is not the most important factor shaping the book that is named for him. One can argue, however, that Isaiah son of Amoz is such an influential figure that, even after his disappearance at the end of Isaiah 39, the scroll has adequate momentum to continue for another twenty-seven chapters. An often-overlooked reference in 8:16 indicates that the character named Isaiah has "disciples," whom he urges to preserve his words for later generations. It is impossible to say the extent to which this description in the text of the scroll matched any particular model of "prophetic schools" outside the text, but this would provide a mechanism by which the prophetic traditions generated by a founding figure might have been preserved and continued to grow for centuries after the death of that figure. Inside the world created by the book of Isaiah, they are specifically assigned this role, whether such a portrayal matches any reality outside the text or not.

A significant tradition in scholarship developed during the twentieth century, often speaking of "Second Isaiah" or "Deutero-Isaiah" as an actual person, an anonymous prophet who continued the work of Isaiah son of Amoz about a century later. There is little sense, however, in which such a person is presented as a narrative character in Isaiah 40–55, other than as a disembodied voice (40:3). The only sustained character in this part of Isaiah is the Servant of YHWH, who appears in four poems spread evenly through the section. This person is characterized as an advocate for justice, a teacher, and a sufferer. Chapter 4 of this book will examine more closely the challenges of understanding this "Servant" as a character and the way the proclamations in this part of the book of Isaiah are entangled with the life of this character.

The situation is very different in the book of Jeremiah, which seems to open with the call narrative of the prophet at a young age, and then follows his prophetic career to a significant extent all the way to the end of the book.[37] The life of Jeremiah is by no means the only force shaping the book, but it is a significant one. Compared to the sparse 16 times that Isaiah's name is mentioned in his book, Jeremiah is mentioned by name 131 times.[38] The most striking aspect of the book of Jeremiah is a series of poems that are spread through Jeremiah 10–20. These poems, often called the Confessions (or Laments) of Jeremiah, present the prophet's private conversations with God and expose his mental and emotional state in a way different from anything else in the prophetic literature of the Old Testament. Jeremiah encounters opposition in a way that Isaiah never does, and this becomes a significant component of the book. He also exhibits more of the strange behavior presented as symbolic actions than does Isaiah.

The character called Ezekiel is present in the book named for him in odd ways. Much of the narrative framework of the book is told in first-person language, so his name does not appear frequently. Ezekiel rarely interacts with another human being in the book, and in his interactions with YHWH, the divine character always calls Ezekiel *ben-ʾadam*, son of a man, or "mortal," as the NRSV translates it. This designation becomes an important part of the development of Ezekiel as a character. Ezekiel is primarily characterized by two kinds of behavior: elaborate visionary experiences, which he describes in great detail, and bizarre symbolic actions. These behaviors are even more textualized than those of Isaiah and Jeremiah, as there is no indication of an audience in Ezekiel's own context inside the book. The audience has become entirely the readers of the book itself.

Of the twelve prophets whose names are attached to portions of the Book of the Twelve, only Hosea, Amos, Jonah, and Haggai appear significantly as narrative characters. Chapter 3 of this book will develop the idea that in the finished form of the Book of the Twelve, these form a collective narrative character who is roughly equal to Isaiah in the frequency of appearance. There are long sections of the Book of the Twelve where there is little or no sense of a narrative character, as in Isaiah. A major difference is the reassertion of a strong narrative presence near the end of the scroll, in Haggai and

Zechariah, a feature not matched in the later portions of the book of Isaiah. In each of the four great prophetic scrolls, the lives of these prophets become entangled with the messages they proclaim. Mary Mills has offered some helpful ways to look at this idea in the cases of Isaiah, Jeremiah, and Ezekiel:

> In all three books, there are sections of utterance delivered as if directly addressed to the reader by an "I" who speaks. This prophetic voice both describes the prophet's own experiences and reports divine utterance in a quotation mode. These various forms of speech are given meaning and context by the framework of the narrated prophetic experience. The interweaving of these two genres is clearest and most consistent in Ezekiel, but the oracles of Isa 1–39 are ultimately grounded in the narration of prophetic vision in Isa 6 and the recorded experiences of Jeremiah are dramatized by the Confessions.[39]

Mills has argued that the narrative superscriptions at the beginnings of all of the prophetic books cast them in the genre of "historical biography."[40] One might respond by wondering if these single verses can carry so much weight, especially when Mills's argument pushes further to claim that "the literary organization encourages readers to approach the books as a form of historical biography."[41] If this really is their intent, then they have failed miserably, especially in the Christian traditions of reading and using the prophetic books, which most often extract small pieces of prophetic utterances and present them devoid of any biblical context. Yet it is important to grasp that Mills is at least half right, that the lives of the prophets are at least trying to surround the theology of their oracles, because their lives testify against so much of that theology. This is an idea perhaps best expressed by Daniel Berrigan in the introduction to his book on Jeremiah:

> For all their moral greatness, we shall not make of the prophets a species of moral superhumans. True, awful events daunt, discourage and dishearten. Terrible misfortune and loss befall Jeremiah, Hosea, Daniel, and Isaiah. Suffering is the price exacted of them in their quest for a fuller and deeper humanity—for others, but for themselves first of all. This realization lurks between the lines. The great ones admit to it. And someone, against all the odds of [YHWH]'s prediction to the contrary, nonetheless hearkens to the word and records it. We are left with that record and with its implication for ourselves: What price the human? They give us one price: to perish, and to have your life and death set down by another.[42]

Perhaps it is the readers who have failed, and that is something this book will attempt to improve upon: this notion of a narrative aspect of a prophetic scroll, even if it does not rise to the level of making the scroll into a historical biography, will be an important tool in that process. In the task of reappropriating prophetic proclamations of impending disaster into words of hope after the disaster, these characters in the books are important resources. As originators of the traditions and literary characters in their final, textual forms, they are present from beginning to end.

THE PLAN OF THIS BOOK

Figure 1 The Prophetic Scrolls and the Story of Israel

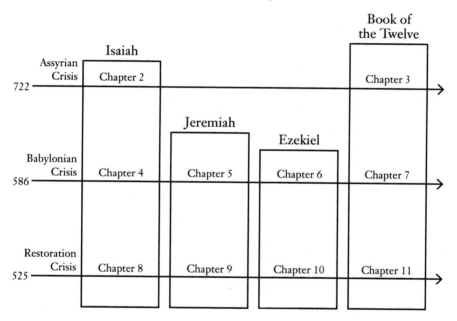

Figure 1 demonstrates how the three major crises in the story of Israel intersect the four prophetic scrolls in the Tanak. Each point of intersection is labeled with the chapter number that addresses it. A modified version of the diagram appears at the beginning of each chapter to remind readers where they are in this picture of how the national story and prophetic proclamation meet.

The preface at the front of this book discusses its goals and how they relate to its organization, but the organization demands some reiteration and expansion at this point. The academic field of biblical studies is often a place of experimentation and rapid change, as it should be. Deciding when significant advances in a particular direction have developed sufficiently that they warrant presentation in an introductory textbook is not an easy call to make. Along with a history of scholarship and a survey of results that would find large agreement among contemporary scholars, a textbook like this one should also make students aware of the growing edge of the discipline, without cluttering the discussion with short-lived fads and half-baked notions. For example, thirty years ago it may have been too early for a textbook like this to give major attention to the idea of prophetic literature as imaginative vision, which was developing in the early work of Walter Brueggemann.[43] On the other hand, any such work produced twenty years ago would have done a severe disservice to readers by neglecting Brueggemann's transformational development. My judgment is that the recent development in our collective scholarship—examining the prophetic literature through the lenses of disaster, trauma, and survival—has reached the stage where it merits inclusion in an introductory textbook. In particular, the tension-filled relationship between the prophets as predisaster preachers and the finished prophetic scrolls as postdisaster literature is certain to be a decisive force in the field for some years to come.[44] A development of this kind demands a complete reexamination of all of our work on the prophetic literature.

Navigating the prophetic literature without falling into the trap of blaming the victims of disaster for their own horrifying fate will require a careful process of tacking between diachronic and synchronic poles. Purely diachronic readings put all victims back into a predisaster context, listening to a preacher threatening judgment that has already come. Purely synchronic readings bring a predisaster preacher into a postdisaster setting, proclaiming a nonsensical message of judgment to a group of beleaguered survivors. The direction in which this book's approach to prophetic literature is heading will require movement back and forth between historical work that places the material in the time and place to which it refers, and literary study that places greater emphasis on how the completed scrolls operate. Performing both tasks at the same time requires the distinctive organization of the book. Chapter 2, for example, has the goal of presenting the claims found in the book of Isaiah concerning the Assyrian crisis of the eighth century, not by merely excerpting a hypothetical eighth-century core of the book, but by reading the parts that refer to the eighth century in the context of the whole book. Chapter 3 will attempt to do the same thing for the Book of the Twelve. The discussions of the book of Isaiah and the Book of the Twelve will be interrupted at the points where the Babylonian period becomes the primary focus.

What makes transformation from predisaster preaching (the historical events and contexts envisioned in the prophetic books) to postdisaster literature (the final literary works known as the books of Isaiah, Jeremiah, Ezekiel, and the Twelve) possible? Perhaps the most important element of the transformation is the presentation of the prophetic characters themselves.

Beginning with the Servant in Isaiah 40–55, prophetic characters embody the suffering that their preaching proclaims. The process may find its clearest expression in the so-called Confessions of Jeremiah, in which the prophet complains that the punishment which should be falling on his wicked enemies is in fact being inflicted upon him because of his faithfulness to YHWH. Ezekiel also embodies the affliction of his prophetic message in his life-altering symbolic actions. The prophets, portrayed as YHWH's most faithful servants, are the ones who suffer most. Through the work of suffering, they switch the identity of the afflicted one from the guilty party being punished by God to the faithful ones who suffer because of their loyalty to YHWH. After chapter 4 addresses the portions of the book of Isaiah most closely associated with the Babylonian period, chapters 5 and 6 will introduce the scrolls of Jeremiah and Ezekiel, both of which begin in the Babylonian period. Eventually this will also require an interruption of these books at points where they turn their attention to the Restoration period. Chapter 7 will then complete the discussion of the Babylonian period by examining the parts of the Book of the Twelve that are primarily related to that set of events.

Chapters 8 through 11 will explore the portions of each of the four prophetic scrolls that are connected to the restoration of Judah in the Persian period. These chapters will also need to return to the discussion of the final shape of each of the scrolls, since this was the period that produced those final forms. Throughout the book there will also be an effort to listen to the separate books of the prophetic literature speaking together as they address different time periods and issues in Israel's story. The final chapter of this book will pull those efforts together to treat the prophetic literature as a chorus of voices, each of which can be discerned individually, but each of which also influences the way we hear the others.

Resources for Further Research

Other Introductions

Heschel, Abraham Joshua. *The Prophets: An Introduction*. Vol. 1. New York: Harper & Row, 1962.

LeClerc, Thomas L. *Introduction to the Prophets: Their Stories, Sayings, and Scrolls*. New York: Paulist Press, 2007.

Petersen, David L. *The Prophetic Literature: An Introduction*. Louisville, KY: Westminster John Knox Press, 2002.

Rad, Gerhard von. *The Message of the Prophets*. Translated by D. G. M. Stalker. New York: Harper & Row, 1967.

Stulman, Louis, and Hyun Chul Paul Kim. *You Are My People: An Introduction to Prophetic Literature*. Nashville: Abingdon Press, 2010.

Sweeney, Marvin A. *The Prophetic Literature*. Nashville: Abingdon Press, 2005.

Specialized Studies

Albertz, Rainer. *Israel in Exile: The History and Literature of the Sixth Century B.C.E.* Translated by David Green. Atlanta: Society of Biblical Literature, 2003.

Brueggemann, Walter. *The Prophetic Imagination.* 2nd ed. Minneapolis: Fortress Press, 2002.

Conrad, Edgar W. *Reading the Latter Prophets: Toward a New Canonical Criticism.* New York: T&T Clark, 2004.

Mills, Mary E. *Alterity, Pain, and Suffering in Isaiah, Jeremiah, and Ezekiel.* New York: T&T Clark, 2007.

Seitz, Christopher R. *Prophecy and Hermeneutics: Toward a New Introduction to the Prophets.* Grand Rapids: Baker Academic, 2007.

Smith-Christopher, Daniel L. *A Biblical Theology of Exile.* Minneapolis: Fortress Press, 2002.

Sweeney, Marvin A. *Reading the Hebrew Bible after the Shoah: Engaging Holocaust Theology.* Minneapolis: Fortress Press, 2008.

Wilson, Robert R. *Prophecy and Society in Ancient Israel.* Philadelphia: Fortress Press, 1980.

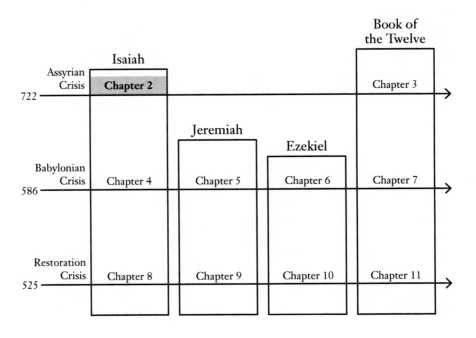

2

The Scroll of Isaiah

Introduction and Response to the Assyrian Crisis

In most manuscript and canonical traditions, the scroll of Isaiah appears first among the prophetic literature, following Kings in the Tanak (the Jewish Bible) and the Song of Songs in the Old Testament (of the Christian Bible).[1] The most logical explanation for this priority of Isaiah is that while prophets such as Hosea and Amos seem to predate Isaiah just slightly, the connection of Isaiah to Jerusalem and its temple may have overridden a purely chronological placement.

Table 2.1 provides a first glance at some of the major features of the book of Isaiah that have been identified by scholars at various times and for a variety of reasons.

Table 2.1 Major Components of the Scroll of Isaiah

Component	*Where*
Superscriptions	1:1; 2:1; 13:1; 14:28
Call Narrative	6:1–13
Royal Narratives	7:1–17; 36:1–39:6
Oracles against the Nations	13:2–23:18
Isaiah Apocalypse	24:1–27:13
Servant Songs	42:1–4; 49:1–6; 50:4–9; 52:13–53:12

A later section will address the literary structure of the book of Isaiah, but it is helpful at the beginning of the chapter to present a broad outline of the book, which table 2.2 does. Some of these divisions coincide with the major components of the book listed in table 2.1.

Table 2.2 Chapter Outline of the Book of Isaiah

Chapters	Description
1–5	Oracles concerning the fate of Jerusalem
6–12	The prophet named Isaiah and Judah's leadership during the Assyrian crisis
13–23	Oracles of judgment against foreign nations
24–27	An apocalyptic (?) vision of the future of Israel and the world
28–35	Oracles of judgment and salvation for Judah and Jerusalem
36–39	The prophet named Isaiah and King Hezekiah
40–55	The suffering and deliverance of Judah during and after the exile
56–66	Life in restored Jerusalem and its new temple[2]

In this book the discussion of Isaiah will take place in this chapter, chapter 4, and chapter 8. Careful observation of the book reveals its composite nature, and the treatment of Isaiah throughout this study will operate from the near consensus within biblical scholarship that the book of Isaiah was produced over the course of about three centuries by a collection of people.[3] Past scholarship has tended to focus either on reconstructing the process of composition and isolating the elements of various stages, or on reading the final form of the book as a unified literary work. The former kind of approach is often labeled *diachronic* because it studies how the book developed "through time," while the latter type is called *synchronic* because it examines the book at only one particular time. Each of these ways of working with the text has had a tendency to ignore, or even reject, the other style, but it is becoming more clear that our understanding of a book like Isaiah requires a combination of the two kinds of reading.[4] The remainder of this chapter will present the literary structure of the book, its spatial and temporal settings, its characters, and what it might be trying to communicate about the experience of Israel in the Assyrian period. These discussions will carefully move back and forth between historical (diachronic) and literary (synchronic) concerns and questions. The "successive restructurings" of Isaiah took place on all sides of a succession of world-altering events for its writers and audiences.[5] No single chronological position allows for a complete view of the book and its vision. Of particular concern for this study will be how the communal disasters and the personal traumas that befell the people of Israel affected their view of the relationship between Israel and its God, YHWH.

THE STRUCTURE OF THE BOOK

The opening discussion in this chapter, including table 2.1, has already pointed to some of the more visible features of the scroll of Isaiah. These features overlap with some of the major turning points of the book, which are important elements of its structure. In this case, it may be best to start at the center of the book, because the divide between Isaiah 39 and 40 is so wide and so striking that it has grabbed the attention of virtually every interpreter. In chapter 39 the narrator describes a strange visit by Babylonian envoys to King Hezekiah of Judah in the final years of the eighth century, supposedly to bring him a gift to celebrate the king's recovery from illness. The most conspicuous aspect of this story is the tour these envoys receive, in which they see everything that belongs to Hezekiah, including the contents of the palace and the temple (39:4). The book of Isaiah never describes the Babylonian invasion of Jerusalem in the early sixth century and the subsequent exile of many of the residents of Judah. Those events lie unspoken in this great gap. The tour seems like a vague replacement for the invasion, an averting of the eyes by the book of Isaiah from the horror of that experience. The introductory chapter of this book has examined the contemporary movement toward understanding the prophetic literature as a response to disaster or trauma. Such approaches might point toward this empty, unspeakable place as a center for the book, a place from which to watch the finished scroll grow outward.

The most important observation of the great divide in the book of Isaiah was made by a German scholar named Bernhard Duhm, early in the twentieth century. Duhm's concerns were primarily historical, and he linked the three major sections of Isaiah—1–39, 40–55, 56–66—to the eighth, sixth, and fifth centuries respectively.[6] This gave birth to the custom of using the phrases First Isaiah, Second Isaiah, and Third Isaiah to talk about these three parts of the book. Such language has sometimes evolved to the point that its users have seemed to be talking about three authors of the book as historical persons. We are on much safer ground, however, to make use of such observations to speak of possible stages of revision of the book and what those might tell us about how the finished book can be read. A further difficulty that has flowed out of the work of Duhm has been the assumption that these subsequent parts were simply added to the book of Isaiah, like more boxcars on a long train. It is more likely that the book of Isaiah was revised many times over the course of about three centuries and that these revisions involved placing new material on the beginning and the end, and also inserting new parts in the middle. The components of the book that have been named "Second" and "Third" Isaiah represent part of what may be the two most obvious of these revisions.

Describing the final structure of Isaiah and proposing a process through which the book may have developed are tasks not as easily separated as some interpreters assume, and movement back and forth between these two activities may allow them to speak productively to each other. Hypotheses about the history of composition of the book can become enormously complex, and the more detailed they grow, the more speculative they become; yet it is possible to portray, in broad strokes, a reasonably certain process for the growth of the book of Isaiah in a way that helps to reveal its literary structure. Like all such proposals, however, the more it presses toward detail, the more uncertain it becomes, a tendency that should urge caution. Arguments concerning small units of text and their origins and precise boundaries of compositional phases are available in other places, but are not suitable for this discussion. Most of the material in the core of the book, chapters 6–39, relates to the Assyrian period. Obvious exceptions are the oracles concerning Babylon in 13–14, the section often called the Isaian Apocalypse in 24–27, and the material in 34–35 that echoes the restoration themes found in 40–55. A foundation remains that begins with Isaiah's call narrative and is framed by his meeting with the two kings of Judah, Ahaz (7) and Hezekiah (37–39).[7] The foundational layer includes all of the places where Isaiah appears as a narrative character in the book. The initial work may be understood as the tradition that Isaiah commands his disciples to "bind up" and carry forward to a later time in 8:16–17.[8] A major stage of revision, near the end of the Babylonian period, would have included adding most, if not all, of 40–55, along with the inserting 13–14 and 34–35.[9] The revision was a response to the end of the Babylonian captivity, as the reference to Cyrus of Persia in Isaiah 45:1 indicates, but the text still wrestles with the pain of the experience and the understanding of it as divine punishment. A final major stage of growth would have involved the placement of 1–5 and 56–66 on the beginning and end, along with the insertion of some new material in the middle, such as 24–27. A primary concern of the last stage would have been the conduct of worship in the Second Temple during the Persian period.[10]

Interpreters have debated the function of Isaiah 1:1 within the book extensively. The primary issue is whether to understand it as an opening for the entire book or just the first chapter. The most important piece of evidence supporting the latter is the presence of a similar superscription at 2:1. On the other hand, these two statements are different, and the use of "vision" in 1:1 seems broader in scope than "word" in 2:1. For many readers, however, the choice has become unnecessary because it is possible for the verse to serve a "dual function." If chapter 1 was written as an opening for the whole book, a likely conclusion, then its first line in 1:1 can also introduce and help frame the whole book.[11] The final form of the book of Isaiah is cast by the superscription in 1:1 as the "vision" of the prophet, and it is a dramatic one. Making sense of such a description in relation to the whole book is a task that Walter Brueggemann's understanding of the prophetic imagination can assist. The idea that prophetic books produce alternative worlds, which help their readers understand and survive the worlds in which they live, provides a way to understand a vision that does not focus on how it matches a reality outside the text. Brueggemann has aptly called the book of Isaiah "an oratorio about the suffering and destiny of Jerusalem."[12] The book moves through days of threat and warnings of divine judgment for Israel's disobedience, and it wavers between this sense of judgment and the possibility of repentance and salvation, but the story is ultimately overtaken by a wave of destruction too severe to look at directly. The horror is perhaps best expressed in the troubling line in 40:2:

> Speak tenderly to Jerusalem,
>   and cry to her
> that she has served her term,
>   that her penalty is paid,
> that she has received from the LORD's hand
>   double for all her sins.

How should Isaiah's audiences, then and now, think about such horror and the weight of it, especially if some claim that the suffering is divine punishment?

Marvin Sweeney has identified the difficulties inherent in "Isaiah's complicity with G-d's judgment."[13] Sweeney's post-Holocaust reading brings the problem into clear relief, but it has always been present. Reading the prophetic literature involves the danger that we end up blaming the victims for the disasters that destroyed their lives. Sweeney's counter to this is to refuse to see the great gap between Isaiah 39 and 40 as the true middle of the book. Instead, he places the dramatic center of the book at the beginning of chapter 34, a move consistent with the proposed stages of textual growth described above. The redeeming and comforting words in 34–35 and 40–55, both of which are part of a major revision of the book, surround the experience of death and destruction, but do not remove the experience. The book of Isaiah highlights painful questions but does not resolve them. Israel may suffer because it does not properly recognize the sovereignty of YHWH, but it was YHWH who engineered the blindness and deafness of Israel in 6:9–10 and who bears responsibility for it.[14] Moreover, the prophet who announces this judgment fails to challenge it. Isaiah does not stand up to YHWH, to challenge YHWH's sense of justice like Abraham and Moses did, so Isaiah becomes complicit.[15] The examination of Isaiah as a character in the book below will address the problems surrounding his culpability further.

Discussion Box 2.1 Disability in the Prophetic Literature

The word "blind," or related words, appears about twenty times in the prophetic literature, more than half of those in Isaiah. The words "deaf" and "lame" also appear several times each. There are additional ways to indicate these conditions without using specific words, as the book of Isaiah does at 6:10. Sometimes, in 35:5 for example, the text seems to promise healing for persons with these conditions. At other times these conditions are used as metaphors for a lack of understanding, faith, and conviction, or for acts of stubbornness and disobedience. Until recent years very few, if any, questions arose about the problematic effects of language about disability. What does it mean to a person who is blind, deaf, or lame to have their disability used as a symbol for a lack of faithfulness or obedience? The appearance of disability studies within the field of biblical studies since the 1990s has sought, among other things, to address this situation, but there is a lot of debate within these studies. One important point of disagreement is between the medical model and the social-functional model of identifying disability. The former tends to focus on physical impairment; the latter considers how people function differently in constructed societies.[16] Use of the social-functional model recognizes that identification of disability changes from one culture to another. The Bible often reflects attitudes toward disability in many cultures, including the ones that produced it, attitudes that include stigmatizing and marginalizing persons with these disabilities.[17] Removing such texts from the Bible is not possible, but perhaps careful attention can lead us to use them in a more constructive way. Instead of playing along with the metaphors, which helps to ingrain practices of stigmatization and marginalization, we can use such texts to expose the realities behind them, and then we can seek for better language to talk about the failures of our faith.

Isaiah 1:1 presents the whole book as a vision, and this aspect is important for understanding how the book operates. Though the book is connected to the story of Israel, time does not govern how it participates in that story. Though its central location is Jerusalem, spatial constraints do not contain the vision. Elements of the vision go back to the creation of the world (40:12) and project forward to its total destruction (27:1–3). The book reports the conversations of human beings in the midst of historical situations at precise locations (7:3), and it addresses unidentified listeners at the far edges of the earth (49:1).[18] Keeping the expansive quality of the book in mind will be a vital part of our interpretive work as we look more closely at its settings.

THE SETTINGS OF THE BOOK

The character named Isaiah is often distinguished from the book bearing his name by the designations "Isaiah son of Amoz" or "Isaiah of Jerusalem." The latter title reveals the sometimes overt, sometimes presumed, setting for the first thirty-nine chapters of the book. The narrative portions within this section are sometimes given more precise settings in or around the city, such as the temple (6:1), the highway to the Fuller's Field (7:3; 36:2), or the royal palace (38:1), but much of the oracular material in Isaiah has no specific narrative setting and identifies no particular audience.

With the shift in subject and tone at Isaiah 40, the setting becomes even more nebulous. The scenery described in this chapter is the wilderness, presumably between Babylon and Jerusalem, where the exiles would need to travel to return. Much of what is in Isaiah 40–55 seems addressed to those planning to make this return (e.g., 48:20), but no precise audience or setting for the delivery of these oracles is described. The final eleven chapters once again seem addressed to a Jerusalem audience (e.g., 59:20; 62:1), with temple worship arising as a frequent theme, but this poetic literature also lacks the kind of narrative framework that would make the identification of a more precise setting difficult.

An examination of place names in the book of Isaiah produces some interesting data, which is presented in table 2.3 on page 34.

The chapter ranges in table 2.3 are quite different in quantity: they are divided to demonstrate where certain place names are clustered in the text and the relatively long gaps in which the place names do not appear or are sparse. Jerusalem and Zion, near synonyms of one another, never disappear for long, but they are noticeably more important at the beginning and end of the book, where this city is the primary setting; the occurrence of Jerusalem and Zion diminishes in 40–55, where the experience of exile is primary and Babylon becomes an important setting. Though Egypt may never be the true setting of any of the events in the book, the name of the place appears with surprising frequency. Egypt continues to evoke the past experience of bondage as new threats of such experience appear, and as a great empire it continues to represent a location of power, one that will ultimately come under the judgment of Israel's God, like all other empires. So Egypt is a setting to which the book of Isaiah often points, even if it never takes the reader there.

Table 2.3 Place Names and Their Distribution in Isaiah

Place (#)	Chapters	Occurrences
Jerusalem (51)	1–10	16
	22–37	16
	40–44	5
	51–52	5
	62–66	9
Zion (48)	1–10	12
	12–18	4
	24–37	14
	40–49	4
	51–52	7
	59–66	7
Babylon/Chaldea (19)[19]	13–23	7
	39–48	12
Egypt (53)	7–11	6
	19–23	32
	27–31	8
	36–37	4
	43–52	3
Assyria (44)	7–11	10
	14–27	12
	30–31	2
	36–38	19
	52	1

The coming and going of all these place names can create a bewildering effect, but a feeling of dislocation may be one goal of the book. Mary Mills has proposed that the book of Isaiah operates in two worlds, "the world of everyday political and social affairs and the world of the supernatural."[20] In the imagination of the prophetic book, the two worlds combine to form a wasteland, a setting repeatedly described in Isaiah (1, 5, 6, 24–27).[21] Thus the settings of Isaiah are (1) the great empires around Jerusalem, both in terms of their political reality and their mythical power; (2) Jerusalem, both as a city reeling from threat and destruction and the visionary focal point of Israel's relationship with YHWH; and (3) the wasteland or wilderness, which represents the distance between the Jerusalem of imagination and the Jerusalem of reality.[22]

THE ROLE OF THE PROPHET WITHIN THE BOOK

The call narrative in 6:1–14 introduces the prophet and the readers of the book to his prophetic task; narratives that include Isaiah as a character in Isaiah 7 and 36–39 frame the remainder of the Assyrian portion of the book. The interaction between Isaiah and YHWH in 6:1–13 has characteristic components that resemble the theophanic experiences of Moses (Exod. 3) and Jeremiah (Jer. 1). In all of these cases the human figure offers some initial resistance to the divine call: the consistency of this component should caution against identifying it as a lack of faith or obedience. Instead, it may be best to understand the resistance as an appropriate display of humility. The purifying act of "one of the seraphs," who touches Isaiah's mouth with an ember from the altar, overcomes the objection that he is "a man of unclean lips" from "a people of unclean lips" (6:5–6). Isaiah must be prepared for the task, and subsequent divine speech makes clear that it is not a task Isaiah or anyone else should accept hastily.

The surprising element of the call narrative in Isaiah 6 is the divine response to Isaiah's eventual agreement to accept the prophetic role. Isaiah 6:1–8 is a frequent focus of attention because of its apparent spirit of volunteerism. In verse 8, Isaiah's line "Here am I; send me!" is famous for its use in hymns and slogans used by religious groups that promote this kind of volunteer spirit. Very little attention, in comparison, is given to 6:9–13, the text in which YHWH informs Isaiah that his work as a prophet will be an exercise in futility:

> "Go and say to this people:
>
> 'Keep listening, but do not comprehend;
>   keep looking but do not understand.'
> Make the mind of this people dull,
>   and stop their ears,
>   and shut their eyes,
> so that they may not look with their eyes,
>   and listen with their ears,
> and comprehend with their minds,
>   and turn and be healed."
>
>   (6:9–10)

It is not just that Isaiah's audience will resist his message; the message itself will also strengthen their resistance. The predictable and predicted failure of Isaiah's mission makes little sense if this is where the entire story of his vocation begins; but as the beginning of an inner story, wrapped in an outer story, the delayed response of Israel and the later re-presentation of the message of Isaiah will play a significant role in the growth of the entire book.

Discussion Box 2.2 The Use of Isaiah 6:9–10 in the Christian Gospels

In the Gospel of Mark, the tradition of Jesus telling parables first appears in chapter 4. When asked by his disciples why he tells puzzling stories, Jesus responds in Mark 4:11–12 by quoting parts of Isaiah 6:9–10. The reasoning behind Jesus' reply seems to be that parables create groups of insiders and outsiders. The insiders hear an explanation of the parable and understand its meaning while outsiders remain perplexed. This use of parables becomes a part of the theme often called the Messianic Secret in the Gospel of Mark, the idea that Jesus is keeping his identity a secret from the majority of people. This part of the Gospel of Mark is included in the Gospels of Matthew (13:14–17) and Luke (8:9–10). In all three of the Synoptic Gospels, the parable tradition, using Isaiah 6:9–10, functions to develop a sense of special privilege for the disciples of Jesus, who receive insider status. The focus in Isaiah 6 seems to be more on the obstinacy of the audience, but eventually the book of Isaiah will reveal that Isaiah has disciples who play the role of carriers of his misunderstood message.

Following the story of his visionary experience, YHWH commands Isaiah to meet with Ahaz, the king of Judah. This story of Isaiah meeting with King Ahaz is matched by his interactions with Hezekiah, the son of Ahaz, in chapters 37–39. The royal narratives serve as a bracket around all of the activity of Isaiah son of Amoz in the eighth century. These stories are intensely political and geographical; without some knowledge of Israelite history, parts of them are nearly incomprehensible to present-day readers. Aside from the names of Isaiah and his son Shear-jashub, no less than thirteen additional proper nouns appear in just the nine verses of 7:1–9. Table 2.4 lists these names of people and places according to their relationships with each other. At this point it becomes apparent that the writer of the book of Isaiah expects the reader to know a great deal about the political situation in the area at the time of this meeting between Isaiah and Ahaz.

Table 2.4 Proper Nouns in Isaiah 7

Nations	Cities	Groups	Kings
Judah	Jerusalem	House of David	Ahaz (son of Jotham)
Aram	Damascus		Rezin
Israel	Samaria	Ephraim	Pekah (son of Remaliah)
			Son of Tabeel

The geopolitical context of this meeting is a conflict that historians label the Syro-Ephraimitic War, an event that will continue to form the backdrop for the book of Isaiah through chapter 8. During the decade of the 730s BCE, the Assyrian Empire was expanding to the southwest, from its capital in Mesopotamia. The natural route toward Egypt, the other major power of the time, would have taken this army along the Fertile Crescent, then southward through the Levant, the passable strip of land just east of the Mediterranean Sea; this route included the nations of Aram (Syria), Israel, and Judah, in that order from north to south. The implication of the story in Isaiah 7 is that Aram and Israel agreed to form an alliance against Assyria and tried to coerce Judah to join them. Further, 7:6 indicates that the kings of these two nations, Rezin and Pekah, had been plotting to overthrow Ahaz and replace him as king of Judah with another leader who would be more cooperative with them. This other person is not named directly but is called "the son of Tabeel" (7:6).

Another important element of this part of Isaiah and the role of the character in the book is the symbolic naming of Isaiah's two sons. As the royal narrative in Isaiah 7 opens, the prophet already has a son, whose name Shear-jashub is commonly translated as "A remnant shall return" (7:3). YHWH commands Isaiah to take this son with him to the meeting with the king, though the relationship between the son's name and the message Isaiah is to give the king is unclear. A second son is born to Isaiah and an unnamed female prophet in 8:3, and YHWH specifically commands that he be named Maher-shalal-hash-baz, which means something like "The spoil speeds, the prey hurries" (8:1). God goes on to provide a precise explanation for this name, which reflects the defeat of Damascus (Syria/Aram) and Samaria (northern kingdom, Israel) by the Assyrian army, so it is the name of the second son, which relates more clearly to the situation Isaiah discusses with Ahaz.

The presence of Isaiah's children in Isaiah 7–8 introduces two important aspects of the role of prophetic characters, both of which will appear again in the prophetic literature.[23] The first is the broader use of symbolic actions or sign-acts, episodes in which the prophet performs instead of just speaking. There will be times when the speech of prophetic figures becomes almost disembodied, to the point that the reader may almost forget that the character is actually present, but the prophetic characters will always be intensely present in their symbolic actions. The second aspect is the intertwining of the prophetic characters' lives with their messages. Like Isaiah, Hosea will also give his children names that are related to his proclamation, but Jeremiah, in a dramatic reversal of this kind of prophetic behavior, will be specifically commanded not to marry and have children as part of his prophetic message (16:1–2). It is unclear how these symbolic actions might have functioned in the lives of these prophets outside of the text. Seldom is any attention given to the setting and audience of these acts, or to any kind of reaction from an audience. The sign-acts are literary elements in the prophetic scrolls now, and one of the important functions they perform is the embodiment of prophetic proclamations in the lives of the prophetic characters and their families.

Discussion Box 2.3 Children in the Old Testament

The roles that children play and the attitudes expressed about them in the Old Testament form a set of issues that have received very little attention within biblical scholarship until the past several years. What little attention they did receive generally played along with the text in viewing them as objects of divine promises or components of covenants. A major development in this area has been the 2013 publication of Naomi Steinberg's book *The World of the Child in the Hebrew Bible*. Steinberg's work begins at an important foundational level by seeking a definition of "child" in various parts of the Old Testament, though there is often little textual data with which to work.[24] How old, for example, are we to imagine Cain and Abel to be when Cain kills Abel? Are they still children in any sense? The only prophetic figure clearly portrayed in childhood is Samuel. Steinberg treats this as an important case because Samuel is given or "loaned" to YHWH at a very young age. What does it mean for God to have possession of a child?[25] The only appearances of specific children in the prophetic literature are the symbolically named offspring of Isaiah and Hosea. If naming is an act of taking possession, then YHWH possesses these children too. This makes the status of children in the prophetic literature as troubling as in the rest of the Old Testament. Are they anything more than instruments or symbols?

The text that follows the meeting between Isaiah and Ahaz at the place called the "upper pool on the highway to the Fuller's Field" sounds like another conversation (Isa. 7:3). The grammar of 7:10 makes it unclear whether the second conversation follows immediately in the same location or takes place later and elsewhere. The subject is still the threat posed to Judah by Aram and Israel. An important and intriguing feature of the prophetic literature becomes fully visible at 7:10 when, in the midst of what seems to have begun as a three-way conversation involving YHWH, Isaiah, and Ahaz, the middle personality vanishes. At 7:10 YHWH speaks directly to Ahaz, and the prophet who has been mediating this message, Isaiah, disappears. It is possible to argue, from an abstract and theological perspective, that the voice of the prophet represents the divine voice, but from a narrative perspective it is difficult to take the disappearance of the human character so lightly. One of the narrative challenges for all of biblical literature is how to embody the divine character, so that God may enter into a story with human characters in ordinary settings. Brueggemann has identified five primary ways in which the divine presence is embodied or mediated in the literature of the Old Testament: torah, king, prophet, cult, and sage. Such mediations are necessary because the direct, immediate presence of God is too dangerous, an observation the Israelites make profoundly at Mount Sinai in Exodus 20:18–21.[26] As a mediating voice for God, one that becomes absorbed in the act of speaking, the prophet is also something like the figure sometimes called "the angel of YHWH," a character sometimes present at the beginning of a theophanic experience. Such is the case in the famous burning-bush episode in which the angel first appears to Moses at Exodus 3:2, but is quickly replaced by the divine presence and the divine voice. Isaiah's own theophanic experience in Isaiah 6 is also initiated by an angelic figure. These angels seem to represent the initial, or outer, edge of God's presence that, once penetrated by the human character, is left behind in favor of more direct divine contact. A narrative feature like this can make the prophets unstable narrative characters, whose presence sometimes becomes unnecessary.

One other important question arises from this story. If both prophet and king are mediators of the divine presence, then a meeting and conversation between a prophet and a king is a strange event. It is, in part at least, a divine self-conversation. It is possible to argue that the monarchy in Israel lost its mediating role at some point, whether this was when antimonarchy prophets like Elijah arose or with the reemergence of YHWH as king, as expressed in Psalms 93–99. Nevertheless, in the context of Isaiah 7, the king must make the political decisions for God's people, and the prophet must communicate God's desire to God's people, including the king. Multiple mediations, interacting with each other, create the possibility for tension within the divine personality, a drama that will play out many times within the prophetic literature, and its visible starting point in this text should remain in our memory as we proceed.

The "sign" of "Immanuel" in Isaiah 7:14 and its use in the Gospel of Matthew often distract from an understanding of the role this text plays in the book of Isaiah (see discussion box 2.4). The sign that Ahaz is so reluctant to ask for is intended as a reassurance that the schemes of Pekah and Rezin will not succeed. It is difficult to understand the scene without assuming that Isaiah is visibly present and active within it, even though 7:10 has placed him in the background. Translations like the NRSV, which inserts Isaiah's name in place of the Hebrew third-person masculine-singular pronoun at the beginning of 7:13, clear up some of the ambiguity, but perhaps the ambiguity is intended. The Hebrew word *hinneh*, with which Isaiah begins his description of the sign in 7:14, is still most often translated as "behold," a word not used by most contemporary English speakers, which subsequently has little meaning. This word is often best understood as a command to "look," and that is a likely sense here. Therefore, one reasonable understanding of this verse is that Isaiah points to a young woman who is present at the scene, and who is pregnant at the time. The sign assures Ahaz that Aram and Israel will soon be destroyed, so he should not be intimidated into joining their alliance. The meaning of the sign, however, presents at least two difficulties. First, what it predicts is not immediate. Another sense of ambiguity in the text is the age at which a child "knows how to refuse the evil and choose the good" (7:16). At the very least, relief from the present problem seems several years away for Ahaz. Second, if the Assyrian Empire is going to conquer Aram and Israel so completely, then Judah is next in line, and nothing will stand in the way of the empire's army as it continues to move south. The defeat of Aram and Israel is both good and bad news for Ahaz and his people. The episode ends with a sequence of four "on that day . . ." statements in 7:18–25, which alert their hearers of God's use of Assyria as a weapon of punishment, but the targets of that punishment remain unclear.

The first-person voice of Isaiah, reporting a personal narrative, reappears at 8:1. Isaiah's call narrative in 6:1–13 has been reported in first-person language, but the intervening stories in 7:1–23 switched to third-person reporting. The shift indicates that even the material within this limited portion of the book of Isaiah comes from a variety of sources; yet in the final form of the book, it is also a feature that contributes to the instability of the prophetic character. Isaiah reports the conception and birth of his second son and his interactions with God that are entangled with these personal experiences. Before a long disappearance, he also reveals in 8:16 that he has disciples, a reference that plays an important role both within the story and in our understanding of prophets outside the text. In the past, it has often been popular to understand the prophets as lone figures, detached from the world, including all human relationships. The command by Isaiah for his disciples to preserve his work for a later time sends the prophet deep into the background again, as the book progresses.

In the superscription at the beginning of the oracles against foreign nations in 13:1, the mention of Isaiah's name reminds the reader to see the book as a vision of Isaiah, but Isaiah does not appear as a narrative character again until 20:2. The brief narrative of Isaiah's symbolic action, walking naked and barefoot for three years, sits in the middle of the oracles against foreign nations. The oracles move around significantly in their historical references,

---

Discussion Box 2.4 Isaiah 7:14 and the "Sign of Immanuel" in Christian Tradition

There is much dispute among interpreters about the meaning of Isaiah 7:14; the root of the controversy is closely related to its use in the New Testament in Matthew 1:21–23. The writer of Matthew used the text from Isaiah to help interpret the meaning of the birth of Jesus, and much of the difficulty lies in the word used to describe the young woman in Isaiah 7:14. While the Hebrew word ʿalmah refers to a young woman, in this case probably a wife of Ahaz, the Greek translation of Isaiah in the Septuagint uses the word *parthenos*, which in biblical literature specifically means "virgin," and this is the version that Matthew quotes. The quotation of the Greek text linked it to the Christian tradition of the "virgin birth" of Jesus. However we understand what the writer of Matthew was doing, it is vital to identify the eighth-century meaning of Isaiah's statement if the text is going to make sense in the book of Isaiah. If Isaiah was talking to Ahaz about a child to be born more than seven centuries later, then the advice is useless to a king trying to lead his people in the midst of a challenging threat.

---

some obviously connecting to the Babylonian period, but the story of Isaiah in 20:1–6 brings the reader back to the Assyrian period. As Isaiah fades away again, his role as the eighth-century point of connection in a book in which time is fluid will continue in only a vague manner until his final dramatic appearance in chapters 37–39.

The royal narrative that brings to an end the book's attention to the Assyrian period and the presence of Isaiah as a narrative character presents a new set of questions because of its connection to the narrative in 2 Kings 18–20. Large swaths of this parallel material match word for word, so either one book was the source for the other, or they share a common source. Most scholars have operated from the assumption that the text is original to Kings and that the book of Isaiah took it from there and adapted it for two primary reasons. The first is that this is precisely the kind of narrative material that makes up the rest of the book of Kings, while it stands out as unusual in Isaiah.[27] Second, the two largest differences between the two accounts are (1) the inclusion of the poem recited by Hezekiah in Isaiah 38:9–20, which is missing from 2 Kings; and (2) the inclusion of the story of Hezekiah's surrender and payment of tribute to Assyria in 2 Kings 18:14–16, an account not in Isaiah. It is somewhat easier to understand why the writer of Isaiah would want to add the prayer and omit the story of surrender than why the writer of Kings would want to do the reverse, but this is not a conclusive argument. The lack of decisive evidence for either view means that the logical strength of the first argument above places the burden of proof on those who would try to argue that the book of Isaiah is the original location of the material. Some interpreters have argued that this material was original to a third and now-missing source, and that the book of Isaiah may have either had direct access to this source or obtained the material through the book of Kings.[28] This seems like a balanced resolution to the problem, as long as we acknowledge that if there was a prior source, it was likely one that looked a lot more like the book of Kings than like the book of Isaiah. Within the approach taken in this book, the most important question may not depend significantly on how we resolve the question of priority. Whatever the origins of the material collected in Isaiah 36–39, what is its purpose in the book?

Any answer to the above question requires attention to the relationship between chapters 36–39 and 7–8. Both of these texts involve a meeting between Isaiah son of Amoz and a king of Judah, the father and son combination of Ahaz and Hezekiah. There are two other very specific links between the two stories. One is the location of the initial event in each, "the upper pool on the highway to the Fuller's Field" (7:3; 36:2), and the other is the use of a sign to confirm the prophetic message to the king (7:13–14; 37:30–32; 38:7–8). It is difficult to miss the point that these two stories are to be read as reflections of one another, particularly since some of the problems associated with the first story are resolved in the second. As noted above, the interaction between Isaiah and Ahaz in chapters 7–8 does nothing to resolve the king's larger problem, and may have even made it worse, so the encroachment of the Assyrian army on Judah and Jerusalem has been hanging over the book of Isaiah throughout the intervening chapters. The threat of the Assyrian messenger (the Rabshakeh), delivered in his meeting with Hezekiah's representatives at the upper pool, sends Hezekiah to Isaiah for counsel, and the meetings between the prophet and this king are significantly different from those involving his father.

In 37:6 Isaiah begins his message to Hezekiah as he had with Ahaz, "Do not be afraid. . . ." After Hezekiah prays, he receives another message from Isaiah assuring deliverance from Assyria, an assurance that is followed by a confirming sign in 37:30–32, but like the sign given to Ahaz, this one will take some time to come into full view, so the sudden demise of the Assyrian army that immediately follows comes as a surprise. The end of the Assyrian advance toward Jerusalem is a stunning text, in its brevity and ferocity. In just two verses, 37:36–37, the book reports the sudden overnight death of 185,000 Assyrian troops and the departure of King Sennacherib to his capital, Nineveh. Elsewhere, in 2 Kings 18:13–16 and Isaiah 36:1–2, reports of the

Assyrian army destroying many Judean cities and trying to force the surrender of Hezekiah have a sense of historical veracity, but how can that be put together with the claim that Israel's God inflicted a miraculous defeat on the Assyrians? Virtually all interpreters have been forced to conclude that there were multiple traditions about Hezekiah and the Assyrian army during the events of 701 BCE. The conflicts between these traditions cannot be resolved historically, however, because the claims in this portion of the book of Isaiah are literary and ideological.[29] In the world being constructed by the book of Isaiah, it may not matter which of the reports is true outside of the text, as long as the story of Judah is allowed to continue.

The first face-to-face meeting between Isaiah and Hezekiah takes place because of Hezekiah's illness in 38:1. Many elements of the story are confusing, and God's behavior toward Hezekiah does not have a clear cause or purpose in the text. Why sentence him to death and then alter the sentence after the prayer, causing Isaiah to have to turn back for an additional meeting? The promise of deliverance from the Assyrians in 38:6 is apparently misplaced because the event has already happened in the previous chapter. Finally, the fatal disease from which God heals Hezekiah in 38:5 becomes simply a boil, for which Isaiah must make a fig compress in 38:21. It is difficult not to draw comparisons between this illness and the Assyrian threat. In both cases God only delays the eventual death or destruction, and the severity of the initial threat and cause of the reprieve are both unclear.

The appearance of Isaiah as a character and the portion of the book of Isaiah addressing the Assyrian period both come to an end in Isaiah 39. The strange little story of the Babylonian envoys is also reported in 2 Kings 20, and it points toward the next crisis in the story of Israel. The difference, as indicated in an earlier discussion, is that Isaiah never directly reports the invasion of the Babylonian army, as 2 Kings does in its final chapter; this shows that Isaiah wants to point beyond the cataclysm. The tour of the envoys thus serves in Isaiah as a stand-in narrative for the invasion. The vision of the book of Isaiah must now compete with a Babylonian vision, which not only sees everything, but also must have all that it sees, for this is the goal of empire. Isaiah's response in 39:5–7 to Hezekiah's answer about the envoys is harsh, and Hezekiah's reply to that response is unsettling in its apparent selfishness. Nevertheless, the idea of "peace and security" at any time, even if temporary, may sound different to a beleaguered and defeated people. With this peaceful space in time and the devastation that will punctuate it hanging together in the air that holds the conversation of prophet and king—a conversation between mediations of the divine, and thus a divine self-conversation—Isaiah son of Amoz vanishes. In chapters 4 and 8 (below), when this book returns to a discussion of the book of Isaiah, it will focus on ways the Servant of YHWH in Isaiah 40–55 and the "servants" of 56–66 may be understood as extensions or developments of this original character.

THE PROCLAMATION OF ISAIAH
CONCERNING THE ASSYRIAN PERIOD

We have examined the structure of the entire book of Isaiah, the settings that appear in the book, and the way the character named Isaiah operates within the book; now it is possible to determine more precisely what the book says about the Assyrian crisis of the late eighth century in Judah. In the previous section the focus on the prophetic character named Isaiah allowed a careful examination of the two royal narratives forming a bracket around the parts of Isaiah that seem to have the eighth century and the Assyrian crisis in view. At the end of chapter 8, the receding of the prophetic character into the book's background may have left readers uncertain of the future. God's interactions with Ahaz, as indicated above, had resolved short-term problems but left long-term ones unattended. The next few chapters of the book of Isaiah begin to address these unresolved issues in three ways. First, two passages promise new leadership for Judah, though these are difficult for Christian readers to read in context. Isaiah 9:1–7 and 11:1–9 have received such heavy use in Christian tradition that their immediate context in Isaiah is obscured. In the midst of the portrayals of Ahaz and Hezekiah, these texts seem to point toward the latter as a model of a faithful and righteous king. While there may be some timeless sense of an ideal king here as well, this immediate sense is the one that would have had meaning for the audience in Isaiah's time. Second, the divine attitude toward Assyria begins to shift here, particularly in 10:5–19. God acknowledges that:

> Ah, Assyria, the rod of my anger—
> the club in their hands is my fury!
> (10:5)

Nevertheless, God also states that Assyria has overstepped its bounds as a divine weapon and has acted arrogantly, so judgment will come upon Assyria when it finishes playing its role. Third, whatever difficulty and destruction may befall Israel and Judah, there will always be a remnant of these nations left that YHWH will restore. All of these elements seem to coalesce in the brief poetic text in 12:1–6. The claim in 12:1 is sufficiently flexible, however, to allow for many different understandings. The timing of "in that day," which echoes 11:10 and 11:11, is ambiguous: even if it refers to the reign of

Hezekiah, it allows for other uses as well. More significantly, the admission of the singer seems uncertain about cause:

> I will give thanks to you, O LORD,
>   for though you were angry with me,
> your anger turned away,
>   and you comforted me.
>
>   (12:1)

The change in divine attitude could be the result of repentance, but that is difficult to reconcile with YHWH's words to Isaiah in 6:9–10. It seems more likely to be a gracious divine choice, but that raises questions about why so many others have suffered destruction before this divine turning. As 10:4 has acknowledged earlier, "His anger has not turned away."

Most interpreters understand the end of chapter 12 as an important division in the book. It may be understood as a "concluding hymn of thanksgiving," and it contains allusions from various psalms and the Song of the Sea in Exodus 15.[30] The text functions as a recapitulation of the previous parts of the book, yet it also functions well in the present position as a transition from Isaiah 11 to the oracles concerning the foreign nations, beginning with Babylon in 13–14.[31] The declaration in 12:6, "great in your midst is the Holy One of Israel," is a statement that fits the idea sometimes labeled "the inviolability of Zion," which is expressed in a number of places in Isaiah, perhaps most forcefully in 31:4–5.[32] The idea apparently developed that, because YHWH dwelled in the temple in Jerusalem, YHWH would never allow the holy city to be invaded or defeated. The experience of the Assyrian period would seem to have affirmed this principle, but the full book of Isaiah would eventually need to deal with this notion's crushing failure.[33] With that idea established for the moment, however, the view of the book of Isaiah is ready to turn outward.

Like the entire book of Isaiah, the series of Oracles against the Nations in 13–23 was the subject of some reshaping in the Babylonian period. The addition of at least the sections that specifically aim the divine anger at Babylon, 13:2–14:23 and 21:1–10, seems fairly certain. This would mean the brief oracle against Assyria in 14:24–27 had been at the head of a list of Israel's older enemies, such as Philistia, Moab, and Damascus. Table 2.5 has a full list of the elements in this section and the nations against whom they proclaim judgment.

The list in table 2.5 demonstrates that Isaiah 10–23 is the focal point of the oracles against foreign nations, but there are such oracles lying outside of the collection. By contrast, there are a few parts of Isaiah 10–23 that do not fit the category, most notably the small narrative about Isaiah in 20:1–6 and the oracle against Judah/Jerusalem in 22:1–25.

Table 2.5 Oracles against the Nations in Isaiah

Text	Nation
10:5–19	Assyria
13:1–22	Babylon
14:3–23	Babylon
14:24–27	Assyria
14:28–32	Philistia
15:1–16:14	Moab
17:1–14	Damascus
18:1–7	Ethiopia
19:1–25	Egypt
21:1–10	Babylon
21:11–12	Dumah (Edom?)
21:13–17	the desert plain (northern Arabia)
22:1–25	Judah/Jerusalem
23:1–18	Tyre
47:1–15	Babylon

Isaiah 24–27 may operate as a conclusion to the collection of oracles concerning the nations or, more generally, to a section that turns its attention outside of Israel. Isaiah 24–27 has often been called the Isaian Apocalypse: it addresses the destruction of the earth, which would include all of the nations in chapters 13–23. A larger discussion of 24–27 will wait until chapter 8 of this book, because of its apparent connections to 56–66 and the Restoration period; yet in the final form of Isaiah, 24–27 plays a role as the climax of YHWH's judgment on the world. Oracles concerning foreign nations serve at least two important purposes in the prophetic books, and the series in Isaiah 13–23 is the first one readers encounter in the canonical progression. First, oracles concerning foreign nations demonstrate the power of Israel's God, YHWH, whose judgment reigns over the entire earth, according to this section. Second, YHWH has used some of the nations, most notably Assyria and Babylon, as tools or weapons to punish Israel. The oracles let Israel and the nations they address know that, from a longer perspective, these weapons of punishment will ultimately suffer the vengeance of YHWH for the role they play in punishing Israel.

Most interpreters see Isaiah 28–33 as a distinct unit that continues where Isaiah 12 left off, and some have argued for a sense of cohesion in the unit, despite its often-fragmented feel. The proclamations of Isaiah here apparently relate to the continued threats of Assyria in the last two decades of the eighth century.[34] The section falls into two parts, the first (Isa. 28–31) built around a series of "woe pronouncements" and the second (32–33) returning to the subject of the future of the monarchy, which was prominent in 9–12. One of the important features of 28–31 and 32–33, which is also the case for 9–12, is that the predominant oracles of judgment are always followed by more positive statements.[35]

Isaiah 34 and 35 may operate as a unified pair of poems. Peter Miscall has helped to illuminate these poems and their relationship by drawing on understandings of fantasy in literature. Miscall labeled the two poems "a nightmare and a dream" and wove them into his approach to the book of Isaiah, which he describes like this:

> I do not read Isaiah as a clear and simplistic morality tale in which Israel is ultimately saved and all other nations are destroyed or subjected to Israel, even though such a morality tale is part of the vision of Isaiah. That is, there are passages that assert it, but they are then contrasted or contradicted by passages that portray prosperity or restoration for all, or at least all who are righteous, who are YHWH's servants. There are also grim passages, such as 2:11, in which YHWH comes in wrath against the world and all humanity.[36]

Whether or not "fantasy" is the right label for the book of Isaiah or parts of it, a reading like this opens up enormous possibilities for the book by detaching it from the demands of a chronological sequence of causes and effects in the world outside of the text, and Isaiah 34–35 plays a crucial role in developing the literary world of the final form of Isaiah, a world that is different from the one readers inhabit.[37] Isaiah 34–35 continues the patterns of tension concerning two themes that have been present throughout the book, destruction and restoration. We will return to this part of Isaiah in chapter 4 of this book because it appears to be a way that a later version of the book of Isaiah reaches back in order to surround catastrophic events with the possibility of salvation and restoration.

ISAIAH INTERRUPTED

The early part of this chapter described the great gap in the book of Isaiah that lies between chapters 39 and 40. While this chapter has examined the literary structure of the whole book of Isaiah and some other aspects of the entire scroll, a more careful reading of its contents must pause here because the book jumps over more than a century and a half. The next chapter will introduce the Book of the Twelve in a similar way and present its proclamation concerning the events of the Assyrian period in the eighth century, allowing us to listen to the two scrolls that address this period together.

Before moving on from Isaiah, a summary of a few important points may be helpful. Within Isaiah 6–39, the book speaks words of judgment concerning both Judah and the northern kingdom, Israel. Isaiah predicts the destruction of the northern kingdom, which takes place within the scope of the life and work of the character named Isaiah. It also celebrates the miraculous rescue of Judah and Jerusalem from a pending Assyrian invasion and generates the idea that YHWH will always protect Jerusalem because of the presence of the temple there. Such proclamations, predictions, and events create some theological challenges. First, in the aftermath of the annihilation of the northern kingdom by the Assyrian army, is it fair to say that all of those who suffered in this event deserved their fate? Second, if the defeat of the north was justified divine punishment, then why was Judah spared even though Isaiah proclaims the disobedience and idolatry of its citizens as well? Third, if destruction does come to Judah and Jerusalem in the future, how would destruction be understood in the light of YHWH's deliverance in the past?

Two subsequent chapters of this book will continue the discussion about the book of Isaiah. Chapter 4 will address what appears to be a major reworking of the book in the wake of the Babylonian crisis, a process that added new material to the book and reframed the existing material, perhaps in response to the kinds of questions raised in the previous paragraph. Chapter 8 will return to the book of Isaiah and its relationship to the struggles of Judah in the restoration process during the Persian era. Again, new circumstances led to the production of more material and the recasting of the parts of Isaiah that already existed. Claims about God's judgment and destruction or deliverance of people in the past may not have made sense or may not have been usable in the light of later circumstances. A rereading of the book of Isaiah in these later periods involved rewriting it as well. In light of subsequent events, old theological claims have to be renegotiated and reframed. Eventually rewriting the book became no longer possible, and it reached a finished form, like the one we have today; yet this did not stop the process of reading and reinterpreting the book that is now ours. Our own reading must be a process of renegotiating theological claims in our own world, a process that models what is happening in the book itself, lest the alternative world that the book of Isaiah struggles to envision becomes co-opted by, and captive to, the powers in control of the world outside the text.

Resources for Further Research

Commentaries

Here and in following chapters, useful commentaries are listed with three classifications:

A. Usable to readers without formal theological education.
B. Assuming significant awareness of issues and terminology in academic biblical studies.
C. Assuming a high level of technical skill and ability to work with biblical languages.

The lines between these categories are not simple and clear, and some commentaries are close to the boundaries. Those comfortable using commentaries which fall into the *C* category may still find valuable ideas with which to interact in commentaries from the other categories.

Blenkinsopp, Joseph. *Isaiah 1–39: A New Translation with Introduction and Commentary*. New York: Doubleday, 2000. (C)

Brueggemann, Walter. *Isaiah 1–39*. Louisville, KY: Westminster John Knox Press, 1998. (A)

Childs, Brevard. *Isaiah: A Commentary*. Louisville, KY: Westminster John Knox Press, 2000. (B)

Tucker, Gene M. "The Book of Isaiah 1–39." In *The New Interpreter's Bible*, edited by Leander E. Keck et al., 6:25–305. Nashville: Abingdon Press, 2001. (B)

Tull, Patricia K. *Isaiah 1–39*. Macon, GA: Mercer University Press, 2010. (B)

Watts, John D. W. *Isaiah 1–33*. Rev. ed. Waco: Word, 2004. (C)

Williamson, H. G. M. *A Critical and Exegetical Commentary on Isaiah 1–27*. Vol. 1. New York: T&T Clark, 2006. (C)

Monographs and Other Studies

Blenkinsopp, Joseph. *Opening the Sealed Book: Interpretations of Isaiah in Late Antiquity*. Grand Rapids: Wm. B. Eerdmans Publishing Co., 2006.

Clements, Ronald E. *Jerusalem and the Nations: Studies in the Book of Isaiah*. Sheffield: Sheffield Phoenix, 2011.

Conrad, Edgar W. *Reading Isaiah*. Minneapolis: Fortress Press, 1991.

Quinn-Miscall, Peter D. *Reading Isaiah: Poetry and Vision*. Louisville, KY: Westminster John Knox Press, 2001.

Sawyer, John F. A. *The Fifth Gospel: Isaiah in the History of Christianity*. Cambridge: Cambridge University Press, 1996.

Seitz, Christopher R. *Zion's Final Destiny: The Development of the Book of Isaiah*. Minneapolis: Fortress Press, 1991.

Book of
the Twelve

Isaiah

Assyrian
Crisis | Chapter 2 | | | **Chapter 3**

722

Jeremiah

Ezekiel

Babylonian
Crisis | Chapter 4 | Chapter 5 | Chapter 6 | Chapter 7

586

Restoration
Crisis | Chapter 8 | Chapter 9 | Chapter 10 | Chapter 11

525

3

The Scroll of the Twelve

Introduction and Response to the Assyrian Crisis

It is still a habit in many places to refer to the collection of "books" from Hosea to Malachi as the Minor Prophets, as opposed to Isaiah, Jeremiah, and Ezekiel, which are Major Prophets. The origins of the phrase are difficult to determine and may go back into late antiquity. When the words are taken in terms of their Latin roots and earlier English usage to mean primarily "large" and "small," such designations are appropriate. In contemporary English, however, *minor* has evolved to mean less significant or less important, and such a designation for this literature is not appropriate. A resolution to the problem of naming the collection exists in the long tradition within Judaism of referring to it as the Book of the Twelve, or simply as the Twelve. Table 3.1 demonstrates that the entire collection is comparable in size to the other three prophetic scrolls. An additional benefit to the collective name is the indication it provides that the Book of the Twelve might be viewed as a literary whole. In Judaism this is the fourth scroll of the Latter Prophets, which balances the four scrolls of the Former Prophets—Joshua, Judges, Samuel, and Kings. In most forms of the Christian Old Testament, the Book of the Twelve has the distinction of bringing the canon to a close.

Table 3.1 Lengths of the Prophetic Scrolls in Verses

Prophetic Scroll	Number of Verses
Isaiah	1,291
Jeremiah	1,364
Ezekiel	1,273
the Book of the Twelve	1,050

The first large interpretive question concerning the Book of the Twelve is whether to read it first as a collection forming a single, unified scroll, or whether the individual identity of each part should have priority. Some interpreters have argued for the latter, because each of twelve little books is self-contained, with a superscription that introduces the prophet.[1] This seems a lot of weight to place on what is, in some cases (e.g., Joel, Nahum, and Habakkuk), the barest of introductions, at least one of which (Malachi) looks like it may have been produced as a means of fitting that component into the collection. The presence of multiple internal superscriptions does not make the Book of the Twelve different from the other three prophetic scrolls. Isaiah has a few internal superscriptions, and Jeremiah and Ezekiel each have many. Only the presence of multiple names is a unique feature. Other interpreters favor placing a unified approach first, and then a move toward examining the smaller parts, as they might tend to do with the other three prophetic scrolls.[2] The mixed results of an inquiry into this question seems to point toward a mixed response, a reading that moves back and forth between emphasis on the components and emphasis on the whole, rather than giving either a distinct priority. One reason for a balanced approach is that the twelve components are so different. Amos and Hosea are large pieces of literature, with their own internal structure and a complex history of composition; but Obadiah, Nahum, and Habakkuk are small pieces of literature that seem to be looking for a larger context in which to fit. The dispute may end up looking like the old question about the bicycle. Do we understand it best by starting with the whole, seeing what a bicycle looks like and what it can do? Or do we start with an examination of the parts and ask what each is for? In this analogy we may discover that the book of Amos is like a wheel, a large complex part that can be studied independently, revealing a lot about its purpose on its own. On the other hand, the little "book" of Obadiah is more like a spoke. By itself it is just a piece of wire and reveals almost nothing of its purpose. A reading process that moves back and forth between parts and the whole seems appropriate and matches the approach this study takes to the other books of the prophetic literature.

A second question arises: when we do begin to look at the full collection, which order of the components should we consider? The order of the units within the Book of the Twelve varies somewhat, depending on the manuscript tradition we examine. The two primary ways of ordering the components are displayed in table 3.2. English Bibles tend to follow the order found in Hebrew manuscripts like the Leningrad Codex and other manuscripts from the Masoretic tradition. The major Greek codices present a slightly different order, with Joel moving down to the fourth position and Micah up to the third, leaving Amos second.[3]

Table 3.2 Sequence of Parts in the Book of the Twelve

Masoretic Manuscripts and English Versions	*Septuagint Manuscripts*
Hosea	Hosea
Joel	Amos
Amos	Micah
Obadiah	Joel
Jonah	Obadiah
Micah	Jonah
Nahum	Nahum
Habakkuk	Habakkuk
Zephaniah	Zephaniah
Haggai	Haggai
Zechariah	Zechariah
Malachi	Malachi

Can we determine the reasoning behind the order? If each of the twelve parts is assigned to the historical period that it primarily addresses, what emerges is an order close to the Masoretic (MT) list on the left in table 3.2, and even closer to the Septuagint (LXX) list on the right, with a couple of exceptions. Zephaniah would move up several positions and Obadiah down a few, while Joel resists any kind of placement in such a scheme. The best conclusion we can reach is that chronology was a significant consideration in the ordering of the Twelve, yet other factors must have played a role.

Factors other than historical chronology may have included the ways that those forming the scroll wanted the audience to read it. Some scholars have argued that the MT order came first and that the LXX moves Hosea, Amos, and Micah together at the front of the list because their superscriptions are so similar, which was a primarily historical concern.[4] Others, however, have claimed that throughout its first three books the order represented in the LXX maintains a focus primarily on the northern kingdom, Israel, and then uses Joel as a transition to an emphasis on the place of Jerusalem among the nations in its Obadiah-Jonah-Nahum sequence. The focus of LXX comes back squarely on Jerusalem in the Habakkuk-Zephaniah-Haggai-Zechariah sequence.[5] This LXX order is earlier because it "indicates an interest in portraying the experience of the northern kingdom of Israel as a model for understanding that of Jerusalem and Judah, whereas the Masoretic sequence focuses on Jerusalem throughout."[6] These are "two very different organizational principles," the latter of which fits better with the concerns of the Persian period and the reestablishment of Jerusalem.[7] The greatest challenge to the argument that the LXX order came first lies in the manuscript evidence itself. The earliest appearance of the MT order is relatively late, in the second century BCE in Judean Desert Scrolls; the LXX ordering of the books is not present in any preserved manuscripts until six or seven centuries later. Those taking this position may counter that most scholars consider the LXX version of Jeremiah found in these manuscripts to be more original than the version in the Masoretic Text.[8] The Jeremiah analogy makes the argument seem plausible, but the manuscripts among the Dead Sea Scrolls confirm the existence of both versions of Jeremiah, in Hebrew and in the first century. Questions concerning which order is older or more original may be unanswerable, but perhaps an examination of how the collection might have come together can shed some light on the issue.

There are some indications that there were earlier stages in the development of the collection. Some readers have proposed an early Hosea-Amos-Micah-Zephaniah complex, a "Book of the Four."[9] These four books have superscriptions that look very similar in form, and their focus is on the destruction of the northern kingdom and the pending Assyrian threat to the kingdom of Judah. Nearly all interpreters agree that there are connections between Haggai and Zechariah 1–8, though some have gone even further in positing an originally independent "Haggai/Zechariah 1–8 corpus."[10] It is difficult, however, to postulate a sequence of events that would have brought these preexisting units together and added the additional books to move the collection toward its present state. What has emerged is the idea of a "Book of the Nine," which did not yet have Joel, Obadiah, and Jonah. The primary support for this, however, is that the positions of Joel, Obadiah, and Jonah are relatively unstable in the manuscript traditions compared to the other nine books. The exclusion of Jonah from the nine, though, seems entirely dependent on it being placed at the end of the collection in the Greek manuscript carrying the Book of the Twelve found among the Dead Sea Scrolls. Yet it is tenuous to place the weight of an argument on one manuscript appearing among a collection that often adjusts texts to fit its own purposes. Moreover, the sense of movement and instability of a particular component can be misperceived. Does Joel move so that it is second in the Masoretic order and fourth in the LXX? Or does it sit still while others move from one side of it to the other? The latter case would lead to the evaluation of Amos and Micah as unstable. The contentious discussion above is intended to illustrate that, beyond a few reasonable propositions, the process of composition of the Book of the Twelve cannot be determined, leaving a clear case for which order should have priority elusive. The discussion below will try to give attention to both ways of ordering the books, yet it will lean toward the Masoretic order because it is used in almost all English Bibles.

One final issue to consider is the status of the book known as Malachi, at the end of the collection. The opening words of this book, "An oracle, the word of YHWH unto Israel" (AT), match the opening words of Zechariah 12 precisely, and these two are a partial match with the opening of Zechariah 9:1. Coupled with the recognition that the word *Malachi* itself could mean "my messenger" instead of being a proper name, these observations point toward the possibility that what is now the "book" of Malachi was at one point the final section of the book of Zechariah, which was broken off and given its own name in order to create a twelfth component.

Despite the canonical distance between them, there are remarkable similarities between the book of Isaiah and the Book of the Twelve. The similarity is apparent from the first verse, as the superscription in Hosea 1:1 closely resembles the one found in Isaiah 1:1. Each of them name the same four Judean kings, while Hosea signals its northern orientation by adding Jeroboam son of Joash as the king of Israel to the book's opening. The Book of the Twelve also spans a similar time period, from the middle of the eighth century to some point in the fifth century, addressing all three of the major crises in the life of Israel. The discussion below will also demonstrate that the Book of the Twelve possesses the same kind of polarity in its movement from judgment to deliverance. If taken as a whole, the various narrative characters, most notably Hosea, Amos, Jonah, and Haggai, come and go with an irregularity similar to Isaiah son of Amoz. There is no way to say with certainty that one of these scrolls deliberately follows the pattern of the other. One can only assert that there seems to be a common understanding of a template for prophetic scrolls that lies behind the two of them. Many aspects of such a template are also present in the scrolls of Jeremiah and Ezekiel.

THE STRUCTURE OF THE BOOK

The components of the Book of the Twelve that specifically address the Assyrian period are Hosea, Amos, Micah, and Nahum. The final three components—Haggai, Zechariah, and Malachi—clearly relate to the period of the Restoration, after the Babylonian captivity; and two of the parts in the center, Habakkuk and Zephaniah, address the Babylonian period. Therefore it is impossible to deny that the chronological sequence of three crises in the life of Israel during the eighth through fifth centuries is a major factor that shapes the collection of materials in this scroll. Nevertheless, it is not a simple chronological movement. Some of the books, especially Joel and Jonah, defy easy placement, and there is chronological development within some of the larger components of the Book of the Twelve. The book of Hosea, for example, can be divided into three major sections. The first of these, Hosea 1–3, is closely related to the prophet's family and seems to be connected almost entirely to the eighth century, consisting primarily of warnings of divine judgment. The second section, Hosea 4–11, raises the possibility of repentance yet recognizes the failure of such a possibility; by the end of this section, the destruction of Israel seems a reality. The final few chapters recognize the brutality of the punishment and offer eventual healing and restoration. It is likely that at least Hosea, Amos, and Micah were the subject of internal revisions in the light of later events.

The introduction to this chapter pointed to some variations in the order of the books and concluded that historical references played a significant role in determining this order but were not the only factor in play. What else may have shaped the collection? One possibility is that the books are arranged in order to develop and emphasize major ideas or themes. Many interpreters have recognized the significance of the idea of "the day of YHWH" in the Book of the Twelve, and table 3.3 demonstrates the distribution of this phrase within the book.

Table 3.3 The Day of YHWH in the Book of the Twelve

Book	References
Joel	1:15; 2:1, 11, 31; 3:14
Amos	5:18 (2 times); 5:20
Obadiah	15
Zephaniah	1:7, 8, 14 (2 times), 18; 2:2, 3
Malachi	4:5

In addition to these seventeen occurrences of the full phrase, the shorter phrases "the day" or "that day" appear dozens of times in the Book of the Twelve, with apparent reference in many of these cases to the day of YHWH.

The function of Joel in the second position may be to introduce this phrase and its attendant concept. A second significant theme in the Book of the Twelve is the fertility of the land.[11] Again, this theme is a major part of the little book of Joel, which begins by describing a locust plague that has stripped the land bare.

It is also possible that the books were so placed to put certain types of literary units in specific places. Another prominent feature in the first half of the book of Isaiah that finds a counterpart in the Book of the Twelve is the Oracles against the Nations. In the Book of the Twelve, this announcement of divine wrath against Israel's enemies is a collective effort. Table 3.4 lists the elements of the Book of the Twelve that fit into this category. The list reveals that the focus of the Book of the Twelve and its threats of divine punishment stay squarely on the Israelites throughout the portions called Hosea and Joel, and that the part called Amos turns the attention of the reader outward. The list of international culprits is familiar, yet unlike Isaiah 13–23, Amos does not include the great empires of the ancient Near East: Egypt, Assyria, and Babylon. Only the smaller, closer neighbors of Israel—Syria (Damascus), the Philistines (Gaza), Tyre, Edom, Ammon, and Moab—are included. The purpose of this geography becomes clear in 2:4 and 2:6 when Judah and Israel are included in the rhythmic pattern of judgment. Thus the idea of oracles against foreign nations is at least partially subverted here.

Table 3.4 Oracles against the Nations in the Book of the Twelve

Location	Nation(s)
Amos 1:3–5	Damascus (Syria/Aram)
Amos 1:6–8	Gaza/Ashdod/Ekron (Philistines)
Amos 1:9–10	Tyre
Amos 1:11–12	Edom
Amos 1:13–15	Ammon
Amos 2:1–3	Moab
Obadiah 1–21	Edom
Jonah 3:4	Nineveh (Assyria)
Nahum 1:1–3:19	Nineveh (Assyria)
Zephaniah 2:1–15	Philistines, Moab, Ammon, Assyria, Ethiopians

This subversion finds another expression in the book of Jonah. The proclamation of Jonah against Nineveh, which is assigned to the prophet by YHWH in 1:2 and 3:2, is pronounced in one short sentence in 3:4. While this is a declaration of pending divine destruction, its end result is the repentance of the Ninevites, which causes God to decide not to destroy them in 3:10. Lest this be the last word, however, the little book of Nahum comes soon after Jonah, completing the sporadic sequence of oracles against the nations by using all three of its chapters to rail against Nineveh. In the Masoretic ordering of the books, which is followed by most English Bibles, Micah sits between Jonah and Nahum to bring attention back to Jerusalem and the threat of divine judgment on Jerusalem in the Assyrian period. The reappearance of a section of oracles against foreign nations later, in Zephaniah, demonstrates that such expressions are not completely restricted to the primary collection within the scroll. Outlying elements like this are present in other prophetic scrolls as well.

THE SETTINGS OF THE BOOK

An examination of the settings in the Book of the Twelve is important for several reasons, not least of which is that this is the only prophetic scroll that takes the reader into the northern kingdom, Israel. The first indication of a northern perspective appears immediately in Hosea 1:1, as discussed above, when the name of Jeroboam son of Joash is included in the superscription along with the Judean kings Uzziah, Jotham, Ahaz, and Hezekiah. The early parts of the Book of the Twelve operate primarily from a northern setting, the primary exception being the book of Joel, which makes multiple references to Zion (Jerusalem). The book of Amos diversifies this setting by opening with a sequence of oracles against foreign nations, including Israel's near neighbors such as Damascus, the Philistine cities, Moab, Ammon, Tyre, and Edom; then it comes back to Israel and Judah. When Amos becomes more focused in its attention, the setting is northern Israel, specifically its worship centers in Samaria, Bethel, and Gilgal. Collectively, the first four components of the Book of the Twelve treat settings in much the same way as the book of Isaiah. The actual positions of the writer and the reader are often ambiguous, and specific place names offer locations that are sometimes only gazed at from afar. Egypt, for example, appears often, in texts like Hosea 9, Amos 9, and Micah 7, where it serves as a recollection of captivity and hardship in the past and a threat of abandonment in the future.

The settings of the little book of Jonah sometimes become more concrete, as is often the case when a prophetic figure steps forward as a narrative character. His location at the beginning of the book is uncertain, but then he travels to the city of Joppa and ends up on a boat in the Mediterranean Sea. We lose track of Jonah's geography when he is swallowed by the fish, then spewed onto "dry land" in an unspecified location, but he quickly travels to the city of Nineveh. Along with Jonah, the book of Nahum also draws attention to the Assyrian Empire and its capital, Nineveh, but this time with vengeful threats of divine destruction pronounced from afar.

The book of Micah makes Jerusalem its primary setting. In the Masoretic ordering of the books, this marks a distinct shift from north to south, which becomes necessary as the Book of the Twelve moves beyond the Assyrian period, during which the northern kingdom of Israel was dispersed. While Nahum is entirely an oracle against Nineveh, it specifically addresses Judah as its audience in 1:15. With the Babylonian and Restoration crises as the primary points of reference for the remainder of the Book of the Twelve, and northern kingdom (Israel) dispersed, Judah and Jerusalem become the primary setting for the remainder of the scroll. The last significant narrative texts, those found in the book of Haggai, are set in Jerusalem, some specifically in the rebuilt temple, which becomes the site for the disputes about worship and priesthood in Malachi.

THE ROLE OF THE PROPHETS WITHIN THE BOOK

The discussion of the prophet(s) as a character in the Book of the Twelve offers a particular challenge in this work because the character is not singular. Of the twelve names that are assigned to portions of this prophetic scroll, four can be said to appear as significant narrative characters: Hosea, Amos, Jonah, and Haggai. There is some slight development of Zechariah as a character, but the other seven appear only as names in superscriptions, six of them only a single time in the first verse of their "book." If taken collectively, this means that the prophetic character in the Book of the Twelve appears about as sporadically as Isaiah, an observation that leads first to the character named Hosea, whose personal story opens the Book of the Twelve, a prophet who has a great deal in common with Isaiah.

The superscription in Hosea 1:1 places Hosea, son of Beeri, in historical context using the same sequence of four Judean kings as Isaiah 1:1, with one northern king, Jeroboam, added as a signal of Hosea's location. Like Isaiah, Hosea has children to whom he gives symbolic names related to his prophetic message, an act that entwines the prophet's vocation and personal life together. One important difference is the identification of the mother of Hosea's children, Gomer, by name; this difference is magnified when the divine voice identifies Gomer as a "wife of whoredom" (1:2). Yet the use of Hosea's family becomes a particular problem because of this and other negative characterizations. In obedience to a divine command, Hosea gives his children names with strong negative connotations. The first, a son, is named for the sight of a massacre, Jezreel (1:4–5); a subsequent daughter and son are given names that signify God's pending punishment of Israel, *Lo-ruhamah* (No mercy) and *Lo-ammi* (Not my people) (1:6–9). The text of Hosea gives no attention to the lives of these children: by no choice of their own, they must carry the weight of these terrible names.

It is common to interpret the first chapter of the book of Hosea as a text that is intended to shock its listeners. If Hosea's primary audience is male, then the portrayal of God as a husband who has been betrayed by an unfaithful spouse, Israel, may have had such a shocking effect. This is a challenge for modern readers, however, because the text promotes brutality and public humiliation (2:1–3) as an appropriate response to this perceived infidelity.

The character named Amos stays far in the background for most of the book named for him. He is introduced in a superscription in 1:1 that places

Discussion Box 3.1 The Marriage Metaphor in Prophetic Literature

The use of the marriage relationship to talk about the relationship between YHWH and Israel has been the subject of intense attention over the last three decades. Before the development of feminist biblical scholarship, this was not the case, unfortunately, as the use of this metaphor was typically accepted without any question of its assumptions or consequences. This gap has been filled by no less than four book-length studies of the phenomenon in 1995 to 2008: *Battered Love: Marriage, Sex, and Violence in the Hebrew Prophets*, by Renita Weems; *The Prostitute and the Prophet: Hosea's Marriage in Literary Perspective*, by Yvonne Sherwood; *Love and Violence: Marriage as Metaphor for the Relationship between YHWH and Israel in the Prophetic Books*, by Gerlinde Baumann; and *Sexual and Marital Metaphors in Hosea, Jeremiah, Isaiah, and Ezekiel*, by Sharon Moughtin-Mumbry. These works, along with many of smaller scope, have focused on the three primary problems related to this literary tool, which appears in several of the prophetic books but is most prominent in Hosea. First, in the metaphorical relationship and the God-Israel relationship that is compared to it, the husband is always presumed to be the innocent and offended party, while all of the fault and guilt for the disrupted relationship is heaped upon the wife. Second, when a metaphor is used repeatedly, the comparison it makes begins to flow in both directions. If God is repeatedly said to be "like a husband," then eventually a husband is understood to be like God.[12] This reversal both strengthens and legitimates a hierarchal relationship already present in most cultures. Third, the use of accusations of infidelity to justify a violent divine response against Israel serves as a justification of spousal abuse both within the text and in contexts in which these texts are read and interpreted, including present-day ones.

In 2009 Julia O'Brien gave major attention to the way this metaphor functions—within a complex of other divine images, including God as "authoritarian father" and "angry warrior"—to create problematic results for readers of the Bible. These images and the common practice of uncritical acceptance of them demands a push-back in the other direction that O'Brien argues may lead to a more engaged and productive reading of the prophetic literature.[13] The issues and problems that arise from this use of a metaphor will arise at a number of points within this book.

him in the north, in Israel at about the same time as Hosea, but as the oracular
material begins in the very next verse, the prophetic voice merges with the
divine voice, as it does in so many other places in the prophetic literature.
The early chapters of Amos are filled with divine first-person statements, so
it is possible for readers to lose sight of the character named Amos altogether;
yet this character makes a dramatic reappearance in the final three chapters
of the book. Amos 7:1 opens this section with first-person narration from
the prophet. Three consecutive visions are introduced with "Thus the Lord
YHWH showed me . . . ,"[14] and they proceed to portray destruction. The
dramatic conclusion to the sequence of visions in 7:9 includes a divine threat:
"I will rise against the house of Jeroboam with the sword." This statement
launches the narrative into a conflict between Amos and Amaziah, the priest
of Bethel. After Amaziah speaks to Jeroboam and Amos, the chapter ends with
Amos prophesying a terrible end for Amaziah, his family, and Israel. When
8:1 opens with an echo of 7:1, "Thus the Lord YHWH showed me . . . ,"
the first-person narrative from an overt Amos continues, and the reader can
expect nothing but a destructive end. Amos 7–9 never brings prophet and
king together in direct dialogue like the royal narratives of the book of Isaiah,
but they communicate through a priest who seems to be a less-than-honest
broker. The appearance of Amos as a narrative character highlights themes
of conflict and destruction, and it raises important questions about the role
and function of a prophet within Israel, particularly in relation to other divine
mediators like kings and prophets. If the reader knows Bethel is about to be
destroyed and the northern monarchy about to end, then Amos's character
enacts the preeminence of the prophet as divine mediator over against the
king.[15] The degree to which Amos's life and his prophetic message become
entangled within the book is minimal, compared to Hosea.

Jonah is arguably the most interesting character in the Book of the Twelve.
The little book in which he is the main human character is a very carefully
structured narrative. In the first and third chapters, Jonah is told by YHWH to
go and proclaim to the people of Nineveh that they are about to be destroyed
because of their wickedness. The first time Jonah does not go, and he ends
up on a boat in a storm, conversing with a group of sailors. To what extent
should we understand Jonah 1–2 as an expanded call narrative that develops
the motif of reluctance of the prophet, like Moses in Exodus 3, Isaiah in Isaiah 6, and Jeremiah in Jeremiah 1? If this is the case, then the story of the
storm and the great fish would become the equivalent of the touching of Isaiah's mouth with an ember, the preparation of the prophet for the task, rather
than a story of disobedience and punishment. In Jonah 3 the prophet follows
the divine command and ends up in Nineveh, where he says only, "Forty days
more, and Nineveh shall be overthrown!" (3:4). Both of these episodes end

with the foreigners worshiping Israel's God and being delivered from their terrible fate. Meanwhile Jonah ends up on the outside: in the belly of a fish in the sea as chapter 2 begins, and outside the city in the shade of a plant as chapter 4 begins. Jonah spends most of these two chapters talking to God. The conversation at the end of the book is grammatically and theologically complex and may point toward a primary purpose for the book. It reveals that, contrary to a frequent assumption, Jonah did not flee the first time because he was afraid to go to Nineveh. Rather, he was afraid that he would be successful and that God would forgive the Ninevites, whom Jonah wanted to see judged: their deliverance makes him so angry that he wants to die (4:9). It is important to remember that there is no instance in all of the prophetic literature of Israelites hearing a message from a prophet about their destruction, then repenting in response, and instead being delivered. This happens only with one of their greatest enemy nations.

There is a lot of dispute about how to understand the book of Jonah. For some readers it is important to understand this as a set of historical events in which a Hebrew prophet spent time inside a fish and traveled to a foreign city to convince them to repent. These readers will emphasize the reference to a Jonah son of Amittai in 2 Kings 14:25, a text that sounds historical in nature. Other readers think the book of Jonah makes more sense as a satirical story about a prophet who wants to be right, wants to see his enemies destroyed, and is resentful of God's mercy. In this case, the character called Jonah may be a stand-in for all prophets or all people who hold such feelings. More important than questions of historicity may be whether this book is primarily about Jonah, the Ninevites, or YHWH. Phyllis Trible's work with the book of Jonah has been highly influential, and she has made the case that the development of the divine character is central to the story. Specifically, the God who starts the story operating by a principle of reciprocity ends the story operating by a principle of pity or compassion. God attacks Jonah with a storm in chapter 1, but tries to persuade him with reason in chapter 4, and the case God makes with this reason is that he should have compassion on the people of Nineveh, rather than giving them what they deserve.[16] This is the way in which Jonah's own life becomes a reflection of his prophetic message. He is also rescued when he prays and is urged by YHWH to view the Ninevites with compassion, as YHWH does.

The book of Jeremiah, specifically the story of Jeremiah's trial in chapter 26, seems to know of a story of Micah of Morosheth, who is used by characters in the story as a parallel to Jeremiah's situation in 26:17–18. These characters quote Micah 3:12 verbatim, but the book of Micah contains no recollection of the interaction with King Hezekiah that Jeremiah 26:19 implies, and Micah never emerges as a narrative character in the book named for him.[17]

A final, major narrative character in the Book of the Twelve is Haggai, a prophet who acts in the midst of the Restoration crisis in Jerusalem in the late sixth century. As table 1.4 in chapter 1 of this book indicates, Haggai appears as a character in Ezra 5–6 during that book's account of the struggle to rebuild the temple in Jerusalem, in the early years after the return from exile. This last overt narrative character of the prophetic literature brings the tradition of such characters full circle when he encounters Zerubbabel on at least two occasions in the book of Haggai. Like Isaiah, Haggai appears as a prophet at the center of the community, an establishment prophet who gets to speak directly to the king and seems to have an official role in the political process. The actions of Haggai may reach back even further in 2:22–23, when he seems to be anointing Zerubbabel, the Davidic heir, as the next king of Judah. This story of a prophet may serve to reconnect the prophetic tradition to the identity of Samuel as an anointer of kings, except that this is a failed anointing. Judah never manages to separate itself from Persian control in order to become an independent monarchy again. This is a subject that will need further treatment in chapter 11 of this book, which treats the proclamation of the Book of the Twelve concerning the Restoration period more directly. Zechariah's name appears four times in his book, but these are all part of prophetic formulas naming him as the recipient of the word of YHWH.[18]

THE PROCLAMATION OF THE TWELVE
CONCERNING THE ASSYRIAN PERIOD

The Book of the Twelve begins in roughly the same historical context as Isaiah, but in a geographical setting that includes the northern nation, Israel. The discussion above reveals that the literary structure of the Twelve and Isaiah may be more alike than they may at first appear, and that the collective character in the Assyrian portions of the Twelve resembles Isaiah in important ways. With both the similarity to Isaiah and its own distinctiveness in mind, we can now listen more precisely to the claims the Book of the Twelve makes about Israel in the mid to late eighth century. The book called **Hosea**, and therefore the entire Book of the Twelve, opens with one of the most intriguing and morally problematic stories in all of the prophetic literature, as the previous section has demonstrated. It is not entirely clear whether we are to understand the first-person account in Hosea 1 as the prophet's initial divine experience, which might be labeled his "call narrative." The divine command to Hosea to marry a woman who seems to be identified as a prostitute takes many readers by surprise and is offensive in many ways, yet this is not a portion of the text that we can simply excise. Because it provides the opening

framework of Hosea and the Book of the Twelve, and because it has helped
to form the voice to which we will continue to listen in the book of Hosea,
this issue must remain in full view. The relationship(s) of Hosea to the one or
two women depicted in chapters 1 and 3 of the book form a frame around the
prophet's initial proclamation concerning Israel in the eighth century.

The book of Hosea is commonly divided into three sections. The first
section, Hosea 1–3, has already received significant treatment because of the
presence of Hosea as a narrative character in these chapters. The large middle
section of the book, Hosea 4–11, needs additional attention here, while discussion of Hosea 12–14 will be reserved for a later chapter because of its
connections to later points in Israel's story. This division into three sections
is demonstrated further in table 3.5. Like Isaiah, the book of Hosea was not
created by simply tacking new parts on the end. Later revisions of the book
also placed material at earlier places in the book, such as 1:11; 3:5; and 8:14.
Like the transition point at 12:1, these earlier portions refer to Judah or the
Davidic dynasty, rather than the eighth-century northern context in which the
prophet named Hosea lived.[19] As we proceed into the middle section, which
has the Assyrian period as its primary context, it is important to remember the
Hosea character who was introduced in the first three chapters.

Table 3.5 Major Divisions of Hosea

Chapters	Description
1–3	Development of Hosea's family and its demonstration of Israel's infidelity to YHWH
4–11	Judgment of Israel, calls for repentance, YHWH's compassion
12–14	Judgment of Judah and Israel, need for repentance, promise of future healing

At Hosea 4:1 a common pattern in prophetic literature appears. The character named Hosea has appeared prominently in the first three chapters of
the book, but here he becomes less visible. The common prophetic formula
"Hear the word of YHWH" begins 4:1, and references to the God of Israel
are most often in third-person language, but first-person divine statements
begin to appear as the chapter progresses. The voice of the prophet is becoming the voice of YHWH, and the prophet as a human character fades into the
background. The direct accusation of Hosea against Israel is a violation of the
second commandment of the Decalogue, according to the way of numbering
them in Jewish tradition. Israel has put other gods before YHWH. Hosea
4:12–19 describes this idolatry in greater detail:

My people consult a piece of wood,
>   and their divining rod gives them oracles.

(v. 12a)

They sacrifice on the tops of the mountains,
>   and make offerings upon the hills,
under oak, poplar, and terebinth,
>   because their shade is good.

(v. 13)

The accusations are not purely about worship, however: this chapter charges Israel with violating numerous other commandments, including those against murder, stealing, and adultery (4:2). According to Hosea, cultic violations are accompanied by social ones. Along with these specific charges of disobedience to the law, references to idolatry, using the metaphor of prostitution ("play the whore," 4:10, etc.), continue to reinforce the framework of marital infidelity introduced in chapters 1–3.

Hosea 5:12–13 places the judgment of Israel and Judah in parallel poetic structure, and the differing fates of the two nations during the Assyrian period present a challenge for reading such a text as a predisaster warning. The final forms of Hosea and the entire Book of the Twelve demonstrate awareness of these differing fates, so that this text is eventually transformed in that context. In this near context, within an eighth-century viewpoint, these verses invite closer examination of a new voice that appears at 6:1. This voice that calls for repentance is difficult to identify. It does not sound like the voice of Hosea himself, who has receded far into the background of the book. Perhaps nowhere more than in the book of Hosea do readers face the temptation to force coherence upon a text, especially as it moves through its mixed messages in chapters 7–14. In its final form this book is a maelstrom of judgment, forgiveness, sin, repentance, anger, and regret; thus it resists easy solutions. The use of the metaphor generates massive moral problems, even while it serves to connect the prophet's life with the prophet's message, offering a path that leads away from the easy formula of retribution. As the book ends, the compassion and healing forgiveness of YHWH become more visible, but brutal suffering as the consequence for disobedience is present even to the end, as in 13:16:[20]

Samaria shall bear her guilt,
>   because she has rebelled against her God;
they shall fall by the sword,
>   their little ones shall be dashed in pieces,
>   and their pregnant women ripped open.

Chapter 11 of this book will return to some small portions of the book of Hosea that seem to be attached to the Restoration period of the fifth century, when the book was probably completed in its current form.

The little book of **Joel** has always presented a challenge for historical approaches to the prophetic literature. There are simply no features in the book to provide historians any sure footing. A literary approach resolves this problem to some degree by accepting Hosea and Amos as the surrounding framework of Joel, thus providing the context for the book that seems to go out of its way to provide no clues to connect it to Israel's narrative. The placement of Joel in the second position in the Book of the Twelve reveals that, for the purposes of this prophetic collection, it attaches to the Assyrian period.[21] Many interpreters have recognized that the phrase "day of YHWH" first appears in Joel and reappears periodically within the collection, as one of the most important theological themes in the Book of the Twelve. Table 3.3, placed earlier in this chapter, contains a list of occurrences of this phrase, which is referred to more often in the shortened forms "the day" and "that day." The overriding theme of the book of Joel is judgment, and it uses this phrase to express that idea, one that fits with Joel's placement early in the Book of the Twelve.

Another central idea in the book of Joel is the fertility of the land of Israel, a continuing emphasis that it introduces to the Book of the Twelve. Unfortunately, this theme often appears in a negative sense, with the agricultural productivity of the land threatened by Israel's idolatrous activity. The book of Joel opens with a description of a locust plague, and the destruction that will come on the "day of YHWH" is depicted as a disaster even worse than this one. The comparison of God's judgment with a natural disaster points toward the importance of reading the prophetic scrolls as literature of disaster. The book of Joel does offer hope and salvation in places, though, and the land is often the focus, even the audience of such promises as in 2:21:

> Do not fear, O soil;
> 　be glad and rejoice,
> 　for the LORD has done great things!

All of this attention to land, fertility, and crops means that weather plays an important role in the book of Joel, in ways that can easily be misunderstood by people who live in very different environments, which is the subject of discussion box 3.2.

The book of Joel also provides an important introduction to the book of **Amos**. The opening line of Amos's first speech is dramatic:

Discussion Box 3.2 Meteorology in the Old Testament

The book of Joel is one of the places in the Old Testament that makes significant use of weather imagery. This imagery is most common in the prophetic literature, and it poses a number of interpretive problems that have been carefully examined by Aloysius Fitzgerald in a book called *The Lord of the East Wind*. Fitzgerald argues that texts using such imagery must be carefully understood in relation to the weather patterns of Palestine, patterns familiar to the writers of the text, not the patterns of the reader's environment. The most important aspect of Palestinian weather is the predominance of winds from the west (off the Mediterranean Sea) during the rainy season and from the east (coming across the Arabian Desert) in the dry season. In between these two seasons are interchange periods in which the wind can shift back and forth in direction.[22] Storms mentioned in the Bible can either be rainstorms from the west or dry, destructive siroccos from the east. The latter came to be associated with divine wrath and judgment, analogous to the hot breath of God. Those who come from places where hurricanes, typhoons, or tornadoes are the primary destructive weather forces might associate rainstorms with destruction, but this is not the case with the weather in Palestine. Fitzgerald further contends that the entire book of Joel "is organized around the shifting meteorological seasons of the year."[23]

> The LORD roars from Zion,
>   and utters his voice from Jerusalem.
>   (1:2a)

This is a repetition of Joel 3:16a and may be one important reason why Joel and Amos are placed next to each other. Here is one example that illustrates the proposal by Nogalski, described above, that the components of the Book of the Twelve are linked together by repeated words and phrases near their beginnings and ends. Thus the opening of the book of Amos may be a specific expression of the "day of YHWH" proclaimed in Joel.

Table 3.4, placed earlier in this chapter, demonstrates the patterns of the Oracles against the Nations in the Book of the Twelve, locating them in Amos, Obadiah, Jonah, Nahum, and Zephaniah. Sweeney has emphasized the significance of these kinds of oracles, particularly in Obadiah, Jonah, and Nahum as a transition from focusing primarily on Israel to a focus on nations around Israel, its enemies. This transitional sequence is more intact

in the LXX sequence of these books than in the Masoretic sequence, in
which Micah intervenes, but they are still concentrated enough to serve this
purpose.[24] As a combination, these Oracles against the Nations walk a challenging path through two very difficult theological issues. As the prophets
of the Assyrian period proclaim their oracles of judgment against Israel, the
presumption—sometimes indirect, sometimes glaringly overt—is that the
Assyrian Empire will be the weapon that YHWH will use to punish the Israelites for their disobedience. The first theological question this raises is how
YHWH can be on the side of another nation in a battle. Surely those people
are no less disobedient. The Oracles against Foreign Nations, in part, assure
that the partnership between YHWH and Assyria is only temporary and that
Assyria will get its punishment soon enough; the book of Isaiah has already
made this point plainly in 10:5–11 and other places. On the other hand, if
this foreign nation is being used by YHWH to perform the task of punishing Israel, then why is this an act for which it should be punished? This element of the Book of the Twelve exposes the disequilibrium created by both
of these questions. The easy formulas of divine retribution do not fit nicely
onto the give-and-take of world events, once Israel as a nation moves fully
onto that stage.

Amos's oracles of judgment against other nations eventually circle around
to Israel and Judah in 2:4–8, and this moves the book of Amos onto its primary subject, the pending destruction of the northern kingdom, Israel. At
this point there is some debate about the organization of the book of Amos.
The seven judgment oracles in 1:3–2:8 are so consistent in form and style that
some interpreters see a new section of less consistent oracles against Israel in
2:9–3:8.[25] Others see enough consistency in form and content to call 2:9–16
a continuation of 1:3–2:8, specifically providing the punishment for Israel
because of its sins pronounced in 2:6–8.[26] The more dramatic shift in form
and content begins at 3:1, which starts with a relatively elaborate introductory formula and proceeds with a series of individual sayings, the first group
of which is a series of riddles in 3:3–8. The delineation of the major sections
of the book of Amos in table 3.6 follows this observation. The condemnation
of Israel continues through the middle of the book of Amos, with a focus
on northern settings like Samaria (3:9; 4:1), Bethel (3:14; 4:4), and Gilgal
(4:4; 5:5).

While the focus stays on the disobedience of Israel and the intent of
YHWH to punish Israel for its sins of idolatry and injustice, it is possible
to see some change in tone between chapters 4 and 5, away from certain
judgment and toward warnings about potential judgment, with some hope of
repentance possible.[27] One place this appears is in 5:4–5:

Table 3.6 Major Sections of Amos

Chapters	Description
1–2	Oracles of judgment against the nations, including Israel and Judah, and the resulting punishment of Israel
3–6	Mixed collection of judgment oracles directed against Israel, focused on northern worship sites and economic injustice
7–9	A collection of Amos's visions and stories of confrontation

> For thus says the LORD to the house of Israel:
> Seek me and live;
> > but do not seek Bethel,
> and do not enter into Gilgal,
> > or cross over to Beer-sheba;
> for Gilgal shall surely go into exile,
> > and Bethel shall come to nothing.

This passage helps point toward one of the great difficulties that a book like Amos creates for itself. Many of the judgment oracles in the book appear to come out of a period of internal prosperity for Israel, in the middle of the eighth century. Much of the condemnation of Israel centers on economic injustice and the mistreatment of the poor (1:6–8; 4:1; 6:4), but when the pronounced punishment for such transgressions is the destruction that comes from the invasion of an imperial army, it hardly seems like an appropriate solution. The poor are likely to be at least, if not more, exposed to the terrors of such an invasion. Thus they would seem to become double victims in this situation. In parts of Amos it is possible to find what may sound like a more selective punishment. For example, 6:4–7 condemns those who "lie on beds of ivory," "eat lambs from the flock," "drink wine from bowls," and "anoint themselves with the finest oils." The passage then concludes with this judgment:

> Therefore they shall now be the first to go into exile,
> > and the revelry of the loungers shall pass away.
> > > > > > (v. 7)

Amos may be less specific about how judgment will come than other prophetic books, but YHWH does say in 6:14, "I am raising up against you a nation," and an armed invasion seems too blunt an instrument for the kind of precise punishment necessary in response to sins committed by a small number of upper-class elites.

The book of **Jonah** received significant attention earlier in this chapter because its narrative character is such a powerful and fascinating presence. In terms of its prophetic proclamation, Jonah is a very confusing book. While the target of Jonah's one oracle, the simple sentence, "Forty days more, and Nineveh shall be overthrown!" (3:4), is a foreign nation, it is unlike the other oracles against the foreign nations in the prophetic literature because it actually has that foreign nation as its audience and narrative setting. Furthermore, though the announcement of destruction seems straightforward and unavoidable, the repentance of the people of Nineveh causes YHWH to reconsider the plan to destroy them. If the readers or hearers of this story are Israelites, then what might the book be proclaiming to them? It might be urging them to forgive foreigners, as YHWH does in the story. The text does not identify the "evil" for which the Ninevites are guilty and does not say whether it includes their oppression of Israel. It might be demonstrating that divine forgiveness is available to Israel if even Nineveh can receive it. The conversation between Jonah and God in Jonah 4 is arranged with intricate care by the writer of the book.[28] The discussion about the life and death of a magical plant is playful, but it is surrounded by subjects that are deadly serious: Jonah contemplates his own fate and the ultimate fate of the people of Nineveh. The plant then becomes the central analogy, allowing God to compare Jonah's feelings about it to God's own feelings about a massive city full of people.[29] There are no easy equations here about who is condemned and who is delivered, and the book invites readers to join Jonah in contemplation with God about these questions. The conflict between the book of Jonah and the prophetic books that announce, and even revel in, YHWH's coming judgment against Nineveh (Isaiah, Amos, and Nahum) is not resolvable. Incoherence will be an internal feature of some prophetic books, like Hosea and Jeremiah, and it is also a feature of the Book of the Twelve at this point.

The book of **Micah** is made up of three distinct sections and demonstrates a long and complex internal composition history.[30] The initial superscription places the prophet named Micah and the beginning of the book in the eighth-century Assyrian crisis by naming three kings of Judah: Jotham, Ahaz, and Hezekiah. Our attention at this point will be on the first section, Micah 1–3, which directly addresses the Assyrian period, though there are signs that at later points the full book was reshaped, not merely with appended text.[31] The internal movement of the book, like most of the prophetic literature, is from destruction to restoration. The book of Micah opens with a divine threat against Samaria, though the audience would seem to be the prophet's own location in Judah, which might be next to face this threat. The accusations against Judah in Micah 2 are concerned with economic injustice, particularly the accumulation of land by wealthy individuals:

They covet fields, and seize them;
    houses, and take them away;
they oppress householder and house,
    people and their inheritance.

(v. 2)

Micah aims his criticism at political and religious leaders in Micah 3 and challenges the false prophets whose words assist these leaders in their corrupt activities. The period leading up to the Assyrian crisis had probably been one of relative security and prosperity; with a lack of outside pressure, some had taken advantage of this situation, politically and economically, to accumulate power and wealth. The reference to "inheritance" in 2:2 is particularly important because it is the word that is used to refer to the allotment of land in the book of Joshua, by tribe, clan, and family. Such an inheritance was the piece of the Promised Land given by YWHW to each Israelite. A specific story of this kind of land accumulation appears in 1 Kings 21, when King Ahab and eventually his wife Jezebel plot to take away the inheritance of a man named Naboth. The action heightened the conflict already present between the Ahab-Jezebel pair and Elijah, and this may be part of the prophetic tradition that Micah thinks is betrayed when he declares in 3:5:

Thus says the LORD concerning the prophets
    who lead my people astray,
who cry "Peace"
    when they have something to eat,
but declare war against those
    who put nothing into their mouths.

Micah 3 ends with the vision of Jerusalem as a "plowed . . . field" and "a heap of ruins." The land and houses that these people coveted and confiscated will be taken away or destroyed by a foreign enemy. Micah 4 begins to look into the distant future, to a restoration of Judah after this destruction, and will be discussed in chapter 11 (below).

The little book called **Nahum** is introduced in its first verse as "an oracle concerning Nineveh," so it falls into the category of Oracles against the Nations. It also means that Israel's engagement with the Assyrian Empire is the part of the story to which most of the book relates. It is important to remember at this point, and at many others, how this study is organizing the prophetic literature. The book of Nahum was almost certainly written in its final form after the exile, perhaps in the fifth century. Its statements about Nineveh likely include an awareness of the destruction of that city in 612 BCE. Nevertheless, the focus on Nineveh attaches this book most closely to those addressing the Assyrian period, and it may be best understood as bringing that part of Israel's story to a close. The coming retribution against Assyria for its role in punishing Israel, which has been proclaimed in Isaiah and Amos, becomes the center of attention for all three chapters of this book. Similar tensions are present in Nahum as in other parts of the prophetic literature that try to address this issue. YHWH chooses to use Assyria as a means of punishing Israel, yet this participation by Assyria in the divine plan makes them the next focus of divine judgment. Amid the proclamations against Assyria, Nahum 1:12–15 declares deliverance and blessing for Judah. The book of Isaiah has provided multiple understandings of the very different impacts of the Assyrian crisis on Israel and Judah, understandings that seem to be in tension with each other, while the book of Amos provides no explanation for this difference at all. Nahum offers very little explanation either, though it is important to remember that it is prose sections of Isaiah, taken from 2 Kings, that do this explaining, and Amos and Nahum do not use such a resource. Is the reader expected to bring awareness of those narratives into the Book of the Twelve, something the writer of Isaiah did for us? Furthermore, the dependence of Nahum on Isaiah is well documented, so that may be another piece of the background to this book that the writer assumes.[32] The promises made to Judah are so powerful in 1:15 that they create another difficulty:[33]

> Look! On the mountains the feet of one
>   who brings good tidings,
>   who proclaims peace!
> Celebrate your festivals, O Judah,
>   fulfill your vows,
> for never again shall the wicked invade you;
>   they are utterly cut off.

If the reference to "the wicked" only concerns Assyria, then this is not a difficulty, but it is easy to see how this good news could be taken as a more general promise of protection, one that would fail Judah when the Babylonians invaded a century and a half later. Some attention has already been given to the apparent conflict between the books of Isaiah and Jeremiah concerning the inviolability of Zion, and Nahum 1:15 can easily be understood as taking Isaiah's side in this debate. The book of Nahum provides no reason why Judah was spared, whether because Judah was less sinful than Israel, or because Judah repented of its disobedience, or because it was purely an act of divine choice.

The final words of the book of Nahum (3:19), which have as strong a claim as any to be the final words of the Book of the Twelve on Assyria and Israel's interaction with that empire, reveal the struggle of human existence:

Discussion Box 3.3 Masculinity and Male Protection

Discussion box 3.1 dealt with the issue of the marriage metaphor in the prophetic literature. A related issue that arises in some texts is the male obligation to protect females. An important extension of this obligation, which sometimes seems to surpass it in importance, is the protection of woman as a symbol for and proof of masculinity.[34] The book of Nahum provides an important example for how this idea operates. In Nahum 3:5, YHWH declares his intent to rape Nineveh:

> I am against you,
>   says the LORD of hosts,
>   and will lift up your skirts over your face;
> and I will let the nations look on your nakedness
>   and kingdoms on your shame.

The purpose of this act is to demonstrate YHWH's masculine power and the corresponding weakness of Assyria's king, who cannot protect his woman, the city, from this sexual assault (cf. "God and Sexual Assault," discussion box 5.2). The use of this imagery, though, is a threat to YHWH's own masculinity, because YHWH was unable to protect Israel from Assyria's earlier attacks. Thus the whole book of Nahum becomes a struggle for masculine power, with feminine objects (cities) used to demonstrate that power through means of sexual assault.[35] Interpretations of these texts that do not maintain an awareness of this discomforting cultural construct threaten to promote all of its assumptions and implications.

> There is no assuaging your hurt,
>   your wound is mortal.
> All who hear the news about you
>   clap their hands over you.
> For who has ever escaped
>   your endless cruelty?

If life is the endless push and shove of political, economic, and military power, then how can we, along with the prophets of ancient Israel, put theological language onto such a process? The punishment of a nation looks just like the acts for which they are being punished—invasion, defeat, brutal death—one disaster after another, each with its resulting trauma. But how do we read this word about Assyria alongside those from Jonah, in which Assyria repents, is forgiven, and receives God's pity? How do we put the world of the prophetic imagination together with the world of lived experience, or at least cope with the distance between them?

THE TWELVE INTERRUPTED

Depending on the order of component parts one follows in the Book of the Twelve, the focus of attention shifts in the fourth or fifth part, the booklet of Obadiah, which rails against Edom for assisting the Babylonians in their invasion of Judah. The shift is temporary: the books of Jonah, Micah, and Nahum in the Masoretic order, and just Jonah and Nahum in the Greek order, turn their attention back to Assyria. This chronological transition is not smooth because other issues have come into play, but eventually, as the Book of the Twelve moves on to Habakkuk and Zephaniah, the Babylonian crisis comes into full view. That will be the subject of chapter 7 of this book, which will return to the Book of the Twelve.

Like the first half of the book of Isaiah, the first half of the Book of the Twelve is dominated by threats of divine punishment, and these are aimed at both Israel and Judah. Unlike Isaiah, the Book of the Twelve offers no explanation for the difference in outcomes of the Assyrian threat for these two nations. This incongruity is even highlighted by the portion of the Book of the Twelve called Micah, which declares the pending judgment of YHWH on Judah in the Assyrian period, a judgment that does not run its course. The open-endedness of Micah's proclamation and the dissonance it creates will hang in the air for about a century before a new sociopolitical crisis provides a stage for a new set of prophetic voices.

Resources for Further Research

Commentaries

Achtemeier, Elizabeth. "Joel: Introduction, Commentary, and Reflections." In *The New Interpreter's Bible*, edited by Leander E. Keck et al., 7:299–336. Nashville: Abingdon Press, 1996. (B)

Anderson, Francis I., and David Noel Freedman. *Micah: A New Translation with Introduction and Commentary*. New Haven: Yale University Press, 2006. (C)

Crenshaw, James L. *Joel: A New Translation with Introduction and Commentary*. New York: Doubleday, 1995. (C)

Gowan, Donald E. "Amos: Introduction, Commentary, and Reflections." In *The New Interpreter's Bible*, edited by Leander E. Keck et al., 7:337–432. Nashville: Abingdon Press, 1996. (B)

Jeremias, Jorg. *The Book of Amos: A Commentary*. Louisville, KY: Westminster John Knox Press, 1996. (B)

Nogalski, James. *The Book of the Twelve: Hosea–Jonah*. Macon, GA: Smyth & Helwys, 2011. (B)

O'Brien, Julia M. *Nahum*. London: Sheffield Academic Press, 2002. (B)

Paul, Shalom M. *Amos: A Commentary on the Book of Amos*. Minneapolis: Fortress Press, 1991. (C)

Sasson, Jack M. *Jonah: A New Translation with Introduction and Commentary*. New York: Doubleday, 1995. (C)

Simundson, Daniel J. *Hosea, Joel, Amos, Obadiah, Jonah, Micah*. Nashville: Abingdon Press, 2005. (A)

————. "Micah: Introduction, Commentary, and Reflections." In *The New Interpreter's Bible*, edited by Leander E. Keck et al., 7:531–90. Nashville: Abingdon Press, 1996. (B)

Sweeney, Marvin A. *The Twelve Prophets*. Vol. 1. Collegeville, MN: Liturgical Press, 2000. (B)

Trible, Phyllis. "Jonah: Introduction, Commentary, and Reflections." In *The New Interpreter's Bible*, edited by Leander E. Keck et al., 7:461–530. Nashville: Abingdon Press, 1996. (B)

Yee, Gale A. "Hosea: Introduction, Commentary, and Reflections." In *The New Interpreter's Bible*, edited by Leander E. Keck et al., 7:195–298. Nashville: Abingdon Press, 1996. (B)

Monographs and Special Studies

Nogalski, James D. *Literary Precursors to the Book of the Twelve*. New York: Walter de Gruyter, 1993.

Nogalski, James D., and Marvin A. Sweeney, eds. *Reading and Hearing the Book of the Twelve*. Atlanta: Society of Biblical Literature, 2000.

Weems, Renita J. *Battered Love: Marriage, Sex, and Violence in the Hebrew Prophets*. Minneapolis: Fortress Press, 1995.

Book of
the Twelve

Isaiah

Assyrian
Crisis | Chapter 2 | | | Chapter 3

722

Jeremiah

Ezekiel

Babylonian
Crisis | Chapter 4 | Chapter 5 | Chapter 6 | Chapter 7

586

Restoration
Crisis | Chapter 8 | Chapter 9 | Chapter 10 | Chapter 11

525

4

The Scroll of Isaiah Continued

Response to the Babylonian Crisis

The clearest division in the book of Isaiah lies between the portions now numbered as chapters 39 and 40. Chapter 2 of this book has already discussed the shape of the book of Isaiah and this division within it. Early attempts within the critical era—which tended to divide Isaiah by using historical criteria, literary style, and theological ideas—often treated Isaiah 1–39 and 40–55, the so-called Proto-Isaiah and Deutero-Isaiah, as separate products of the Assyrian and Babylonian periods respectively. The common assumption was that the writer of the second part placed the two units together end to end. More recent and more nuanced analyses have treated the Deutero-Isaiah phase as a revision of the book during the sixth century that not only added new material on the end, but also reshaped the existing material, adding small and medium-sized portions in many parts of the work. Table 4.1 on page 78 presents a list of pieces that may have been added in this stage of the revision. For the purposes of the discussion here, it is more important to observe that these sections seem to address the Babylonian period than it is to establish dates for their composition or their addition to the developing scroll of Isaiah.

These sections contemplate two large theological issues, looking back on the events of the sixth century and forward to the possibilities of a new era. First, how can the people of Judah think about the Babylonian Empire, which, even though now defeated, was the instrument of divine punishment for them? Second, what is the possibility of a future for people returning to Judah, a future still dominated by the failure and disaster of the past?

Table 4.1 Portions of Isaiah Addressing the Babylonian Crisis

Portion	Description
13:1–14:23	This opening section of the Oracles against the Nations condemns Babylon.
21	A poem near the end of the Oracles against the Nations that also seems to address Babylon, forming a Babylonian bracket around the collection.[1]
34–35	In this section the poems have many connections to Isaiah 40.
40–55	The classic Deutero-Isaiah, filled with a diverse collection of material pondering the future of Judah and Jerusalem after the exile.

THE PROCLAMATION OF ISAIAH CONCERNING THE BABYLONIAN PERIOD

The Oracles against Foreign Nations in the first half of Isaiah turned the attention of the book onto territories and people outside Judah and Jerusalem, particularly the old nemeses and adversaries of Israel such as Egypt, Moab, Ammon, the Philistines, and Assyria. A list like this needed reframing after the experiences of Judah at the hands of the Babylonians in the sixth century, and this is at least part of what Isaiah 13–14 and 21 attempt to do. The earlier version of the book of Isaiah already provided a pathway for this revision to follow in its halting portrayal of Assyria as the instrument of divine punishment in 10:5–19, and the retaliation against Assyria finds an echo in 14:24–27. The two oracles announcing the destruction of Babylon by YHWH—the nation in 13:2–22 and its king in 14:3–23—also surround a brief but powerful statement about the restoration of Israel in 14:1–2.

Chapter 2 of this book already gave some attention to Isaiah 34–35, because of the inclusion of these texts among the parts of Isaiah that directly address the Assyrian period, but it also acknowledged their affinity to 40–55. These poems, which address themes of destruction and restoration, extend back into the earlier part of the book in order to renegotiate the claims of an earlier version of the book of Isaiah, in light of events that lie between chapters 34–35 and 40–55, including the miraculous rescue of Judah from the Assyrian advance of the eighth century and the devastating destruction of Judah by the Babylonian army in the early sixth century. The book of Isaiah had developed the idea that YHWH would always protect Jerusalem because the city was the location of the temple, YHWH's house, yet the eighth-century portions of the book of Isaiah threaten all Israel with divine judgment because

Discussion Box 4.1 Isaiah 14:12–21 and the "Fall of Satan"

Isaiah 14:12–21 is another text that Christian tradition has lifted out of Isaiah and used so extensively for another purpose that it can be a distraction from a careful reading of the book. The precise person to whom the term "Day Star" refers and to whom the taunt is directed is uncertain. Numerous proposals have arisen, with the general sense prevailing that the taunt at one stage was directed toward an Assyrian king, but has been adapted to address a Babylonian one. The general sense of imperial arrogance may be more important than naming a specific king, and such a choice would follow what the text itself does.[2] There also appear to be mythological motifs in the taunt poem, deriving from a complex ancient Near Eastern background. Perhaps it was this nature of the text and its background that invited an extension of the mythological reading in later Christian interpretations. The Latin translation of the word rendered "Day Star" in most English versions is "Lucifer," and the King James followed this path and brought that proper noun into English.[3] The idea of rebellious angels who live and act on earth appears in some Jewish literature of the Hellenistic period. The book called *Jubilees*, for example, retells the book of Genesis and includes a mysterious figure called Mastema, who does things such as challenge Abraham to sacrifice Isaac.[4] In the book called *1 Enoch*, a character named Shemihaza leads a band of heavenly beings from heaven to earth to produce offspring with human women, in a story that reflects Genesis 6:1–4.[5] These ideas are probably reflected in the New Testament in passages like Luke 10:18 and Revelation 12:9. All of this tradition comes together in the poetry of Dante Alighieri (*The Divine Comedy*) in the fourteenth century and of John Milton (*Paradise Lost*) in the seventeenth century, popularizing the idea of a Satanic fall, which eventually had little to do with what is going on in Isaiah 14.[6]

of disobedience to YHWH through acts of injustice and idolatry. These two ideas seem to be in direct conflict with each other. From the perspective of Isaiah 38, as the Assyrian portion of the book is drawing to a close, the conflict appears to be resolved in favor of divine protection for Jerusalem, but it is not clear why the city was delivered. Isaiah 36:1 reports that Sennacherib and his army captured "all the fortified cities of Judah," but it does not explain why Jerusalem is not among those cities. The parallel text in 2 Kings 18 reports that Hezekiah paid tribute to Sennacherib in order to prevent the invasion of Jerusalem, but the book of Isaiah excludes this detail.[7] The spokesperson of Sennacherib, the Rabshakeh, even makes the astounding claim in Isaiah 36:10 that "YHWH said to me, Go up against this land, and destroy it." The book of Isaiah offers two pieces of information about the rescue of Jerusalem that readers should probably see as connected. First, Isaiah 37 portrays a distraught Hezekiah, praying in sackcloth or mourning clothes, but it is unclear whether Hezekiah's actions denote repentance.[8] His words to Isaiah in 37:3–4 and to YHWH in 37:16–20 focus on the haughty and presumptuous behavior of the Assyrians and the potential dishonor this brings to YHWH and the people of Judah. The story in Isaiah 37 ends with the entire army of Assyria, 185,000 troops, dying mysteriously in the night and Sennacherib fleeing back to his home. But Isaiah had sent a message to Hezekiah in 37:6–7 that promised Sennacherib would flee because he would "hear a rumor."[9] The Assyrian threat to Jerusalem ended in 701 with only one thing certain, that Jerusalem and its king had survived, even if just barely, but the book of Isaiah presents ambiguous information about how and why the escape occurred.

Isaiah 39 changes the tone of this part of the book: Isaiah proclaims that the rescue of Jerusalem is temporary. A new enemy, Babylon, is on the rise, and Jerusalem will not escape the next invasion, even though it is in the distant future. In light of this, the book of Isaiah must redefine YHWH's care for Jerusalem across a long period of time and a confusing mixture of events. The poems in Isaiah 34–35 are as circumspect as Isaiah 39 about the actual invasion and destruction of Jerusalem. The "ransomed of the LORD shall return," according to 35:10, but from what they are ransomed and why they need to return are aspects kept outside the reader's view. A "wilderness," a "dry land," and a "desert" appear in 35:1, and 35:8 places a "highway . . . for God's people" there. The wilderness and the desert become visible again in 40:3, and they contain "a highway for our God."[10] It appears that Israel and its God will meet in this place, perhaps in a scene reminiscent of the meeting at Mount Sinai. Intervening events have called into question YHWH's power, so much of the remainder of Isaiah 40 must reassert this power by portraying YHWH as the creator of the world. Isaiah 41 takes the next step in reasserting the biblical story by recalling the selection of Israel, through Abraham (41:8). Once the texts have reestablished YHWH's care for Jerusalem and YHWH's power to exert that care, the other issue needing renegotiation is the suffering that results from the enactment of divine punishment. The initial signal of this task is in 40:2, but the work requires the entry of a new character in the story.

The Servant Poems in Isaiah 42, 49, 50, and 52–53 play at least two very important roles within the book. First, the Servant figure takes Isaiah's place as an occasional character around whom this part of the book can organize itself. The lack of a precise identity for the Servant has led to a great deal of speculative interpretation through the centuries; yet if we take the lack of identity seriously, as a deliberate choice of the book, then readers should not assign this Servant any specific identity, beyond the vague designation as "Israel" in 49:3. The value of such imprecision is that it keeps the task of the Servant open to be fulfilled by many different persons at later moments in the reading and interpretation of the book. The second role this character plays is to help transform the understanding of suffering from being entirely the result of divine punishment, to being part of the task of God's righteous one(s). Again, ambiguous identity gives this idea a flexibility that resists boundaries. Both tasks may become clearer with an exploration of the content of the Servant Poems. Table 4.2 presents the boundaries of the poems and some of their key aspects.

Table 4.2 The Servant Poems, Their Speakers, Their Central Ideas

Isaiah	Speaker	Central idea
42:1–4	YHWH	Teaching of justice
49:1–6	The Servant	Expansion of service beyond the boundaries of Israel
50:4–9	The Servant	The Servant suffers for his teaching task
52:13–53:12	YHWH	The Servant's suffering redeems others

Some commentators who count chapters 40–55 as a discrete unit that is also well integrated into the full book of Isaiah also see a division at the end of 48 that separates 40–55 into two parts.[11] This means that the second Servant Poem opens a new section of the book, with the Servant as the speaker. An overt link between the first and second poems bridges these two sections of the book and brings attention back to the question of settings. The word "coastlands" is a favorite of the book of Isaiah. The Hebrew word typically translated that way in 42:4 and 49:1 appears thirty-six times in the entire Old Testament, seventeen of them in Isaiah, and nine of the seventeen in chapters 40–55.[12] In the last line of the first Servant Poem, YHWH declares about the Servant, "The coastlands wait for his teaching [lit., *torah*]" (42:4), and the first time the Servant speaks, in the opening line of the second poem, he proclaims, "Listen to me, O coastlands" (49:1). The section in chapter 2 of this book called "The Settings of the Book" introduced the idea of a "wasteland" as an imaginary setting of Isaiah, a space in between the everyday world and the supernatural world.[13] Isaiah 40–55 is a text in which the idea of being between places is most poignant. The possibility of returning to Jerusalem is present, but not yet realized. A physical wilderness and a wilderness of the imagination lie between the audience and the possibility of return, and the wilderness represents a combination of brutal struggle and creative power. If a reader feels dislocated, disoriented, or even lost, such a feeling is appropriate to the structure and content of Isaiah in this section. This space reflects the experience of the audience in this part of Israel's story, and it is the wide, uncertain space into which the Servant speaks.[14]

The lack of a specific setting and audience, along with elements of the second of the Servant Poems, are factors that raise questions about the limits of the prophet's mission, the role of Israel in the world, and the scope of divine redemptive activity. The two different kinds of answers to such questions are sometimes called "universalism" and "particularism." Does God's care about all human beings extend salvation to everyone alike, or is God's concern focused on one particular group of people? If the latter, then who can claim to be the group, and how does the group determine its identity and its boundaries? The intense debate over issues of particularity and universality in Isaiah, especially in chapters 40–55, are the result of inherent tensions and ambiguities within the text, and it should not be the goal of interpreters to resolve these.[15] It may seem entirely odd that a group whose own place in the world is so uncertain might be contemplating a more expansive view of its identity and its Deity. On the other hand, the group of Israelites returning from captivity in Babylon had lived through a very international experience. They were not the only group taken captive to Babylon, and they were not the only group freed by Cyrus of Persia to return to their homeland. If they understood Cyrus to be YHWH's anointed instrument to free them from Babylonian captivity, then how could Cyrus's emancipation of other groups not be YHWH's work too? The Israelites in Babylon had a lot in common with these other people, perhaps as much or more than they had in common with the other citizens of Judah who had remained there during the two or three generations of time that they had been gone.

In the previous paragraph the reference to Cyrus of Persia points to a need to explore the role of this character in Isaiah 40–55 more carefully. While the unnamed Servant is the central character in this part of the book, Cyrus is the only character mentioned by name. His name appears only twice in Isaiah, in 44:28 and 45:1,[16] but Cyrus appears elsewhere in the Old Testament, most prominently at the end of 2 Chronicles and the beginning of Ezra. These books contain two different versions of a royal decree issued by this character, freeing the Judahites to return to their homeland and promising to sponsor their efforts, including the rebuilding of the temple in Jerusalem. The historicity of this decree is a matter of dispute (see discussion box 4.3 below), but the ideas expressed about Cyrus in 2 Chronicles and Ezra are consistent with the way the book of Isaiah views him. There are two very important images of

Discussion Box 4.2 The Use of the Servant
Poems in the New Testament

The Servant Poems in Isaiah 40–55 present another occasion in which reading the book of Isaiah is difficult for Christian readers because of later use of these texts. Matthew 12:18–21 quotes a version of Isaiah 42:1–4 to explain why Jesus asks those he has cured to be silent about it. In his explanation of the mission to the Gentiles in Acts 13:47, Paul quotes a version of Isaiah 49:6. Most significantly, parts of the fourth servant poem are quoted in numerous places in the New Testament, including Matthew 8:17; Acts 8:32–33; and 1 Peter 2:22. Some readers see many more vague allusions to this text, and later Christian interpretation has gone much further in connecting Jesus to the Suffering Servant of the fourth servant song. In the aftermath of seeing their teacher brutally executed, it is not surprising that the early followers of Jesus looked to the Servant in Isaiah as a way of understanding their experience and finding purpose in it. At some point, interpreters made a different move and started arguing that the Servant Poems in Isaiah were actually predictions of Jesus five or six centuries earlier, and Jesus became the Servant about whom the book of Isaiah spoke. Such a claim of proof falls apart when we realize that Jesus' followers who wrote the New Testament knew the book of Isaiah well and borrowed its language to talk about Jesus. The attention to predictions and proofs obscures the much more important point that, according to the stories in the Gospels, Jesus stood in a long line of suffering servants, both before and after him, and identified with this experience of innocent suffering and its redemptive value. One need not claim that Jesus is "the" Suffering Servant for him to be "a" suffering servant, and for his followers to be called to imitate such behavior.

Cyrus that appear alongside the two occurrences of his name in Isaiah 44 and 45. In 44:28, YHWH says of Cyrus, "He is my shepherd," and the narrator of 45:1 calls Cyrus YHWH's "anointed." This latter description is a translation of the Hebrew word that is often simply transliterated as "messiah." The references to Cyrus as shepherd and anointed one seem unmistakably Davidic, though it seems strange to bestow such ideals upon a foreign king. It is possible that such powerful language was part of a debate with the Judahite community about whether to make an effort to reestablish the Davidic monarchy or to live within the imperial power of Cyrus. Taking the latter position

Discussion Box 4.3 The Cyrus Cylinder

An artifact known as the Cyrus Cylinder has received a lot of attention, notably as it was on an exhibition tour in the United States during 2013. A replica of the cylinder is kept in the United Nations Building in New York because it is often understood and described as the world's oldest declaration of human rights. Such portrayals may be overly dramatic, but it is an important artifact because of its age and its relationship to important world events. In 1879 an archaeological expedition sponsored by the British Museum found the Cyrus Cylinder at the site of ancient Babylon; that museum then claimed ownership and took possession of it. This ancient clay cylinder (nearly 9 inches long and 4 inches in diameter), now in several pieces, is universally recognized as an authentic document from the reign of Cyrus the Great of Persia, in the sixth century, but there are significant disagreements about its meaning. Among the writings on the cylinder are grants of freedom to certain groups of people to return to their homelands, rebuild there, and reestablish their religious instructions. The list of places includes only locations in Mesopotamia, so Israel and its nearby neighbors are not included, yet the ideas are consistent with what the books of the Old Testament say that Cyrus did for the Israelites. It is also unclear to what extent Cyrus was a tolerant, progressive humanitarian or a king with a somewhat different idea about how to run an empire in the most profitable way.

would put the book of Isaiah at odds with books like Haggai and Zechariah, which promote the possible reign of Zerubbabel, a surviving Davidic heir.[17]

The involvement of Isaiah 40–55 in such an argument (over whether to reestablish Judahite kingship) would fit with the idea that it sought to bridge a gap between the world of its own imaginative vision and the world of politics and economics in which it lived. This tension is embodied in the text that places the description of Cyrus between the first and second of the Servant Poems.

The third and fourth of the Servant Poems shift to address the other difficult issue with which Isaiah 40–55 must contend in the wake of the experience of exile: human suffering. The second servant poem had opened the second half of Isaiah 40–55 by allowing the Servant to speak (49:1–6). In the very next chapter, the Servant is allowed to speak again and elaborate further on his experience and his task. Much of the material that lies between 49:1–6 and 50:4–9 is commentary on the Servant, who has just spoken.[18] After this section in which the comfort of YWHW in the midst of struggle is the primary theme, the Servant speaks openly and specifically about his own suffering. The most important aspect of this description is that the suffering is not the result of disobedience to YHWH. To the contrary, it is because of the Servant's faithful obedience to his task that he suffers. This constitutes an important move away from the standard retribution theology in much of the Old Testament, which large portions of the prophetic literature embrace.[19] The Servant's experience is transforming the understanding of suffering in the book of Isaiah, and suffering is now the fate of those who are faithful to YHWH, but this raises the very difficult question of why the faithful should suffer. After the third poem (50:4–9), the remainder of Isaiah 50 and most of 51–52 speak primarily of the blessings that Israel is about to enjoy and the rejoicing that will be the response to those blessings. If the connection between the suffering of the Servant and these blessings is uncertain for a while, the final servant poem, in 52:13–53:12, makes it clear.

This time YHWH is speaking about the Servant, as in the first poem. There may have been no request in the third servant poem for the suffering to be relieved, but now there is a divine declaration that it will be. The third poem made a step forward by not making the common association of suffering with shame, yet 52:13 makes another stunning advance in relation to that theme. Now the Servant will be honored because of his suffering. It may be puzzling to many readers why the chapter break between Isaiah 52 and 53 occurs in the middle of the poem typically designated as the fourth servant song. Chapter and verse numbers were added to different parts of the Bible during the thirteenth to fifteenth centuries of the Common Era, so it is a relatively recent phenomenon. It is not difficult to see what may have confused those putting in the divisions at what is now 53:1, because a new voice appears here. After three verses of speech from God in 52:13–15, a collective group responds in first-person plural in 53:1–6. The identity of the speaker(s) is not clear in 53:7–10, but the divine voice returns to close the poem in verses 11–12, reminding the audience that the object of all of this speech is "my servant" (v. 11). The startling recognition happens at verse 4, when the audience realizes that the Servant has suffered on their behalf and that this suffering makes their redemption possible. This idea of redemptive or vicarious suffering will appear occasionally in other prophetic books, so it will arise again. The concept is not without its difficulties. The statement in 53:5 by the audience reverts back to the idea of punishment, even though the one being punished has not committed the offense. This problem becomes even more acute in 53:10, which says, "Yet it was the will of the LORD to crush him with pain." This text may be returning back to the problem of divine punishment as a blunt instrument, one that looks problematic in retrospect.

Another important aspect of this suffering that has been a matter of dispute is its source. Given the context in the book of Isaiah, it seems most likely that the suffering the Servant experiences is at the hands of outsiders, specifically the Babylonian Empire. The suffering of the Servant in Isaiah 50–53 is the same as the suffering of Jerusalem, so painfully named in 40:1–2. Like the identity of the Servant, the identity of the Servant's oppressors remains vague, and this seems deliberate as well. The book of Isaiah is moving toward an important transition, from the pains of captivity to the struggles of freedom. For this reason, however, some interpreters argue that this is already a portrayal of suffering during the Restoration period and with an internal cause.[20] Chapter 8 of this book (below) will continue the discussion of Isaiah 56–66 and will present the possibility that internal conflict within the community of restored Judah lies behind some parts of the final section of Isaiah. Such conflict may also be present behind the scenes in the book of Ezekiel and in the Book of the Twelve, in places like Haggai and Malachi. It is true that there are some prophetic figures in the prophetic literature who suffer at the hands of their own people. Jeremiah is a perhaps the most important example of this kind of suffering. Nevertheless, at this point in the development of the story that the book of Isaiah is telling, the suffering of the Israelites throughout the period of the exile appears to be the primary subject, even if the book is already looking forward to the next phase of the story, when Israel's struggle will be of a different kind. The remaining parts of Isaiah 40–55 continue to recall the pain of divine abandonment in the experience of defeat, so this context should not be overlooked in understanding the nature of the Servant's suffering.

As we reach the end of Isaiah 40–55, we should notice that the language of marriage appears again in Isaiah 54:5–8. There was extensive discussion of this subject in chapter 3 of this book (above) because of its centrality to the book of Hosea, and it will become prominent again in both Jeremiah and Ezekiel, so the subject will arise again in later chapters. In the overwhelming number of instances, this language is negative, focusing on the disobedience and idolatry of Israel as analogous to the adultery of a wife. While that assumption is present in these verses, the restoration of the marriage is the primary theme. When YHWH actually speaks in 54:7–8, it is to acknowledge that he has abandoned her out of anger but is now filled with compassion. It is possible to read this passage in a number of ways, and one of the senses that may come through in this speech is a sense of divine regret about this abandonment.[21] The restored relationship with the female figure, who represents the city of Jerusalem, becomes complete in Isaiah 55, as the portion of the book that is connected to the Babylonian period comes to a close. The book of Isaiah has moved in a number of important directions, as highlighted in

Discussion Box 4.4 Misreading Prophetic Texts

It should be obvious by now that it is not the position of this book that there is a single, correct reading of any prophetic text. This raises the question of whether certain readings are likely incorrect and, if so, why? Hardly a week goes by that I do not hear someone quote or paraphrase Isaiah 55:8. This is usually in response to the way I perform my professional task, the constructing of biblical theology. Isaiah 55:8 says:

> For my thoughts are not your thoughts,
>   nor are your ways my ways,
>   says the LORD.

Those I hear quoting this verse are typically responding in a negative manner to the asking of hard questions both about and to God. Their implication is that human beings are not to engage in such questioning because God forbids it, in order to maintain distance between God and human beings. We are not supposed to ask why God is the way God is, nor why God acts the way God acts.

This is an ideal illustration of the danger of memorizing individual verses of Scripture, a practice ingrained in many of us during our childhood, Sunday school days. Isaiah 55:8 is actually one part of a longer poem in Isaiah 55:6–9. The whole poem reads like this:

> Seek the LORD when he is encountered,
>   call out when he is near.
> Wicked ones shall abandon their way,
>   and troubled ones their thoughts.
> They shall return to the Lord and he will be merciful to them,
>   unto our God and he will be great to forgive.
> For my thoughts are not your thoughts,
>   and my ways are not your ways,
>   a saying of the LORD.
> For heaven is higher than earth,
>   therefore my ways are higher than your ways,
>   and my thoughts than your thoughts.[22]

The meaning of the whole poem is exactly the opposite of the meaning that those who quote just 55:8 often try to imply. Because God's ways of being and acting and thinking are better than ours, the book of Isaiah calls us to try to discover what God's ways are. We are supposed to ask hard questions and struggle to understand God.

this chapter. While Israel is still the primary recipient of the divine covenant (55:3), there is an extension of the blessings of this covenant to other nations (v. 4). The turning away of God's face and the abandonment of Israel in the exilic experience have ended, and Israel's God is near and approachable (vv. 6–9). The character called the Servant has played an important role in negotiating the meaning of suffering throughout this section in order to help reach this theological destination.

Suffering has changed from a means that God uses to identify obedience and disobedience, to an experience that identifies God's faithful servant, and further to a redemptive act the Servant performs for the whole nation. The Servant has progressed from a teacher of justice, to one who suffers for his message of justice, and further to one whose suffering helps bring about justice. As this progression takes place, it becomes more difficult to think of the Servant as an individual. The trauma of destruction and captivity during the sixth century did not fall on one person, or even on a few people, but primarily onto the two or three generations alive at the time. Isaiah acknowledges that Judah's punishment is delayed, most directly in 39:5–7. There is no claim at that point in Isaiah that those who will receive the punishment are any guiltier than those who came before them, and other parts of the Old Testament debate the issue of blame vociferously. The Deuteronomistic History presents King Manasseh of Judah as the worst culprit, when blame for the exile comes straight from the mouth of YHWH in 2 Kings 21:10–15. Chronicles shifts blame away from Manasseh with a story of his repentance in 2 Chronicles 33:10–17, and it tries to spread the blame across all of Israelite society and throughout many generations in 36:11–16. At the same time, 36:17–21 acknowledges, even if obliquely, that an undue share of the punishment falls on the generations alive at the time of the Babylonian invasion. It is difficult not to see these people, particularly the young persons slaughtered within the Jerusalem temple in 36:17, as at least one manifestation of Isaiah's Suffering Servant.

ISAIAH INTERRUPTED AGAIN

The remainder of Isaiah, chapters 56–66—along with other portions like 1–5 and 24–27, all of which look most closely related to the restoration of Judah in the Persian period—will be the subject of chapter 8 of this book. The book of Isaiah has arrived at an understanding of the destruction of Jerusalem and the exilic experience, though it is not an entirely comfortable interpretation. The completion of Isaiah's vision requires the inclusion of the restoration story. The greatest theological challenge for the book of Isaiah is whether the vision will be enough. How can such a story of suffering and redemption come to an end? Already in Isaiah 40–55, the book is expanding its vision and pointing beyond Israel geographically and ethnically. Jerusalem will always be the centerpiece of the vision, but the scroll may continue to test Jerusalem's boundaries in terms of time and space.

Before coming back to Isaiah in the Restoration period, however, it is important to bring in the other prophetic voices that speak along with it about the Babylonian period. Two entirely new voices, Jeremiah and Ezekiel, come into play here and will sometimes join in harmony with Isaiah or complement Isaiah by filling its silent moments. Jeremiah, for example, will look the horror of the Babylonian invasion straight in the eyes, countering Isaiah's reticence on the subject. The book of Ezekiel will portray a prophet whose life is not merely entangled in his prophetic vocation, like Isaiah's, but completely absorbed by it. At other times we may find dissonance among the voices of Isaiah, Jeremiah, and Ezekiel. In the next few chapters (below), it will take some time to listen to the two new voices individually before we are able to listen to them well with Isaiah.

Resources for Further Research

Commentaries

Blenkinsopp, Joseph. *Isaiah 40–55: A New Translation with Commentary*. New Haven: Yale University Press, 2002. (C)

Goldingay, John, and David Payne. *Isaiah 40–55: A Critical and Exegetical Commentary*. 2 vols. New York: T&T Clark, 2007. (C)

Seitz, Christopher R. "The Book of Isaiah 40–66: Introduction, Commentary, and Reflections." In *The New Interpreter's Bible*, edited by Leander Keck et al., 6:307–552. Nashville: Abingdon Press, 2001. (B)

Monographs and Special Studies

Baumann, Gerlinde. *Love and Violence: Marriage as Metaphor for the Relationship between YHWH and Israel in the Prophetic Books*. Collegeville, MN: Liturgical Press, 2003.

Kim, Hyun Chun Paul. *Ambiguity, Tension, and Multiplicity in Deutero-Isaiah*. New York: Peter Lang, 2003.

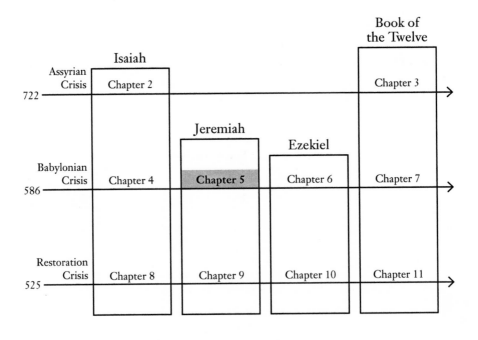

5

The Scroll of Jeremiah

Introduction and Response to the Babylonian Crisis

There may be no more powerful image in all of Christian theology than Daniel Berrigan's description of the world as a wound on the body of God. That he uses the image to form the title of his book about Jeremiah is a warning from the outset that readers of Jeremiah may well be wounded. The character named Jeremiah and the book named for him arise from the anguish of the Babylonian crisis in the sixth century BCE. The traditional identification of Jeremiah as the "weeping prophet," so powerfully depicted in portraits by Michelangelo and Rembrandt, aptly recognizes the way this scroll engages the pain of disaster and destruction.

The scroll called Jeremiah opens as most readers might expect, by introducing the prophetic character for which it is named and reporting the initial divine experience that establishes his task. When compared with the book of Isaiah, Jeremiah comes far closer to being a presentation of its primary character's career, yet the Jeremiah tradition provides other challenges for those who study it as a complete literary work. Perhaps the most significant challenge is that the book is extant in two different forms. The Greek version of the book, found in the fifth-century Christian Bibles that represent the Septuagint, is considerably shorter than the Hebrew version used to translate the major English versions of Jeremiah, and it places the chapters in a different order. The Oracles against Foreign Nations, which make up chapters 46–51 in the Hebrew version, appear in chapters 26–31 in the Greek version, and the internal order of the oracles is different as well. For a long time scholars assumed that the Hebrew book of Jeremiah, found in the Masoretic manuscripts, represented the older version of the book, and that the text tradition in the Greek manuscripts was a later revision. This assumption seemed logical simply because the book was written in Hebrew before it was translated into Greek, but the prevailing opinion among scholars has switched in recent decades, and most now think that the Hebrew precursor to the Greek version of Jeremiah was the older form of the book. The older, shorter Hebrew version no longer exists, however, and is only available in its Greek translation. This situation is significant because it reveals that the traditions behind the prophetic scrolls were sometimes quite fluid. Different groups that had access to the Jeremiah materials put them together in different ways, a possibility displayed in the evidence concerning Jeremiah among the Dead Sea Scrolls. Six fragmentary copies of Jeremiah were found among the scrolls: two of them appear to be closer to the Hebrew precursor of the Greek text, and four are closer to the Masoretic Hebrew text.[1] It is easy to assume that the further back in time we go, the more narrow the biblical tradition becomes, until we reach a single point in time when a book was first written. The reality may be quite the opposite, though: the further back we go, the more diverse the traditions become, and no single "first writing" of a book like Jeremiah ever happened. The earliest portions of Jeremiah emerged amid the Babylonian crisis, a time of enormous upheaval in Judah, and the book addresses the dividing of Judah into at least three separate communities, one remaining in a defeated Judah, one fleeing to Egypt, and one taken captive to Babylon. Scribes collected and shaped the material during a period when a defeated and destroyed nation struggled to understand its fate, and the formation of Jeremiah may have been part of the ground on which such a debate was held. If this is true, then readers make a mistake if they study the composition process and the final form of the book in isolation from each other.[2]

THE STRUCTURE OF THE BOOK

After looking at parts of the book of Isaiah and the Book of the Twelve, most of the components that make up the book of Jeremiah will look quite familiar. There are superscriptions, oracles, and narratives about the prophet. Table 5.1 lists some of the major components. There is also a similarity in the design of the book as a whole. The first half of the book has an overall negative tone, despite some positive elements, but in the middle of the book a shift toward hope and salvation takes place, giving the book a polarity similar to Isaiah and the Twelve.

Jeremiah's call narrative is in the logical place, at the beginning of the book, and it also serves as a programmatic statement for the entire scroll. After Jeremiah makes the customary objection to his divine selection in 1:6, which is overcome by a divine touch in 1:9, his task is defined by using a sequence of six infinitive verb forms in 1:10:

Table 5.1 Major Components of the Book of Jeremiah

Component	Jeremiah
Superscriptions	1:1; 2:1; 3:6; 7:1; 10:1; 11:1; 14:1; 21:1; 22:11; 25:1; 26:1; 27:1; 28:1[3]
Call Narrative	1:4–19
Oracles of Judgment	chapters 2–6
The Temple Sermon	chapter 7
Jeremiah's Confessions	11:18–23; 12:1–4 (6); 15:10–21; 17:14–18; 18:18–23; 20:7–18
Symbolic Actions	13:1–11; 16:1–9; 19:1–15; 27:1–28:17; 32:1–15; 36:1–32
The Book of Consolation	chapters 30–33
Oracles against the Nations	chapters 46–51
The Fall of Jerusalem	chapter 52 (narrative apparently from 2 Kings 24)

> See, today I appoint you over nations and over kingdoms,
>> to pluck up and to pull down,
>> to destroy and to overthrow,
>> to build and to plant.

The polarity of the book that is described above, created by a shift in dominance from negative statements of judgment to positive statements of restoration, is reflected in this collection of six verbs, four negative and two positive. This collection of verbs, in whole or in part, is repeated at various locations in the book, as illustrated in table 5.2 below.

Careful examination of these recurrences shows a shift toward the last two, more positive actions, or negations of the negative ones. The two positive verbs, build and plant, sometimes appear with the nouns "houses" and "vineyards," visible symbols of belonging and prosperity.

Jeremiah's call narrative precedes a long collection of oracular and sermonic material, containing relatively little narrative framework. Even though Jeremiah is a far more overt figure in his book than Isaiah in his book or the prophets in the Book of the Twelve, he often fades into the background and become a disembodied voice. Much of the material in Jeremiah 2–6 exhibits such a pattern before the brief narrative introducing the Temple Sermon brings Jeremiah back into clear view. Still, the report in chapter 7 is the divine revelation of the content of the Temple Sermon to Jeremiah, not the actual preaching event. The interaction between YHWH and Jeremiah dominates the first half of the book of Jeremiah, and the little narrative in 19:14–15

Table 5.2 Repeated Uses of Elements of 1:10 in the Rest of Jeremiah

Jeremiah	Element
12:14	pluck up (2)
12:15	pluck up
18:7	pluck up, pull down,[4] destroy[5]
18:9	build, plant
24:6	build, plant, *not* pluck up
29:5	build, plant
29:28	build, plant
31:4	build
31:5	plant
31:28	all six
31:40	*not* plucked up, *not* overthrown
32:41	plant
42:10	build, *not* overthrow, plant, *not* pluck up
45:4	overthrow,[6] built, pluck up, planted

becomes his first explicit public appearance.[7] Readers must assume all of the settings and audiences of the prophetic proclamations up until that point, but the text provides some assistance on that point, as Jeremiah 7–20 presents a prophetic drama in which multiple voices participate. The different voices can be difficult to distinguish, however, so at every point readers must ask who is speaking. Among the speakers, along with Jeremiah and YHWH, are the people of Israel and the city of Jerusalem itself, personified here and elsewhere as a grieving woman.[8]

Nearly all interpreters notice a major shift in the book of Jeremiah at the beginning of chapter 26. This shift includes a change to predominately prose-narrative material, compared to a slight majority of poetry in 1–25, and the use of repeated historical superscriptions at 26:1; 27:1; 28:1; 32:1; 34:1; 35:1; 36:1; 40:1; and 45:1. The second half of the book begins with the story of the trial of Jeremiah, which appears to revisit the Temple Sermon in Jeremiah 7. This is one of the many indicators that the book of Jeremiah does not present its material in a straightforward, chronological manner. Jeremiah 7 reports the divine command to the prophet to preach the Temple Sermon and presents the text of the sermon within the divine speech, but it does not report the actual preaching of the sermon, nor any reaction from an audience, yet the latter seems to be the subject of Jeremiah 26. After a divine command to speak and a brief summary of a sermon in 26:4–6, a group of priests and prophets instigate the crowd against Jeremiah, leading to his arrest and trial. The trial will be treated in more detail in the next section, but at this point it is important to recognize that parts of Jeremiah 26–52 are parallel to parts of 1–25 and provide additional narrative framework for some of the speech units present in earlier parts of the book. This observation leads to many more perceptions about the movement of the book of Jeremiah, which does not appear to take any simple direction. The section near the center of the book, often called the "Little Book of Consolation" (Jer. 30–33), does not function as a complete and thorough pivot from judgment and destruction to salvation and restoration. All of these themes are present on either side of this section. In light of what looks like a positive turn in chapters 30–33, the sudden turn back to primarily negative proclamations in 34–45 may even come as a shock to the system of the reader, and the jolt may indicate one of the most important effects of placing the Oracles against the Nations in 46–51.[9] If God's judgment and defeat of Israel's enemies may be seen as Israel's vindication, then the book is able to make one more positive move. The Masoretic version of the book, which English translations follow, also places the oracle against Babylon last in the collection in chapters 46–51, so that it is beside the story of Jerusalem's destruction in 52. If the more common conclusion is that the version reflected in the LXX is the earlier order, with the Oracles against the Nations in the middle of the book, then a rearrangement like the one found in the Masoretic version may be a sign that the earlier version was dissatisfying for some early readers.

Scholarship on the book of Jeremiah has reached a near consensus on a general process for the development of the book, though there are many disagreements about the details, the possible dates, and the persons involved. The process began with the oral proclamations of Jeremiah himself, some of which others eventually wrote down and collected. The person identified as Baruch within the book of Jeremiah, or someone like him, then added the biographical materials about Jeremiah as a framework for the oracles. Later an editor added a set of prose sermons, which reflect the theology of the book of Deuteronomy; finally another editor, again with a Deuteronomic perspective, produced the final scroll. It is possible to combine these final two stages as the simultaneous work of one person or a group of editors. At some point, however, the process diverged, producing the two significantly different final forms described above. Kathleen O'Connor, whose work on the book of Jeremiah will be central to the approach taken in this book, has described a process similar to this and has named it "how the book became unreadable."[10] While she does not object to the basic outlines of such a process, she is less concerned about working out the details of that process:

> But I am not trying to figure out how the book came to be. I am trying
> to gain a glimpse of what the book might have meant for its early read-
> ers, survivors of the Babylonian disaster and their offspring, the ones
> who did not know if they would ever again be God's chosen people.
> Using trauma and disaster studies, I want to ask how the book helps
> them survive. Its literary confusion contributes to that survival.[11]

This final statement and the approach to Jeremiah to which it points are
very much in alignment with the approach this book will take to reading Jeremiah and, in some ways, all of the prophetic scrolls. I am not as certain,
however, that the two questions at the beginning of that statement can be
separated. The first readers of the book of Jeremiah and the compilers of
the book were overlapping groups. The instability of the text of Jeremiah,
which seems to have lasted into the period when the copies among the Dead
Sea Scrolls were produced, indicates that reading the book of Jeremiah and
putting it together were processes that occurred together for a long time.
Reading the book of Jeremiah was an act of survival, as O'Connor has so powerfully demonstrated, but forming the text was an act of survival too.

Some interpreters have even imagined the earliest form of the "book" of
Jeremiah as a basket full of broken pieces of pottery, each with a portion of the
book written on it. Writing on broken pottery was a common practice in the
ancient world, so this is not an unrealistic image. The important point is that
putting together the full book of Jeremiah would have been a creative act that
could have been done in multiple ways, even by the same person at different
times.[12] This is an apt image in many ways, for it fits the culture in which the
book was produced, it fits the sense of brokenness that inhabits the book and
agonizes with its main character, and it matches one of the central images of
the book: the broken jug of Jeremiah 19:1–15.

THE SETTINGS OF THE BOOK

The primary setting of the book of Jeremiah is obviously the city of Jerusalem in the late seventh and early sixth centuries, but this simple identification becomes complicated in two ways. First, the nature of Jerusalem changes
so drastically within the course of the story that the book of Jeremiah tells
it becomes a different setting, more than once. Second, one of the turning
points that alters the nature of Jerusalem so severely is the deportation of
some of its citizens to Babylon in about 597. This event moved part of Jeremiah's audience to a new location, and that location became an important
additional setting of the book. Jeremiah's Letter to the Exiles in 29:4–23 may
be the most visible sign of this, because a letter, as a literary device embedded

within a story, carries the reader from sender to recipient, changing the setting of the story. There are also many other signs that parts of the book were even being formed within the exiled community there, developing the traditions established by Jeremiah.[13]

Table 5.3 Events of the Babylonian Crisis Significant for Jeremiah

BCE	Event
641	King Josiah of Judah begins to reign.
612	Nineveh's fall to the Babylonians.
609	Death of King Josiah of Judah.
609	Jehoiakim, son of Josiah, begins to reign.
605	King Nebuchadnezzar of Babylon comes to the throne.
598	Jehoiachin of Judah begins to reign.
597	First deportation of Israelites to Babylon.
597	Zedekiah of Judah begins to reign.
586	Destruction of Jerusalem and the second deportation.

Returning to the chronology of Jerusalem during the story of Jeremiah, we can identify four different phases in the life of the city and in the life of Jeremiah as one of its citizens. The superscription at the beginning of the book places the first stage of Jeremiah's career within the years of the reforms of King Josiah. The great king was revitalizing the worship of YHWH and returning Judah to obedience to the law, according to a scroll mysteriously "found" in the temple during its renovation. Jeremiah seems to refer to this scroll in 15:16.[14] Josiah was tragically killed, however, in a battle against the Egyptians, and one of his sons, Jehoiakim, was placed on the throne by Pharaoh Neco. The death of the king and the assertion of Egyptian control changed Jeremiah's setting and his relationship to it. This change led to a conflict with the political and religious leadership of Judah, which resulted in Jeremiah's trial, depicted in chapter 26. The opposition to any cooperation with Egypt is one of Jeremiah's most consistent positions (e.g., 42:15–19). A third phase in the nature of Jerusalem came about with the expansion of the Babylonian Empire. After several years of putting pressure on Judah, in 597 the Babylonians made Zedekiah king and exiled some of Judah's citizens to Babylon, while others fled to Egypt. This split Jeremiah's audience into at least three settings and altered his setting in Jerusalem again. In contrast to his views on Egypt, Jeremiah preached cooperation with Babylon, and he urged those already taken captive there to make a life for themselves and accept the exile as deserved punishment (e.g., 29:5). The book of Jeremiah takes its reading audience beyond the destruction of Jerusalem by the Babylonian army in

586. This event is described in Jeremiah 52, the last chapter of the book, in a text taken almost verbatim from 2 Kings 25, but earlier sections of the book (e.g., 40–42) address the people remaining in Judah after the invasion.

Aside from Jerusalem, Babylon, and Egypt, the book of Jeremiah also points to other settings, even if it may not take the audience there. Like Isaiah and the Book of the Twelve, Jeremiah has a section of Oracles against Foreign Nations. In the Masoretic version of the book and all English versions, these oracles are in chapters 46–51 and address Egypt, Babylon, Philistia, Moab, Ammon, Edom, Damascus, and Elam. As the book of Jeremiah progresses, its Jerusalem setting becomes diminished and its scope becomes more international. The book's address to multiple settings reflects the broken nature of Israel, which is a central theme of the book of Jeremiah.

THE ROLE OF THE PROPHET WITHIN THE BOOK

An important transformation takes place in the book of Jeremiah at the end of chapter 11 and the beginning of chapter 12. Up until this point, the book has consisted primarily of Jeremiah's proclamations of judgment against Judah and Jerusalem. Occasionally there is some narrative framework, such as in the opening verse of the Temple Sermon in 7:1–2, but most of these oracles are disembodied. Jeremiah was introduced as a character at the beginning of the book, but it is left largely to the reader to connect that person with the primary voice that speaks for the next ten chapters. The sequence of poems that are identified as the Confessions (or Laments or Complaints) of Jeremiah are delineated in table 5.4. There is no other place in the prophetic literature where the audience overhears this kind of intense, personal conversation between the prophet and YHWH. Some interpreters have drawn connections between the Confessions of Jeremiah and the Servant Songs of Isaiah, particularly the middle two poems, where the Servant speaks. The similarities between these two groups of poems are very important, yet it is also important to notice how they differ. The strongest point of connection comes at Isaiah 49:4.[15] This is the one verse in the Servant Songs where it sounds as if the Servant may be talking to YHWH. In the second servant song this verse serves as a moment for the redefining of the Servant's task, expanding it to an international scope, so it does not provide us with the same sustained view of the relationship between the Servant and YHWH as the Confessions of Jeremiah do. Moreover, the vague identity of the Servant hinders this kind of an understanding of individual struggle and turmoil. Even though these two voices are different and speak differently, we need to listen to them together on at least one particular issue. The Confessions of Jeremiah and the Servant

Songs of Isaiah make similar theological moves concerning the understanding of suffering, which put them in tension with much of Israelite tradition, including much of what is in other parts of the books of Isaiah and Jeremiah. Most of the book of Jeremiah assumes that suffering is divine punishment for disobedience, but the Confessions of Jeremiah, like the third and fourth servant songs in Isaiah, reveal that this can be a false assumption. Jeremiah's own experience disproves it, and that is the problem about which he is most often complaining to YHWH. The expected move in response to his suffering might be repentance, but he never does this because he knows he is innocent.[16]

The role of this theological shift in the book of Jeremiah is a matter of debate. It is possible to see this as the development of a parallel between the experience of YHWH and the experience of Jeremiah. Israel's rejection of YHWH is a frequent subject in Jeremiah 1–10, and YHWH sometimes expresses pain and anguish over this.[17] If this is the case, then the mistreatment of Jeremiah is becoming one more act of disobedience for which Judah will eventually suffer divine punishment. While this might be instructive or vindicating for Jeremiah himself, what does it do for readers of the book? A more important claim might be that the suffering of Jeremiah reveals that in the grinding brutality of national politics and disaster, some who suffer are innocent, and the readers of the book may locate themselves there.

Table 5.4 The Confessions of Jeremiah and Their Primary Ideas*

Jeremiah	Primary Idea(s)
11:18–23	Scheming against Jeremiah
12:1–4 (6)	The prosperity of the wicked
15:10–12	Regret over being born
15:15–21	Jeremiah's loyalty and his pain
17:14–18	Request to be saved from persecution
18:18–23	Revenge against those who plot against him
20:7–13	Inability to keep silent and revenge against persecutors
20:14–18	Wishing he had not been born

* Interpreters identify anywhere from five to eight of these poems. The list of eight above includes three pairs of poems that are adjacent to one another. Any combination of these pairs might be considered as a single poem, thus reducing the number of individual confessions.

The primary ideas, also identified in table 5.4, indicate that the task of being YHWH's prophet at such a time and place is having a brutal effect on Jeremiah. The life of the prophet and his message are becoming intertwined in this part of the book. It looks as though he is becoming the victim of the message of judgment he was commanded to proclaim. Other elements of this section of Jeremiah also play a role in the prophet's embodiment of his own message, perhaps the most significant of which is the command from YHWH in 16:1–2 that Jeremiah not marry and have children. The reason provided in the following verses is that children born during this time will soon be dying in the terrible events to come, but this also leaves Jeremiah more intensely alone in his task. In a bizarre sequence in 13:1–11, YHWH commands Jeremiah to buy a new undergarment, wear it for some time, then go and bury it in the bank of the Euphrates River. Later YHWH commands him to return and dig up the garment, which he finds to be rotted. There is some interpretation of this sign-act provided:

> Just so I will ruin the pride of Judah and the great pride of Jerusalem. This evil people, who refuse to hear my words, who stubbornly follow their own will and have gone after other gods to serve them and worship them, shall be like this loincloth, which is good for nothing. For as the loincloth clings to one's loins, so I made the whole house of Israel and the whole house of Judah cling to me. (13:9b–11a)

It is all but impossible to imagine any kind of narrative audience for such a symbolic action, and it hardly seems necessary for Jeremiah himself to receive whatever confirmation this experience might provide; but with this act placed in the book of Jeremiah, the readers become the audience. The effect is to join the person of Jeremiah even more closely with his message, to the extent that even his clothing is involved.

The fourth confession in the list in table 5.4 is closely connected to the symbolic action of Jeremiah that immediately follows it in 16:1–12. This is another symbolic action that would seem difficult, perhaps impossible, for an actual audience to observe, because it is negative in nature. YHWH's command to Jeremiah not to marry and have children is the opposite of the command given to Isaiah and Hosea, who are both commanded to have children and give them symbolic names that play a role in the prophetic message. Even though, in the book of Jeremiah, this command eventually leads to a conversation with the people in 16:10–13, it is difficult to see how a long-term avoidance of the behaviors of marrying and having children would lead to such a moment. This is a place where a symbolic action works much better as a literary unit and where the pattern of hearing God's words to Jeremiah (16:2–4) allows the reader to understand things that could not be grasped by an observing audience, whether inside or outside of the text.

The fifth, sixth, and seventh confessions listed in table 5.4 share some common ideas. Jeremiah's complaints here also include requests, and this is a point at which we might begin to see the Jeremiah character in the book as a reflection or microcosm of the nation of Judah. The most frequent idea in these three poems is the desire to see YHWH take vengeance upon those who are oppressing or persecuting him. For the character named Jeremiah, this kind of oppression would be an internal matter, because his opponents are those within the political, religious, and social power structure who do not like his preaching. For the nation of Judah, the oppressor can be understood in three ways. Most directly, their enemy or oppressor in this period is Babylon, the nation that controls them and will ultimately besiege and destroy them and take them captive. In another sense, their oppressor is YHWH, who, according to the preaching of Jeremiah, is using the Babylonian Empire to punish them for their sins of idolatry and injustice. A third way of looking at their oppression, through the eyes of the powerless members of the society, is to see the leadership as the cause of YHWH's punishment, using the Babylonian Empire as a tool, which would identify the leaders as the oppressors of the ordinary people. This would align such ordinary citizens of Judah with Jeremiah, all those who suffer at the hands of the political and religious establishment. The combination of these three perspectives, particularly the last one, makes the book of Jeremiah a tangled web of sin, judgment, punishment, and suffering. The roles of all involved, the people of Judah, the leadership of Judah, Jeremiah, YHWH, and the Babylonians, are shifting and multifaceted.[18]

The final confession, in 20:14–18, is the most despairing: Jeremiah wishes that he had not been born, a sentiment that echoes the first poetic speech of Job in Job 3. Just prior to this, in 20:1–3, a priest named Pashhur has beaten Jeremiah and placed him in stocks at one of the city gates. After his release, Jeremiah gives this priest a new name, "Terror-all-around," but in 20:10 it sounds as if this name has been turned back onto Jeremiah himself. According to the seventh confession, Jeremiah is caught in a bind, unable to keep silent, but unable to speak without becoming the object of scorn and ridicule. From the midst of this no-win situation, he cries out:

> Cursed be the day
>   on which I was born!
> . . . .
> Why did I come forth from the womb
>   to see toil and sorrow,
>   and spend my days in shame?
>   (20:14a, 18)

Many interpreters have identified a layer in the composition of the book of Jeremiah that is heavily influenced by the so-called Deuteronomistic view, which will receive more attention in the next section. Central to this understanding is the system of retribution that seems to have all parties in its grip in the story the book of Jeremiah is telling, but seems to be cracking under its own weight in the book itself. Jeremiah complains that this system is not working since he suffers undeservedly for his obedience to YWHW as a prophet. Jeremiah is about to proclaim the most straightforward declaration in the entire book about the coming destruction at the hands of Nebuchadnezzar in 21:1–10, but the Babylonians are not righteous, so why are they being rewarded with victory? In 21:7, Jeremiah must insist that YHWH is giving Judah "into the hands of King Nebuchadnezzar" (also spelled Nebuchadrezzar), because the only alternative is to believe that the gods of Babylon are stronger than Israel's God. As the first half of the book of Jeremiah comes to a close, the prophet continues to play a role in this drama: he sees the vision of the two baskets of figs in 24:1–2, and he takes the "cup of wrath" from the hand of YHWH in 25:15–17 in order to make "all the nations . . . drink it."

While Jeremiah is explicitly present in the first half of the book, as the speaker of the confessions and as the proclaimer of oracles and sermons, it is difficult to connect much of this material precisely to the life and career of Jeremiah the prophet. Even though this part of the book is filled with superscriptions and introductory formulas, they lack precise dates; this is a situation that changes abruptly in Jeremiah 25, which begins by placing the narrative "in the fourth year of King Jehoiakim."[19] In 25:3, Jeremiah also reminds readers that at this point he has been a prophet of YHWH for twenty-three years. The use of precise dates serves to connect the last chapter of Jeremiah 1–25 with 26–52, though this second half of the book opens with a dated superscription that is four years earlier than the one in 25:1. After the first half of the book comes to a conclusion with a divine announcement of disaster for all the nations, the book of Jeremiah backs up these four years to tell the story of Jeremiah more precisely.

The more explicitly biographical material about Jeremiah begins at Jeremiah 26. Two large sections, chapters 26–29 and 34–35, form a bracket around the Book of Consolation in 30–33. Jeremiah 26 tells the story of Jeremiah's trial, which seems to be the result of his preaching the Temple Sermon, the text of which is in Jeremiah 7. The internal agony of Jeremiah expressed in his Confessions finds its clearest context in this story. The superscription in 26:1 provides chronological setting for the story "at the beginning of the reign of King Jehoiakim," which would place it around 609. Jehoiakim was placed on the throne by Pharaoh Neco, so Jeremiah's opposition to any kind of dependence upon or cooperation with Egypt would have put them in conflict with each other. While chapter 2 of this book (above) portrayed conversations between Isaiah and Kings Ahaz and Hezekiah as partly divine self-conversations, because king and prophet are both divine mediators, the sense of a king as a divine mediator in the book of Jeremiah seems to have died with Josiah, leaving that aspect of prophetic royal interaction difficult to see in Jeremiah by this point. In Jeremiah 26:5–9 it is specifically the prophet's comparison of the Jerusalem temple's future to the story of Shiloh that creates the tension. It is not clear anywhere in the Old Testament exactly what had happened to Shiloh, but it is easy enough to assume that it had been abandoned as a worship site when the northern nation, Israel, was defeated by the Assyrians in the eighth century. Psalm 78:60 and Jeremiah 7:12–14 both make reference to the divine abandonment of Shiloh, which was the traditional home of the ark of the covenant before it was moved to Jerusalem by David. The subsequent trial of Jeremiah is an intricately told story, involving a number of characters, including two other prophets. One of these prophets is Micah of Morosheth (26:18), who is invoked by some of the elders who speak in Jeremiah's defense, quoting Micah 3:12. Their argument is that because Micah predicted the destruction of Jerusalem and was not executed by King Hezekiah, Jeremiah should not be executed for making the same prediction a century or so later. In 26:20–23 the narrator tells of another prophet named Uriah, who was executed by Jehoiakim for prophesying against Jerusalem. Jeremiah's life seems to hang in the balance, between these two prophetic figures and their dramatically different fates, until he is finally rescued by a person identified as Ahikam in 26:24.[20]

Opposition to Jeremiah continues in chapters 27–28, this time from another prophet named Hananiah. The conflict between these two prophets is centered around the symbol of the yoke and begins with a sign-act in which Jeremiah makes a yoke and puts it on himself, symbolizing the coming oppression of Judah and its neighbors by Babylon. Jeremiah's proclamation indicates the presence of prophetic opponents in 27:14, though Hananiah son of Azzur does not appear by name until 28:1. Jeremiah and Hananiah do not disagree about YHWH's punishment of Israel through the oppression of "the yoke of the king of Babylon," but they disagree concerning the length and extent of that punishment. In the year 594, Hananiah is declaring the punishment to be nearly over and seems to be promoting a revolt against Babylon among the citizens of Judah between the times of the two deportations (see table 5.3). Jeremiah places the confrontation between the two prophets in the temple, in front of an audience that includes "the priests and all the people" (27:16; 28:1). It becomes even more dramatic when Hananiah takes the yoke off Jeremiah's neck and breaks it, symbolizing the breaking of the yoke of Babylon (28:10). This kind of confrontation must have presented great difficulties for the audience. Hananiah's message would obviously have been more appealing than Jeremiah's, and it was consistent with the kinds of things some great prophets, such as Isaiah, said at certain times. Would the difficulty and lack of popularity of Jeremiah's message be enough to make it seem more likely to be true, since he would not have had any other motive to preach such a message?[21] But he was the old "Terror-all-around," Mister gloom-and-doom (cf. 20:3; etc.), who seemed to revel in predictions of disaster the way some prophets in every era do. The scene is even more important because it becomes a mirror image of the trial of Jeremiah in chapter 26, when Jeremiah pronounces a death sentence on Hananiah in 28:16. Unlike Jeremiah, however, no voices come forward to defend and protect Hananiah, and the next verse reports his death, but no cause of death is provided. Did Jeremiah or his supporters kill Hananiah?

Following this dramatic victory, Jeremiah broadens his audience. The letter that he writes to the exiles in chapter 29 carries the prophetic disagreement to Babylon. The argument is crucial for those who are living there in captivity, as the content of the letter makes clear. If the captivity in Babylon is nearly over, then the exiles should begin preparing to return to Judah. On the other hand, if it is to last for seven decades, as Jeremiah contends, then the appropriate response is to settle in and make a life for themselves there as best they can. This is exactly what Jeremiah urges them to do in the letter, and he does so by using the two positive verbs from the end of the list of six infinitives that have defined his proclamation from the beginning of the book in 1:10. He tells them to "build houses" and "plant gardens" (29:5), and with that statement the captivity and the restoration that will eventually follow it become inextricably bound. There are prophets in Babylon preaching otherwise, just as Hananiah has been doing in Jerusalem, and Jeremiah denounces them by name in 29:21, 31. There is no report on the outcome of this prophetic conflict other than the pronouncement of a death sentence for Shemaiah in 29:32; yet if read in parallel with the Jeremiah-Hananiah conflict in chapters 27–28, the prospects for the prophets Ahab, Zedekiah, and Shemaiah do not look good.

The biographical material on Jeremiah in the second half of the book is interrupted by the Book of Consolation in chapters 30–33. Because this text connects most closely to the restoration of Judah, it will be treated in chapter 9 of this work (below). This section does include some important actions by Jeremiah, including Jeremiah's purchase of a field and his prayer following the transaction, but these actions also have more to do with the later story of the restoration of Judah. The chronology of the Babylonian period resumes in 34:1 with a sequence of divine messages to Jeremiah while Nebuchadnezzar's army is surrounding Jerusalem.

A large biographical section about Jeremiah is held together by reports concerning a scroll written for Jeremiah by Baruch son of Neriah in Jeremiah 36 and 45. Baruch is mentioned by name about two dozen times in the book

---

Discussion Box 5.1 Relationship between
Jeremiah and the Book of Lamentations

In the Tanak, the book of Lamentations is one of the five Festival Scrolls in the third section, called the Writings; in Jewish tradition it is linked to the Ninth of Ab, the day that commemorates the destruction of the temples in Jerusalem. The Christian Old Testament spreads these five little scrolls out into various places in the canon, and Lamentations has ended up immediately after Jeremiah. Connections between the two books go back into ancient time and appear to rely, at least in part, on the assumption that the occasion described in 2 Chronicles 35:25, during which Jeremiah "uttered a lament for Josiah," was the origin of the book of Lamentations. Lamentations is a sequence of poems concerning the suffering of the people of Jerusalem during the three-year siege by the Babylonian army. The extent to which Jeremiah would have experienced this suffering and been able to write about it is uncertain, but the grief expressed in them is consistent with the traditional image of Jeremiah as the "weeping prophet." Rembrandt's classic painting *Jeremiah Weeping over the Fall of Jerusalem* brings this event and this description of the prophet together in a riveting image. Even if Jeremiah knew enough from direct observation, indirect reports, and his own imagination, this is only part of an argument that Jeremiah could have written the book, not that he did. In the end, it is much more important to recognize the emotional connections and tensions between the two books than to construct arguments about authorship with so little evidence available.

---

of Jeremiah, and more than half of these are in chapter 36. This part of the book is filled with stories about Jeremiah as the victim of oppression and captivity, from which he routinely manages to escape. Table 5.5 on page 106 lists these episodes, including those that appear prior to this part of the book.

It seems unlikely that this collection of stories appears here simply to fulfill the desire of the reading audience to know some details about the life of Jeremiah. If interest in Jeremiah's biography was such an issue, then it hardly makes sense that the story of his life simply ends in Egypt, unresolved, in chapter 44.[22] It is much more likely that the life of Jeremiah matched, and therefore enhanced, his prophetic message. Jeremiah was accused, subjected to judgment, and taken captive just like the people of Judah. He agonized over his fate and cried out to God about the unfairness of it, just as many of them must have done.[23] Jeremiah's harsh interaction with the Judahite

Table 5.5 The Hardships of Jeremiah

Jeremiah	Hardship
20:1–6	Jeremiah placed in stocks at the city gate
26:1–24	Jeremiah arrested and put on trial for preaching the Temple Sermon
32:1–5	Jeremiah imprisoned in the court of the guard
37:11–21	Jeremiah imprisoned in the cistern house and the court of the guard
38:1–6	Jeremiah held captive in a muddy cistern
40:1–4	Jeremiah bound with fetters
43–44	Jeremiah taken in exile to Egypt

refugees in Egypt in chapter 44 is the last time we see him, chronologically, as a narrative character. Beyond that text, he appears by name several more times as a speaker. The announcement to Baruch in chapter 45 is given a time and setting much earlier in Jeremiah's career, and the superscriptions within the oracles against foreign nations do not contain designations of time and setting. Thus the character named Jeremiah fades away, leaving behind an unsettled feeling, but this is fitting. The nation of Judah is in an unsettled position and will be so for a long time, as massive world events grind away on it. Perhaps the promise of persistence to Baruch in 45:5, so obviously moved out of chronological sequence, is the best the reader can hold on to for the nation as a whole.

THE PROCLAMATION OF JEREMIAH
CONCERNING THE BABYLONIAN PERIOD

The discussion so far in this chapter has established a historical and geographical setting for the book called Jeremiah, outlined some ways of understanding the literary structure of the whole book, and observed how Jeremiah operates as a character within it. Those three elements offer a framework to explore more precisely what the book has to say about the experience of Israel in the late seventh and early sixth centuries. The image of a Babylonian invasion appears early in the book of Jeremiah, in the image of the "boiling pot, tilted away from the north" that he sees as part of his call narrative in 1:13. Jeremiah 1–20 contains a lot of material related to the character Jeremiah, which was described in the prior section. Most of the remainder of this part of the book consists of judgment oracles against Judah, and at many places these oracles assume that the destruction of Judah is inevitable. Jeremiah 6, for example, is a lengthy poem that ends with a statement of divine rejection against Judah.

Jeremiah 10 describes Judah's idolatry and commands the audience to listen for "a great commotion [coming] from the land of the north to make the cities of Judah a desolation" (10:22). At other times, however, Jeremiah makes it sound as if repentance and reconciliation are still possible. In 3:12, Jeremiah is ordered by YHWH to say, "Return, faithless Israel. . . . I will not look on you in anger, for I am merciful." And in 17:19–23 Jeremiah stands at "the People's Gate," urging a recommitment to the Sabbath.

The sense of movement back and forth in several aspects of the book of Jeremiah might best be compared to the idea of "resonance," particularly as that term is used in the field of chemistry, to explain a substance that alternates back and forth between two possible forms in a way that allows it to act like both forms at the same time, like a hybrid substance. The punishment of Judah is both inevitable yet avoidable by means of repentance. The destruction of Jerusalem is both in the future and in the past. The word of YHWH to the Israelites is both doom and hope. It is little wonder that in the past some interpreters have called the book of Jeremiah things like a "hopeless hodgepodge."[24] It is not linear or consistent. There are ways to explain this situation by using a reconstruction of the book's composition process. The idea that materials expressing the views of opposing groups found their way into the book is compelling.[25] The situation this produces for readers of the finished scroll, however, is one of confusion and internal dissonance. One advantage of the set of changes in the world that are often labeled "postmodernism" is that a lack of consistency or linear coherence is no longer viewed as sloppy or careless, but can be an artful and effective way of expressing complex ideas and experiences. Postmodern observers are more comfortable with, and may even desire, other ways of putting a story together. Many modern films like *Magnolia, Memento, Batman Begins, Michael Clayton, Watchmen,* and *Slumdog Millionaire* provide good examples of this phenomenon. These films use shifts in perspective and nonchronological storytelling to add conflict and suspense to their plots and to emphasize certain elements that might not emerge as powerfully in a straightforward report of a narrative. The book of Jeremiah does not force a kind of coherence onto the experience of Israel that does not fit that experience, so a search for meaning must proceed in a different manner.[26]

Amid dominant messages of condemnation, some different notes are sounded in the early chapters of Jeremiah. One of those is the expression of grief, such as the one found in 4:19–31. The identity of the speaker in these verses is not always clear. The phrase "My anguish, my anguish! I writhe in pain!" does not immediately identify its speaker, but the statement in verse 22, "For my people are foolish," is typically understood as one coming from "Lady Zion," the city of Jerusalem depicted as a woman. In verse 27 the divine voice responds, and it is difficult to tell whether God joins in the grief, but certainly the text acknowledges the pain in 4:31. The divine observation of pain and mourning appears again in 9:17–22, but it is still unclear how YWHW feels about this. The grieving people also waver in their emotions, sometimes expressing understanding and acceptance of their punishment, as in 10:19:

> Woe is me because of my hurt!
>   My wound is severe.
> But I said, "Truly this is my punishment,
>   and I must bear it."

There are other times, however, when it seems to be too great or unjust, and they protest:

> Correct me, O Lord, but in just measure;
>   not in your anger, or you will bring me to nothing.
>   (10:24)

While the coming Babylonian invasion is treated metaphorically or symbolically, using the vision of the boiling pot in 1:13–19 or the act of breaking the clay jug in 19:1–15, it is also described in a more direct manner in several places in the book. Prominent, poetic versions of this prediction appear in 4:5–31; 6:1–30; and 10:17–25. In each of these cases, the character named Jeremiah has receded into the background. The descriptions of the invasion include the naming of weapons and other instruments of war, including horses and chariots (4:13), ramp (6:6), bow and javelin (6:23), and sword (6:25). Each of these texts specifically describes ancient military tactics in a siege (4:16; 6:6; 10:17), which involved surrounding a walled city with an army, not allowing anyone or anything to go in or out, and waiting for the population to be weakened by hunger, thirst, and disease. At the point when the population could no longer defend itself, the invading army would breach the wall, using ramps and/or battering rams. These brutal texts in Jeremiah also describe the extent of the destruction in vivid detail.   •

Interpreters who have sought to identify multiple layers of composition in Jeremiah have often described a set of "Deuteronomistic prose sayings." These sayings are certain parts of the book that sound not only like Deuteronomy, but also like the books of Joshua, Judges, Samuel, and Kings, often labeled the Deuteronomistic History. Among the most commonly identified sayings in this layer of the scroll are 7:1–8:3; 11:1–17; and 25:1–11.[29] The saying in 25:11 introduces the "cup of wrath" oracle that concludes Jeremiah 1–25. While the harsh divine judgment of this oracle fits well within the themes forming the first half of the book, some elements seem out of place,

---

Discussion Box 5.2 God and Sexual Assault

The issue of the prophets' use of the marriage metaphor arose in chapter 3 of this book (above) and will appear again in chapter 6. The metaphor is also in Jeremiah 2–3, but an even more troubling image appears in Jeremiah 13:20–27. Here YHWH declares that he will rape Israel. The most pointed text is verse 26:

> I myself will lift up your skirts over your face,
> and your shame will be seen.

Some interpreters try to understand this as a divine threat to strip Judah/Jerusalem naked in public, still a violent act of sexual abuse, but O'Connor's argument that this is explicit rape language prevails against such efforts to soften the text.[27] O'Connor's own attempt to come to grips with the horror of this passage is to present the choice that the people of Judah had before them concerning YHWH. He was either defeated by the gods of Babylon, or was acting in and through the Babylonian army to destroy, punish, and rape Jerusalem. She characterizes the choice of YHWH as rapist as "provisional thinking about God" that "restores the capacity to speak what cannot be spoken."[28] As readers, we are horrified, but perhaps that is the point, for us to catch a sense of the horror experienced by Jeremiah and his audience. That this literary move creates enormous theological problems makes it a good fit for the book of Jeremiah.

---

especially the list of foreign nations and kings in 25:19–26. This is a good place to remember that the book of Jeremiah exists in two versions, as the introductory material in this chapter described. In the Greek version, the collection of Oracles against the Nations begins in the middle of what is chapter 25 in the Hebrew version, which is used to produce all English versions. The list in 25:19–26 and the worldwide disaster that follows would be a fitting conclusion to the oracles concerning foreign nations, so they may be a relic of the earlier order of the book.[30] In the Hebrew/English order, the oracles against the foreign nations must wait their turn to play a specific function at the end of the book.

The preceding section on Jeremiah as a character looked at much of Jeremiah 26–45 because of the heavily biographical nature of those chapters. The material that lies in the center of these chapters, Jeremiah 30–33, will await discussion in chapter 9 of this book, because of the connections to the restoration of Judah. One more fascinating text needs some attention before moving on to the conclusion of the book, and that is the report about a group of people called the "Rechabites" in Jeremiah 35. The precise identity and origins of this group are not available to us, but their significance in the book of Jeremiah rests on the commands they report were given them by their founding figure, Jonadab son of Rechab. Two such commands are identified: "Never drink wine" (v. 6); "Live in tents," "not . . . houses" (vv. 7, 9–10).[31] Jeremiah's test of the Rechabites in the temple reveals that they have remained faithful to the first command, and it allows them to explain the reasons for a temporary compromise on the second. The immediate threat of the Babylonian army has made it impossible for them to live outside the city in tents. When this episode closes with a blessing of the Rechabites and a divine promise of their survival, the result is that the demands of YHWH do not look rigid or unreasonable, thus removing the possibility of such a complaint from any of Jeremiah's audiences.[32] Jeremiah can then use the example of the Rechabites to condemn the unfaithfulness of Judah (v. 17).

If the emerging majority opinion among scholars of the book of Jeremiah is correct, counting the Greek order of the material as older than the Hebrew/English order, then the function of the oracles against the nations in chapters 46–51 commands careful attention because it reflects a deliberate reshaping of the Jeremiah tradition.

Table 5.6 Oracles against the Nations in Jeremiah

Nation	Jeremiah
Egypt	46:1–24
The Philistines	47:1–7
Moab	48:1–47
The Ammonites	49:1–6
Edom	49:7–22
Damascus	49:23–27
Kedar and Hazor	49:28–33
Elam	49:34–39
Babylon	50:1–51:58

Along with the movement of the whole collection of oracles concerning foreign nations to the end of Jeremiah, there is also an internal shift in order, moving the oracle against Babylon from second position in the Greek text, following the one against Egypt, to the last position (see table 5.6). Not only does the collection itself form part of the climax of the Hebrew version, but also the judgment of Babylon is in the climactic position among them. The rearrangement places the judgment of Babylon in Hebrew and English versions in Jeremiah 50–51, right next to the story of the Babylonian invasion in Jeremiah 52, which Jeremiah takes from 2 Kings 25. If Jeremiah's life parallels the life of the people of Judah, as an earlier section of this chapter explained, then the death of Babylon in chapters 50–51 is parallel to the death of Hananiah, Jeremiah's greatest personal opponent, in 28:17. The book of Jeremiah sees future hope, and the more pleasant aspect of this is a future restoration for Judah, but it also includes divine vengeance against Judah's enemies. One text that softens the vengeance is 49:39, where YHWH promises to "restore the fortunes of Elam" after inflicting punishment upon them. This is the final word about all the foreign nations, except for Babylon.

The scroll of Isaiah seems incomplete in its proclamation concerning the Babylonian period. In light of the destruction of the northern kingdom during the Assyrian period, and the miraculous salvation of Judah at the end of the eighth century, the destruction of Judah and Jerusalem by the Babylonians creates some cognitive dissonance. The positive result of the tension is a focus on the restoration of Judah in Isaiah 40–55, and the book of Isaiah makes great advances toward understanding the redemptive value of suffering, while ignoring the events that inflicted the suffering almost entirely. The scroll of Jeremiah more than fills the void in powerful, sometimes brutal, fashion. The voice of Jeremiah may clash with the Isaiah tradition, but the suffering of Jeremiah himself, because of his faithfulness to the prophetic task, finds harmony with the Servant Poems in Isaiah. The second half of the book of Jeremiah addresses many different groups and individuals in different ways. Judgment and destruction are the loudest elements, but the positive portrayals of, and promises to, people like Ahikam (26:24), Baruch (45:1–5), the Rechabites (35:1–19), and the Elamites (49:39) differentiate degrees of guilt and innocence and offer differing consequences.

JEREMIAH INTERRUPTED

The book of Jeremiah does not contain a clean break between the portions of the book that address the Babylonian period and those that address the Restoration period. The nonchronological nature of the book allows the destruction of Jerusalem in the early sixth century to embrace the entire book, even though there are materials that address the late sixth and fifth centuries. The famous section in chapters 30–33 stands out most clearly among such texts, but there are earlier passages in the book, such as 16:14–21 and 23:1–8, which also address the rebuilding of Judah and Jerusalem. Texts like these, whose horizon is the Restoration period, will be the subject of chapter 9 of this book.

It is important that the restoration of Judah lies in the center of the book and not just at its end, because the harsh judgment throughout Jeremiah may cause us to forget that, from the beginning, the ultimate goal is a restored Judah—but does the end justify and adequately explain the means? The great challenge of the book persists, when we view it from the same direction as did the first readers of the finished book in the Persian period, though at a greater distance. Is everyone to blame for the suffering they experience? Do the citizens of Judah get what they deserve, collectively and individually?[33] The book of Jeremiah cannot fully resolve the predisaster versus postdisaster tension it creates, but perhaps it can point us in the direction of the right kinds of questions we need to continue to ask in the midst of a wounded world. This is a question that Ezekiel, whose book is the subject of the next chapter, poses in profound and creative ways. When chapters 9 and 10 resume the discussion of Jeremiah and Ezekiel, delineation of guilt and punishment will become a primary question.

Resources for Further Research

Commentaries

Allen, Leslie C. *Jeremiah: A Commentary*. Louisville, KY: Westminster John Knox Press, 2008. (B)

Fretheim, Terrence E. *Jeremiah*. Macon, GA: Smyth & Helwys, 2002. (B)

Holladay, William L. *Jeremiah*. 2 vols. Minneapolis: Fortress Press, 1986–89. (C)

Lundbom, Jack R. *Jeremiah 1–20: A New Translation with Commentary*. New York: Doubleday, 1999. (C)

Miller, Patrick D. "The Book of Jeremiah." In *The New Interpreter's Bible*, edited by Leander E. Keck et al., 6:553–927. Nashville: Abingdon Press, 2001. (B)

Stulman, Louis. *Jeremiah*. Nashville: Abingdon Press, 2005. (A)

Monographs and Special Studies

Biddle, Mark E. *Polyphony and Symphony in Prophetic Literature: Rereading Jeremiah 7–20*. Macon, GA: Mercer University Press, 1996.

Brueggemann, Walter. *The Theology of the Book of Jeremiah*. Cambridge: Cambridge University Press, 2007.

Nicholson, Ernest W. *Preaching to the Exiles: A Study of the Prose Tradition in Jeremiah*. Oxford: Blackwell, 1970.

O'Brien, Julia. *Challenging Prophetic Metaphor*. Louisville, KY: Westminster John Knox Press, 2008.

O'Connor, Kathleen M. *Jeremiah: Pain and Promise*. Minneapolis: Fortress Press, 2011.

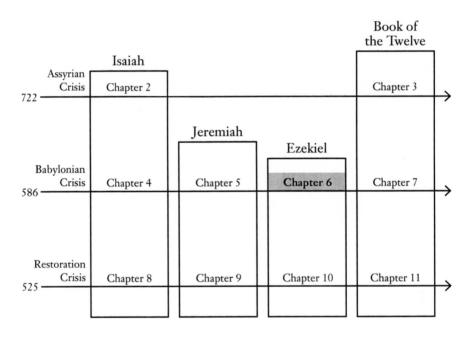

6

The Scroll of Ezekiel

Introduction and Response to the Babylonian Crisis

The character named Ezekiel and the book that goes by his name serve as reminders that while there are many common patterns and connections between the prophetic scrolls, each of them is also unique. From the opening superscription this uniqueness is apparent, as Ezekiel speaks in first person and provides us with a specific day and location for the opening event. The text becomes confusing when the first-person superscription in 1:1, which seems to be introducing a vision, leads to a third-person superscription that supplies the reader with Ezekiel's name and a different identification of the date (1:2–3). The other voice also informs the reader that Ezekiel is a priest and uses the mysterious phrase "the hand of YHWH was on him there." The description of Ezekiel's famous *merkabah* vision, beginning in 1:4, in first-person language, makes the third-person superscription in 1:2–3 feel like an intrusion, but without it we would not know to whom we are listening.

The vision Ezekiel describes, which tradition has labeled using the Hebrew word for chariot, *merkabah*, is stunning in its beauty and complexity. Nothing like it appears in the prophetic literature up to this point, because no other vision has been so elaborate in its symbolic description. Isaiah sees YHWH and the heavenly beings accompanying the divine being, but there is no attempt to say what the divine being looks like, and no attempt to hide God's appearance behind symbolism. YHWH directs Jeremiah to see things that have symbolic meanings, but they are ordinary objects—a branch of an almond tree, a boiling pot of water—so they may not be visions at all. Ezekiel's vision is so extraordinary that elements of it have become iconic. The four creatures of 1:10 are a complex of symbols later utilized by the writer of the New Testament book of Revelation (4:7), and these four creatures—an angel, a lion, an ox, and an eagle—became symbols for the four Gospels in Christian tradition.

The wheels within wheels in Ezekiel 1:15–21 have inspired a classic gospel song, an early attempt to fly, and wild theories about UFOs.

The strange qualities of both the person named Ezekiel and the book named for him have led to widely divergent understandings of the relationship between the two and, specifically, of how and when the book came to be written in the form we possess. The extensive use of precisely dated introductory formulas has led some interpreters to assume that the final form of the book is closely connected to a historical figure named Ezekiel, but the book of Ezekiel pays almost no attention to any kind of audience for Ezekiel's proclamations or performances in the text. This may mean that the material in the book originated as literature, rather than as public proclamations and performances, and thus some interpreters have promoted the idea of Ezekiel as primarily a writer and the producer of the book in something like its present form.[1] Other interpreters see enormous distance between (1) the literary character named Ezekiel, who is beset by wild visions and commanded by God to perform bizarre symbolic actions, and (2) the careful and orderly narrator of the book, who presents the character.[2] The book of Ezekiel may not exhibit the exact combination of clues found in other scrolls that some of its contents originated in spoken form and that it slowly grew into its current written form; but the idea that it came to exist as a prophetic scroll in an entirely different way than the other three would require significantly more evidence than proponents of the idea have presented.[3]

The text of Ezekiel is not present in two obviously different forms, like the book of Jeremiah, but the Hebrew text that is translated in all English versions exhibits considerable problems, and there are some differences between the Greek and Hebrew text as large as whole verses found in one and not the other. Recently a Greek manuscript of Ezekiel known as Papyrus 967 has generated significant discussion. The existence of the manuscript came to light over a period of several decades during the twentieth century, sometimes a few pages at a time.[4] Some recent research points toward the possibility that this Greek manuscript was produced from a Hebrew form of the book

Table 6.1 Significant Events for Ezekiel in the Babylonian Period

BCE	Event
597	The first deportation of Judahites to Babylon
593	The date of Ezekiel's initial vision (1:4–28a)
586	The fall of Jerusalem and the second deportation
585	Ezekiel hears of the fall of Jerusalem from a messenger (33:21)
573	The date of Ezekiel's final vision (chaps. 40–48)

of Ezekiel substantially different from the one that we have, but it is too early to draw firm conclusions about such a proposal.[5] The text treated here and in chapter 10 of this book will be the Hebrew version of the book, which is typically translated into English versions of Ezekiel.

THE STRUCTURE OF THE BOOK

Like the books of Isaiah and Jeremiah, Ezekiel is a complex, composite work that has a sense of movement from judgment to salvation, and the book has a distinct turning point in the middle at Ezekiel 33. Perhaps the most obvious and unique feature is the framework formed by the visions that begin and end the book and two more elaborate vision reports between them. The four major vision accounts are situated in Ezekiel 1–3, 8–10, 37, and 40–48. The first, second, and fourth visions go together because all three contain "the appearance of the likeness of the glory of the LORD." The vision framework and the intensive use of formulas with precise dates have led the majority of scholars to conclude that Ezekiel is a very carefully ordered book. After the apparent disorder found in so much of the prophetic literature so far, such a conclusion may be quite welcome, yet may also be a bit premature.

There have been some significant attempts to understand the fourteen chronological formulas in the book as deliberate literary, structural devices.[6]

Table 6.2 Chronological Notations in Ezekiel

Ezekiel	Chronological Note
1:1	30th year of (?), 4th month, 5th day
1:2	5th year of Jehoiachin's exile, 4th month, 5th day
8:1	6th year, 6th month, 5th day (of Jehoiachin's exile)
20:1	7th year, 5th month, 10th day
24:1	9th year, 10th month, 10th day
26:1	11th year, (?) month, 1st day
29:1	10th year, 10th month, 12th day
29:17	27th year, 1st month, 1st day
30:20	11th year, 1st month, 7th day
31:1	11th year, 3rd month, 1st day
32:1	12th year, 12th month, 1st day
32:17	12th year, 1st month, 15th day
33:21	12th year, 10th month, 5th day
40:1	25th year, (1st?) month, 10th day

The very uneven distribution of the markers makes the proposal awkward as a grand organizational scheme, but it is important to pay attention to the formulas and the role they play in the text.[7] For example, each of the visions of the "glory of YHWH" begins with one of the dated formulas in 1:1; 8:1; and 40:1. The dates generally follow a chronological order through the book, though the date in 26:1 comes slightly later than those in 29:1; 30:20; and 31:1. The one extreme violation of the chronological sequence is the date in 29:17, some sixteen years after the ones on either side, but this is the introduction to Ezekiel's revised oracle against Tyre, which looks like an insertion an editor added after the original oracle did not come true.[8] Finally, the dates place the vision of the restored temple long after all of the other chronological events, which occur within a fairly brief period of about seven years.

The discussion below and in chapter 10 (below) will present a number of additional reasons to conclude that the scroll of Ezekiel continued to develop into the Persian period. Most interpreters accept the general observation that the book of Ezekiel takes a significant turn at chapter 33, where it begins to speak more of mercy and restoration and moves toward the final two visions. The primary dispute concerning the broad outlines of the book is whether to consider the collection of oracles concerning foreign nations in chapters 25–32 as a conclusion to the first half of the book, an introduction to the second half of the book, or a transition between the two halves. The discussion of Ezekiel's proclamation below will treat this question in more detail and will identify points of connection between the oracles concerning foreign nations and both halves of the book, making the transitional option the best choice.

THE SETTINGS OF THE BOOK

The geographical settings in Ezekiel have been a matter of lively discussion and debate. In the opening superscription, the prophet locates himself in Babylon, "by the river Chebar," a location of great theological importance, because Ezekiel is about to elaborate a grand vision of divine presence. Hence he wants to declare that the divine presence is in Babylon, with the exiled community. In 3:14–15, Ezekiel reports being carried to the Babylonian setting by "the spirit," or wind, but there had been no report of him leaving after chapter 1. In 3:22 the spirit forces Ezekiel into an unnamed valley, where the vision from chapter 1 appears to him again. At times in the sequence of strange events and behaviors that Ezekiel describes in chapters 4–12, he seems to be in Jerusalem. There are several ways to respond to the confusing shifts in location. Some have proposed that YHWH physically transported Ezekiel to various places during the time between the two deportations of Judahites to Babylon, between 597 and 586.[9] Walther Eichrodt famously insisted that Ezekiel resided in Babylon, ministering among the exiles, and that Ezekiel addressed the prophetic words concerning Jerusalem to an exilic audience in Babylon. Eichrodt argued against two fronts in the scholarship of his day: One of these views held that Ezekiel had "two spheres of activity," Jerusalem and Babylon, and the written book of Ezekiel wove the two spheres together. The other view characterized Ezekiel as a "prophet without a people," who spoke to a Jerusalem audience while in Babylon. Instead, Eichrodt insisted that the exiles were Ezekiel's audience and Jerusalem was his primary subject because Jerusalem's fate was a topic of intense concern to him and his audience, even though they were not living there.[10]

Much of the dispute about Ezekiel's location seems unnecessary if the book is understood, like the other prophetic scrolls, to present an alternative world of the imagination. In 3:12–14 Ezekiel reports that "the spirit lifted me up and bore me away" to be with the exiles in Babylon, "by the river Chebar." The description is very much like the vision in chapter 10, when Ezekiel sees the glory of YHWH rise up out of the temple and depart from Jerusalem. Similarly, the spirit lifts Ezekiel and brings him to the "east gate" of the temple in 11:1. In 3:22–23, Ezekiel goes out into a valley, apparently under his own power, but because YHWH commanded him to, though the valley is unidentified. As Ezekiel begins his collection of symbolic actions in chapters 4–5 the location is not clear, but the presumed context of the acts is Jerusalem, so many readers assume he is there. Ezekiel moves around a lot, just as the glory of YHWH and YHWH's spirit do. The lack of an audience in the book, a void filled by readers, means the physical location of the "historical Ezekiel" is of little, if any, importance. Specific movements to and from specific or implied locations can be literary devices that take the reader to the appropriate place to see and hear Ezekiel, and to see and hear with him. Literary settings need not be tied to real-world limitations of time and space.

The arguments above indicate the complexity and strangeness of the book of Ezekiel, particularly as it relates to space and location. The contents of Ezekiel provide a lot of chronological cues, but some aspects of the book of Ezekiel are not chronological in nature. For example, the vision in Ezekiel 8–10 of the glory of YHWH leaving the temple in Jerusalem seems to be prior to the vision of that glory in Babylon in Ezekiel 1. Most modern interpreters respond to these observations by accepting that the book is not trying to operate within the spatial and temporal restraints of ordinary life. Rather, the entire book presents itself as an imaginative vision, moving the reader wherever the reader needs to be to hear and see the prophet present the word of YHWH.

Ezekiel's final two visions offer additional examples. The famous vision of the valley of bones in Ezekiel 37 takes place in an unnamed valley, like the (same?) one he visited in 3:22. The spirit transports the prophet in Ezekiel 37 as it transported him to the river Chebar in 3:14. The spirit's activity and the prophet's movement connect the parts of the book, not in temporal or spatial ways, but in terms of the nature of Ezekiel's experience, the contents of the vision, and the proclamation to the audience, the readers of the book. The last nine chapters of the book of Ezekiel are a vision of a new temple in a restored Jerusalem, after the exile. Once again, at 40:2, the vision relocates the prophet in time and space. The temple that he sees is not a structure that can exist in ordinary time and space, but an elaborate vision.

THE ROLE OF THE PROPHET WITHIN THE BOOK

It has been impossible to avoid references to the person named Ezekiel while discussing the structure of the book and the settings in which events happen, because these aspects are so intimately connected. The book of Ezekiel speaks in the first-person voice of Ezekiel and the third-person voice of a narrator, though the first is far more common. Ezekiel's name appears only twice in the book, at 1:3 and 24:24. One of the more striking features of the book's language is the way the divine character consistently addresses the prophet. The literal Hebrew expression is "Son of man," and most English translations use this phrase. The New Revised Standard Version chose to use the term "Mortal" instead, in part to avoid heavily gendered language referring to human beings. The additional idea that the phrase intends primarily to remind the character named Ezekiel in the text, and the reader who is encountering the text, that Ezekiel is human is probably correct, and the choice of "Mortal" reflects this well. Using "Son of man" presents one further problem because Jesus often uses the Greek version of the phrase in the New Testament Gospels to refer to himself, but it is unlikely that Jesus or the writers of the Gospels were making any reference to Ezekiel.[11]

In much of the vision material, Ezekiel recedes into the background, but his presence is not as far away as some of the other prophets because the extensive use of first-person language keeps him overt. First-person verbs, in places like 1:4, 15, 24, and 27, frequently remind the reader that Ezekiel is seeing and hearing these phenomena and invite us to see and hear with the prophet. Speculation about the psychology of Ezekiel has been fairly common during the past century. Because the level of detail in the visions is unprecedented in the Old Testament, and so far removed from ordinary human existence, it is natural to wonder what the prophet's mental state may have been on such occasions. Certain questions about Ezekiel's mental state find some footing in the text and the way it presents the character named Ezekiel because the use of the phrase "the hand of YHWH" to describe a force that takes control of Ezekiel appears so prominently. In the prophetic literature outside Ezekiel, only Isaiah uses the phrase, and in all five occurrences in Isaiah "the hand of YHWH" is a metaphor for God's strength or presence accomplishing something. The seven texts that use the phrase in Ezekiel to describe an action of YHWH directly on the prophet are unique in the prophetic literature. The narrator uses the phrase one time (1:3), and the other six uses appear in first-person statements by Ezekiel. In most cases the divine action transports Ezekiel to another place (3:14, 22; 37:1; and 40:1), and each of the major visions of Ezekiel opens with such an experience. In two cases (3:26; 33:22) the experience renders Ezekiel unable to speak until the hand of YHWH departs. The episode in 33:21–22 represents a rare case in the book of Ezekiel when another person, here described as "a fugitive" who comes to report the fall of Jerusalem, speaks to Ezekiel. These reports, taken together, make it reasonable to assume that the Ezekiel character enters an altered mental state on such occasions. Whether the person named Ezekiel, outside of the text, suffered from some kind of condition that caused what we might call seizures or trances is of little importance. What is important is that from a literary perspective readers are being invited into these experiences, to have them along with the character named Ezekiel in the book. "The hand of YHWH was upon me there" becomes a means of joining the senses of Ezekiel with the senses of the readers, so that we can see and hear with him

One other aspect of Ezekiel 1–3 that deserves attention is the way it may function as a call narrative for Ezekiel. While some of the elements of a call narrative are missing, and the presence of the vision distracts from this purpose, other parts of the text support the idea. YHWH gives Ezekiel a lot of instructions in chapters 2–3 that are more general in nature and seem to be related to his whole prophetic career. These include the striking instruction to eat the scroll in 3:1–3, an act involving the preparation of Ezekiel's mouth, similar to Isaiah 6:7 and Jeremiah 1:9. Perhaps the most disconcerting aspect of the commissioning is the divine threat to Ezekiel in 3:18 and 20 that if he fails at his prophetic task, and God subsequently punishes the Israelites, God will hold him responsible: "Their blood I will require at your hand." It is rare in the Israelite prophetic tradition for a prophet to be accountable for the response of his intended audience. In Isaiah 6:9–13, YHWH predicts the failure of Isaiah's work, but there is no sense that Isaiah is responsible. On the contrary, Isaiah's faithful proclamation will bring about their lack of faithful response, but the responsibility belongs to the audience, not to the prophet. Ezekiel's fate, on the other hand, is completely tied up with the fate of his

Discussion Box 6.1 Prophecy and Mental Illness

The idea of mental illness is relatively modern. For most of human history, persons who acted consistently outside of the norm were considered to be affected by spirits or other types of supernatural forces. Modern psychology has made enormous progress in understanding the human mind and behavior, but is any of that knowledge helpful in the task of interpreting ancient texts like the prophetic scrolls of the Old Testament? The use of psychology in attempts to understand the book of Ezekiel has a relatively long and controversial history, beginning with an article written by August Klostermann in 1877. The title of that article can be roughly translated into English as the rather innocuous "Ezekiel: A Contribution to a Better Appreciation of His Person and His Writing." In the article, Klostermann described Ezekiel's condition by using the somewhat vague term "catalepsy," which would have included loss of ability to move (Ezek. 4:1–8) and speak (33:22).[12] This idea lay dormant across a very important time period that included the groundbreaking work of Sigmund Freud and Carl Jung. Psychoanalysis of Ezekiel was then picked up by Edwin Broome, whose 1946 article "Ezekiel's Abnormal Personality" met primarily with ridicule from biblical scholars.[13] The general criticism was that psychoanalyzing a person across such a large span of time and space is a useless enterprise. This is a valid issue to raise, but some of these interpreters seem to have been offended by the idea that mental illness could have played a role in prophecy and seek to defend Ezekiel against what they perceived as an accusation. The psychological proposals of Broome received a vigorous rehabilitation in a 1993 book by David Halperin, whose primary conclusion involved interpreting the vision in Ezekiel 8:7–12 as an expression of "dread and loathing of female sexuality," a condition that he used to explain many of the strange features of the book of Ezekiel.[14] An additional question on this issue, in light of the approach taken in this book, is whether any attempts to understand Ezekiel from a psychological perspective are still valid if we understand him primarily as a literary character, rather than as a person in the sixth-century world outside of the text. It is easy to dismiss such questions on grounds of lack of evidence, but it is difficult to avoid one final question: What would we think of a person we saw acting like Ezekiel in our own world?

audience.[15] The responsibility placed upon Ezekiel becomes even more confusing when he is bound by cords in 3:25 "so that you cannot go out among the people," and he becomes mute in 3:26 "so that you shall be speechless and unable to reprove them." The final verse of Ezekiel 3 seeks to clarify this, contending that Ezekiel will be able to speak only when YHWH opens the prophet's mouth, which may mean that Ezekiel will become incapable of any ordinary human conversation.[16]

Questions about Ezekiel's behavior in connection with his visionary experiences invite examination of another kind of experience that often afflicted him. Other prophets we have already examined performed symbolic actions, or sign-acts, but none of those did so in ways as strange as Ezekiel. When the account of the first vision ends, the book carries the Ezekiel character into an intense sequence of symbolic actions. It is difficult to know how readers are to understand the sequence and how the sign-acts are related to each other. There are no chronological markers in Ezekiel 4–5. The introductory phrase "And you . . ." (AT), followed by an imperative verb form, marks out five different acts, beginning in 4:1, 3, 4, 9, and 5:1, but some of the acts seem necessarily to coincide.[17] The text weaves some explanation of the meaning of these actions into the divine commands, but there are more comprehensive explanations in separate sections like 4:16–17 and 5:5–17. Without such explanations the divine speeches provide, the acts might seem incomprehensible, which raises questions about any understanding of the acts as performances for real audiences outside the text.

The first two sign-acts, 4:1–2 and 4:3, go together, assuming the city that Ezekiel is to portray on a brick in the first sign-act is also the city he uses along with an iron plate in the second. Together they establish the Babylonian siege of Jerusalem as the setting and the separation of the prophet (God?) from the city in its distress. The next two acts are considerably more elaborate and also closely related to each other, and they place more significant physical demands on the prophet than the first two. The divine command for Ezekiel to lie on each of his sides for a particular number of days is curious for many reasons, among which is the apparent inclusion of the northern kingdom of Israel, long since vanished, in the drama he enacts. Ezekiel 4:5 says that the 390 days Ezekiel lies on his left side correspond to 390 years of punishment for Israel, though it is not clear what actual years these might match, or why the particular number is chosen. The forty days of lying on his right side to depict the punishment of Judah has no explanation either. The fourth sign-act takes place at the same time that Ezekiel is lying on his sides: it describes the diet and food-preparation regimen Ezekiel must follow during this period. Interpreters have understood the strange nature of the food and its limited quantity in two ways. Those who connect the food preparation more closely to the siege portrayal in 4:1–3 emphasize the shortage of food that characterized conditions inside Jerusalem during the siege. Others make the more apparent connection between the exile and eating and emphasize the lack of choice and freedom in eating during captivity or forced relocation, a point 4:13 seems to make explicit.[18] When Ezekiel objects to the command to cook his food over a fire made with human dung (4:12), YHWH compromises and allows him to use cow dung instead (v. 15). Curiously, Ezekiel's objection has to do with eating something unclean, using the language that designates certain animals as unclean and forbidden, and it is unclear why the fuel used for the fire, though repulsive, would cause such impurity.[19] The revision indicates that the divine punishment of Israel is not unreasonable and that parts of it may be open to negotiation and modification, but such an important point would seem to require a more sustained explanation. The final sign-act in the sequence (5:1–12) involves Ezekiel shaving his head and face, so that the hair can be divided into three portions he can burn, chop with a sword, or scatter. The few hairs Ezekiel preserves and sews into the hem of his garment (5:3) may be one of the early, subtle indications of future restoration in Ezekiel.

There is no report of the performance of these acts, only the divine instruction to perform them, a feature that may serve to save space, but it compels us to acknowledge that these acts are, in some ways, unperformable. Is Ezekiel really to lie down in public on his sides, continuously, for 430 days? Perhaps the description of the cooking and eating indicates that he is only to lie down each day at mealtime, but how is he to build the fire and prepare the food while tied up with cords (4:8)? If he is to lie down continuously, then from where will this supply of food, water, and cow dung come? These kinds of questions help to indicate the importance of understanding the book of Ezekiel as a literary presentation that is not required to match with a reality outside the text.[20]

The issue surrounding all of the actions is the degree to which they inflict the prophetic message of judgment on the body of the prophetic character named Ezekiel. This phenomenon joins Ezekiel with the Servant in Isaiah 40–55, with Hosea, and with Jeremiah, who become the innocent victims of their own proclamation. The coming judgment will inflict enormous trauma on the Israelites, and the book of Ezekiel will make the common prophetic claim that at least some of it is deserved; yet the Babylonian siege and invasion of Jerusalem will undoubtedly inflict collateral damage on the innocent, and we may see Ezekiel himself as the first example of such an innocent victim.

After the second vision—in chapters 8–11, a text that follows the pattern of 1–3 by using the eyes and ears of the character named Ezekiel to allow readers to see and hear with him—12:1–20 invites the reader to look at Ezekiel again, as in chapters 4–5. Like the earlier collection of sign-acts, this one includes the divine commands to Ezekiel to perform the actions, but when YHWH tells Ezekiel to pack his "exile's baggage" (12:3), something different happens. First, though the text never portrays or describes the audience members, it acknowledges them repeatedly. Four times during the commands to pack his bags, depart from his home, and dig through a wall, YHWH tells Ezekiel to perform the sign-act "in their sight" (4:3, 4, 5, 6). In addition, 12:7 provides a first-person report of Ezekiel's performance of the acts "in their sight." Second, verses 8–9 describe a response when YHWH speaks to Ezekiel, implying that someone has seen the performance and asked, "What are you doing?" The question gives YHWH an opportunity to provide Ezekiel with an answer to such a question in verses 11–16, which leads into an extended set of instructions to the prophet.[21]

The book of Ezekiel makes only one reference to the family of the prophetic character, aside from the mention of his father's name in 1:3, and it is a troubling little story. As the opening half of the book is nearing a close, YHWH speaks to Ezekiel in 24:16: "Mortal, with one blow I am about to take away from you the delight of your eyes; yet you shall not mourn or weep, nor shall your tears run down." At this point it is not clear what Ezekiel is going to lose, nor whether controlling these somewhat involuntary manifestations of grief is his responsibility, through effort, or something that YHWH will control. The continuing instructions about not mourning are matters of human choice, but failing to do them would violate cultural convention. The loss comes with a shock in verse 18, in which Ezekiel reports the death of his wife in first-person language, along with the plain statement, "I did as I was commanded." Ezekiel's behavior is the cause for questions from a group of people in verse 19; in the following verses Ezekiel responds that when the loss of Jerusalem comes, along with the death of family members, they are to follow his example and not mourn. Ezekiel's response to his wife's death becomes a different sort of symbolic action, because an event that YHWH apparently causes triggers the action. This is a rare case in Ezekiel when an audience sees the symbolic action and responds to it. The analogy is painfully strained, though, because the text reports no wrongdoing on the part of Ezekiel or his wife that could merit the punishment, so there is no apparent reason for his wife's death beyond the divine need to demonstrate a point. As Ezekiel 1–24 comes to a close, therefore, we see the ultimate entanglement of the prophetic character with his message. Ezekiel's unnamed wife must give her life for his vocation, and he must lose "the delight of his eyes." The payment of the ultimate price by an innocent person raises significant questions about the understanding of disaster as punishment for sin. While Ezekiel's words often claim such a transaction, his own experience defies and interrogates such a claim, like Jeremiah and the Servant in Isaiah 40–55.

Much of the content of Ezekiel's final two visions, in chapters 37 and 40–48, will await discussion in chapter 10 of this book, but the presence and function of Ezekiel as a narrative character requires some attention here. For most of the second half of Ezekiel, the prophet is only minimally present as a narrative character. He continues to introduce prophetic oracles with the first-person formula, "The word of YHWH came to me. . . ." The command to Ezekiel to "set your face," which occurs six times in chapters 1–24, and three more times in the collection of Oracles against Foreign Nations in 25–32, appears only twice more, in 35:2 and 38:2. Both visions begin with the statement, "the hand of the LORD was/came upon me," in 37:1 and 40:1. In both cases the spirit transports Ezekiel, in 37:1 to a valley, and in 40:2 to "the land of Israel." Both visions require significant personal involvement from Ezekiel. In chapter 37 he must speak to the bones and to the wind in order to bring together the elements for reconstituting the Israelite army. The vision is followed immediately in 37:15–23 by the divine command to Ezekiel to write "for Judah" and "for Joseph" on two sticks. In the vision of the new temple in chapters 40–48, Ezekiel must be moved around constantly so he can observe all the necessary measurements for the new structure. Eventually Ezekiel finds himself observing measurements for allotment of the land to the tribes of Israel. The final first-person pronouns from the Ezekiel character appear in 47:7–8, as he reports seeing all of the trees along the banks of the river and being told by God where the river is flowing. The character named Ezekiel then fades from view, the land allotment continues, and YHWH seems to speak directly to the reader. Like all of the other named prophets in the prophetic literature, there is no report of Ezekiel's death, a void that will be considered in chapter 12 of this book.

THE PROCLAMATION OF EZEKIEL
CONCERNING THE BABYLONIAN PERIOD

The nature of the book of Ezekiel and the prophet for which it is named presents unique challenges to readers. The discussion above has explored the literary structure of the book and the narrative role of the prophet within it, along with the complex array of settings created by the book's emphasis on visionary experience. The distinctive way the book and the prophet within it communicate about the experience of Israel in the early sixth century should now be more visible. After the intense visionary experience and the initial sequence of symbolic actions in Ezekiel 1–5, the book enters into a brief interlude made up of oracular material in 6–7, in which Ezekiel is acknowledged as the recipient of the word of YHWH (6:1; 7:1), but he fades from direct view for much of the divine pronouncement of these oracles. The "oracle against the mountains" in 6:3–14 is important because it is matched by a reversal text in Ezekiel 35, which will receive attention in chapter 10 of this book because of its focus on restoration.[22] The oracle against the mountains repeats a lot of the oracle in 5:5–17 that had been connected to Ezekiel's symbolic actions, but now it is directed against the geographical features of the land. The inclusion of "the ravines and the valleys" along with "the mountains and the hills" (6:3) makes it possible that this is an extension of judgment onto the entire land, a central part of YHWH's covenant with Israel.[23] Yet the mountains and hills get more attention, and the prevalent references to idol worship in this passage highlight the frequent association of false worship with "high places" in the Old Testament (Num. 33:52, 1 Kgs. 14:23). Mountains have also been positive aspects of Israelite tradition, from Mount Moriah in Genesis 22 to Mount Sinai to Mount Zion, so their pollution by idols is a particular challenge. That the mountains are condemned for what people do on them may be taken as entirely metaphorical, but this may be another place where the prophetic literature points to the tendency for judgment and punishment to fall indiscriminately.

The explanations related to Ezekiel's performances in 12:1–7 continue through the end of chapter 12 and begin to push the narrative character into the background. A phrase that has appeared four times in Ezekiel 1–11, "The word of YHWH came to me . . . ," appears five times in Ezekiel 12 alone (the full distribution of this phrase is illustrated in table 6.3).

The pattern at the end of Ezekiel 12 prepares the reader for a long section of the book in which the prophetic character's presence is limited to this regular pattern of introducing prophetic oracles. In chapters 13–24 this phrase appears an additional twenty times, indicating that this part of the book is dominated by divine speech. The section begins with a condemnation of false prophets in 13:2–23. These prophets are denounced for "prophesying out of their own imagination" (vv. 2, 17) and for using means of "divination" (vv. 7, 9).

Table 6.3 "The word of YHWH came to me . . ."
in the Book of Ezekiel

Ezekiel	"The word of YHWH came to me"
1–11	4 times
12–24	25 times
25–30	10 times (introducing each of the Oracles against the Nations)
31–38	10 times
39–48	0 times

Thus Ezekiel's constant declarations of "the word of YHWH came to me . . ."
draw a sharp contrast between himself and these individuals, whose words
come either from themselves or from some magical means (see discussion box
6.2 on divination).

The beginning of Ezekiel 14 highlights the very limited way in which other
human characters participate in the narrative of Ezekiel. This is the second
of three occasions on which a group of elders has come to Ezekiel and "sat
down before [him]." In none of the three cases does the expected conversation between Ezekiel and these elders take place. In 8:1 the elders are sitting
in front of Ezekiel when the "hand of YHWH" seizes him and the description of his second vision begins. The text does not mention these elders again
and does not specify the purpose of their presence. Perhaps the best we can
speculate is that they are there to witness Ezekiel entering his visionary state.
In 14:1–2 the arrival of the elders accompanies the arrival of the "word of

---

Discussion Box 6.2 Means of Divination in Ancient Near Eastern Prophecy

It is common to draw a distinction between the "true prophets" of Israel
and the "false prophets" of Israel and surrounding nations based on the
latter's use of certain mechanical means of determining the divine will
that may come under the general category of "divination." The tech-
nique specifically mentioned in Ezekiel 13 involves smearing white-
wash on a wall (vv. 10–16). Other methods in the ancient Near East
included the interpretation of patterns in animal livers (hepatoscopy),
patterns in dropped or shaken arrows, patterns in mixtures of water
and oil, and the use of devices described as "lots" (cf. Ezek. 21:21–23).
Along with other prophetic books, Ezekiel generally condemns tech-
niques of divination, like the condemnations in Deuteronomy 18:9–14
(see Isa. 3:2; Jer. 14:14; Mic. 3:7; Zech. 10:2). Sometimes the Old Testament presents the use of lots or other devices as acceptable, such
the use of "Urim and Thummim" by Israelite priests (see Exod. 28:30;
Num. 27:21; Deut. 33:8; 1 Sam. 14:41; Ezra 2:63). Lots are also used
in Joshua 7 to identify Achan as the transgressor of holy war legislation.
Ezekiel does not deny the efficacy of divination and seems to approve
the use of such methods by Nebuchadrezzar in 21:18–23. The problem
with methods of divination is not that they do not work, but that they
are foreign practices, in which Israel should not engage.[24] They have
been replaced by prophets who speak the word of YHWH.

YHWH" to Ezekiel. It is possible that the first oracle Ezekiel receives—which begins, "Mortal, these men . . . " (14:3)—makes reference to the elders, but that is not necessarily so. The oracles continue with frequent introductory formulas of various kinds, but the text does not report any of Ezekiel's speech to the elders, and it does not describe their departure, so the purpose of their presence is not clear. The third occasion (20:1) is similar: the elders come and sit before Ezekiel, whom God provides with oracles to speak to them, but there is no description of Ezekiel's speech or the elders' response.

Ezekiel 16 and 23 are two of the more problematic texts in this section. Both texts use the marriage metaphor and are sexually charged (see earlier comments on this issue re Hosea, in chap. 3 of this book, esp. discussion box 3.1). While there are obvious similarities to the use of the marriage metaphor in Hosea 1–3, the differences in Ezekiel are significant. First, there is no apparent connection to Ezekiel's own life. As the previous section has illustrated, the death of Ezekiel's wife was a component of one of his symbolic actions , but the text draws no parallel between her and the women portrayed as wives of YHWH in Ezekiel 16 and 23. In Hosea, the metaphor portrays a marriage between YHWH and the northern nation, Israel; Ezekiel 16 portrays a marriage with the city of Jerusalem; and in Ezekiel 23, YHWH is married to two sisters named Oholah and Oholibah, who are identified as the cities of Jerusalem and Samaria. This difference leads to a new set of images to speak of both the beauty and punishment of the unfaithful wives. In Hosea, the imagery is primarily concerned with fertility and agriculture, while in Ezekiel the images are both more international and urban, involving architecture and commerce.[25]

The opening of Ezekiel 16 is troubling and confusing: YHWH describes finding Jerusalem like an abandoned infant, naked and still covered in blood. At that point, in verse 6, God does no more than command the baby to "Live!" Later, YHWH spies her again, still naked and bloody, but now grown and sexually attractive, so he cleans her, adorns her, and marries her. The remainder of the chapter is filled with lurid descriptions of her "[playing] the whore" (e.g., 16:15). Ezekiel 16:35–37 is a central text:

> Therefore, O whore, hear the word of the LORD: Thus says the Lord GOD, Because your lust was poured out and your nakedness uncovered in your whoring with your lovers, and because of all your abominable idols, and because of the blood of your children that you gave to them, therefore, I will gather all your lovers, with whom you took pleasure, all those you loved and all those you hated; I will gather them against you from all around, and will uncover your nakedness to them, so that they may see all your nakedness.

This text and its continuation bring together all the elements of the metaphor: idolatry and sexual infidelity, shaming and exposure, and the stoning of an adulteress and the destruction of a city. Many interpreters argue that the purpose of this literary choice is to shock, and it is no doubt shocking, but it is also necessary to continue to ask, What are the costs of choosing to shock in this way?

If "seeing/uncovering the nakedness" is mostly a euphemism (as explained in discussion box 6.3) and so used in texts like Ezekiel 16:37 and 23:29, then YHWH does more than publicly strip these women: YHWH offers them up to be raped, a reality that would have been a part of the pending invasion of Jerusalem by the Babylonian army. If Ezekiel 16 is shocking, then it is difficult to find the word to describe chapter 23. It is the most brazenly sexual text in all of the Bible, to the extent that it has even been labeled "pornoprophetics."[27] This text adds the polygamous angle, with YHWH being married to two sisters, and speaks specifically of them bearing sons and daughters for YHWH (23:4). Neither the accused women, nor the cities they represent,

---

Discussion Box 6.3 The Meaning of
"Seeing the Nakedness" in the Old Testament

The first time the phrase "seeing/uncovering the nakedness" appears in the Bible is in the strange story of Noah's family just after the flood. In Genesis 9:22 the narrator reports that Noah's youngest son, Ham, "saw the nakedness of his father." The reference seems cryptic there, because the resulting punishment falls not on Ham, but on his son Canaan, and is all out of proportion to the literal meaning of the offense. The phrase becomes prominent again in Leviticus 18:6–18, where all of the prohibitions against incest using this phrase make it obvious that "uncovering the nakedness" means having sexual relations and, more specifically, that the "nakedness of your father" represents the sexual relationship between the father and his wife (18:8). If this apparent use of a euphemism is taken back to the cryptic text in Genesis 9, then many of the difficulties with that text can be resolved. Canaan, the son of Ham, is punished severely because Ham had sexual relations with his father's wife (his own mother?), and Canaan was the product of this incestuous union.[26] In various forms this phrase is used many times in Ezekiel 16 and 23, and several more times elsewhere in the prophetic literature (Isa. 47:3; 57:8; Hos. 2:9; Nah. 3:5; Hab. 2:15). It may not always be a euphemism carrying such a meaning, but it is always necessary to try out this possibility, to see if it yields helpful interpretive results.

get to speak in response in these texts; nevertheless, the book of Lamentations is filled with the speech of a defeated city personified as a woman, and objections may occasionally come from other voices in Ezekiel, such as in 8:12.[28] The portrait of God that these texts present is enormously challenging for modern readers. They are ignored or skipped over not just because of their sexually explicit descriptions, but also for theological difficulties. These chapters show us what it means to claim that a military invasion is an act of divine punishment. If the conclusion is intolerable, then we must go back and question the premise. The explicit brutality of Ezekiel 16 and 23 will not let us get away with a vague ideal of retributive justice.

One of the major issues in all of the prophetic literature, the tension between individual and corporate responsibility for sin, finally receives direct address in Ezekiel 18. The entry point of this discussion is YHWH's reference to a proverb: "The parents have eaten sour grapes, and the children's teeth are set on edge" (18:2).[29] YHWH goes on to refute this claim specifically, commanding that this proverb not be used any more in Israel and insisting that "it is only the person who sins that shall die" (v. 4). Such a claim is surprising in light of the strong tradition in the Old Testament of inherited guilt, exhibited most prominently in the oft-repeated saying from Exodus 34:6–7, as in these lines:

> Forgiving iniquity and transgression and sin,
>   yet by no means clearing the guilty,
> but visiting the iniquity of the parents
>   upon the children
>   and the children's children
>   to the third and the fourth generation

This text from Exodus contains within itself enormous tension on the subject of judgment and forgiveness, and this is a tension over which the prophets often agonize. The ideas of inherited and corporate guilt solve many theological problems in the Old Testament, but they are likely to create as many more, and the book of Ezekiel seems to be coming to that realization. If guilt can be assessed corporately or inherited, then obedience and repentance cannot guarantee divine favor, and Israel's God is not reliable. Ezekiel 18 ends with a call to repentance in verse 32, "Turn, then, and live." The God who says this declares, "I have no pleasure in the death of anyone" (18:32). This text in the first half of Ezekiel is an early pointer to the theme of restoration in the second half of the book, so we will return to it in chapter 10 of this book.

At first glance, the Oracles against the Nations in Ezekiel 25–32 appears to be in a similar position as in the book of Isaiah (13–23) and the Greek tradition of the book of Jeremiah (25:14–31:44 LXX; cf. 46–51 NRSV), but closer examination reveals that this section may be playing more of a transitional or pivotal role at the center of the scroll in Ezekiel. The chapters prior to this are focused almost entirely on divine judgment of Judah, and Ezekiel 33 begins a new emphasis on divine mercy. It is not clear how such a pivot in divine action is related to the judgment of the nations, but Ezekiel understands the problem of foreign alliances and their resulting idolatry to be at the core of Judah's problem of disobedience.[30] Restoring Judah may require the removal of these nations, yet that removal, like many other parts of the book of Ezekiel, only works as an act of the imagination. Table 6.4 illustrates that the list of foreign nations here is similar to Isaiah, Jeremiah, and Amos, with greater emphasis on Tyre as the most notable distinction.

Table 6.4 The Oracles against Foreign Nations in Ezekiel

Ezekiel	Nation
25:1–7	Ammonites
25:8–11	Moab
25:12–14	Edom
25:15–17	Philistines
26:1–28:19	Tyre
28:20–23	Sidon
29:1–30:26	Egypt
31:1–18	Egypt (by comparison to Assyria)
32:1–32	Egypt

The most shocking aspect of this list may be the absence of Babylon. It is not that the Babylonians are missing from Ezekiel's oracles against foreign nations, for they are mentioned eight times in the section, but all of these references to Babylon focus on its role as the means by which YHWH will punish all the other nations, just as YHWH will punish Judah. Thus, unlike Jeremiah, Ezekiel does not choose to use vengeance on Babylon as an element of the restoration, satisfying as that might have been to the book's original audience.

Ezekiel's fixation on Tyre requires some special attention because of its length and character. The nearly three full chapters concerning Tyre are a collection by themselves. The introductory formulas in verses 1, 7, 15, and 19 divide Ezekiel 26 into four oracles against Tyre. Other historical sources indicate Nebuchadrezzar of Babylon attacked Tyre at about the same time he invaded Judah and attacked Jerusalem, but the history of this engagement is complex and need not match the contents of Ezekiel 26. Nebuchadrezzar is mentioned by name in 26:7, and the final verse of the chapter powerfully asserts the end result of his work against Tyre: "I will bring you to a dreadful end; and you shall be no more" (v. 21a). Ezekiel 27 functions like a judgment oracle in the context of Ezekiel, even though it is technically a lament for the nation. The problem is that Nebuchadrezzar never defeated Tyre, and this may be the source of Ezekiel's obsession. The latest date in the whole book is in 29:17, some sixteen years later than the date the initial Tyre oracles provide, when Ezekiel finally gives up hope that Tyre will collapse and revises his oracles of judgment against it (see 29:18).[31]

The Tyre material is followed by a collection of oracles concerning Egypt that is equal in complexity and approximate length, but perhaps this is not so surprising given the long and complex engagement that Israel had with this ancient superpower. Like Tyre, the fate of Egypt is also baffling for Ezekiel. In the revised Tyre oracle in 29:17–20, Ezekiel proclaims that YHWH will give Egypt to Nebuchadrezzar because of the failure to deliver victory over Tyre to him, but the Babylonian king did not fully conquer Egypt either. Another important connection between the Tyre and Egypt traditions in Ezekiel is the use of mythical elements. In denouncing the King of Tyre in 28:11–14, Ezekiel places him in the garden of Eden, perhaps even as an angel. The use of this mythical metaphor is complex: one role it plays in the text is to highlight the failure of this king, who was given so much but used it irresponsibly.[32] In Ezekiel 31, Egypt is described as a great tree, which is also placed in Eden in verses 8–9. The oracle also connects Egypt to Assyria, a great empire that had been destroyed fairly recently. By the end of this oracle, the great tree has been sent down to the pit, or Sheol. As was the case with Tyre, one function of the mythical elements, Eden and Sheol in this case, is to provide an illustration of the distance between the greatness that Egypt obtained and the destiny to which it is headed.

One way to bring the discussion of Ezekiel to a preliminary close may be to observe the important role that "spirit" plays in the scroll. Many interpreters of Ezekiel have noticed the prominence of the word "spirit" in the book and have wondered if the idea of the divine spirit or "spirit of YWHW" is an integral part of what the book is trying to communicate. The New Revised Standard Version uses "spirit" twenty-five times in Ezekiel, but counts like this can vary because the Hebrew word for "spirit" can also mean "wind" or "breath," so the count will vary from version to version depending on the translators. Sometimes the word can mean two or even all three of these at the same time. When Ezekiel prophesies to the "breath" in 37:9–10, it comes as a wind through the valley and enters the bodies that have reassembled; thus the wind/breath is related to the animating power or "spirit" of YHWH that God promises to put into the people in 37:14. By contrast, the word "spirit" appears only once in the NRSV of Jeremiah (51:11), and this is clearly not a reference to the divine spirit. "Spirit" appears in the book of Isaiah and the Book of the Twelve with frequencies comparable to that found in Ezekiel, but the way it is used in those books looks different from its use in Ezekiel, though this is a somewhat subjective evaluation. What appears to be different in Ezekiel is the connection between the divine spirit and the prophetic task, particularly the understanding of the spirit of YHWH as the inspirational force behind prophetic activity.[33] The famous passage in Isaiah 11:1–2, for example, uses the word "spirit" four times, but these all refer to YHWH's interaction with the ideal king, not with the prophet. When the spirit becomes a human capacity—as it does in Ezekiel 11:19; 18:31; and 36:26—it creates new symbolic possibilities.[34] This means that, though the proclamation of the book of Ezekiel is closely connected to the body of the character called Ezekiel, the scroll is not limited in time and space, but is able to move beyond such limitations in its vision of the covenant between YHWH and Israel.

EZEKIEL INTERRUPTED

The discussion of the oracles against foreign nations in Ezekiel 25–31 (above) presented them as a transitional device in the scroll of Ezekiel. Within the visionary world of Ezekiel, the judgment of the nations punctuates the judgment of Israel and also opens up the possibility for the restoration of Judah. This will allow the scroll of Ezekiel to move on and consider the life of Judah and its inhabitants after the exile. Several important ideas have developed in the discussion of Ezekiel that will be helpful to carry forward. First, the framework of visions in the scroll of Ezekiel has established a visionary character for the book as a whole. While the character named Ezekiel, who is placed in an early sixth-century context, is central to the function of the book, he has been liberated from a fixed time and place in order to operate in a world of the imagination, where the reader can still encounter him after the exile, even if not in as physical a form. Second, the afflictions of Ezekiel, which came upon him as a part of his faithful response to the divine calling, offers a way to understand suffering in a way other than the simple equation of sin and punishment. In this experience, Ezekiel is aligned with Hosea, Jeremiah, and the Servant of Isaiah 40–55. Third, the Tyre tradition that stands out so starkly at the center of the book presents an example of the reinterpretation of past proclamation based on later events. When Ezekiel comes back to his failed prediction about Tyre more than a decade later, perhaps he is inviting readers to come back to proclamations of the past and continue to measure them against the present in a continuing struggle for new understanding. When we come back to Ezekiel in chapter 10 of this book, its vision for a restored Judah in the Persian period will demand this kind of rigorous imagination that envisions the future and reenvisions the past.

Resources for Further Research

Commentaries

Bowen, Nancy R. *Ezekiel*. Nashville: Abingdon Press, 2010. (A)

Clements, Ronald E. *Ezekiel*. Louisville, KY: Westminster John Knox Press, 1996. (A)

Darr, Katheryn Pfisterer. "The Book of Ezekiel: Introduction, Commentary, and Reflections." In *The New Interpreter's Bible*, edited by Leander E. Keck et al., 6:1073–1607. Nashville: Abingdon Press, 2001. (B)

Eichrodt, Walther. *Ezekiel: A Commentary*. Translated by Cosslett Quin. Philadelphia: Westminster Press, 1970. (B)

Greenberg, Moshe. *Ezekiel 1–20: A New Translation with Introduction and Commentary*. Garden City, NY: Doubleday, 1983. (C)

Joyce, Paul M. *Ezekiel: A Commentary*. London: T&T Clark, 2007. (B)

Odell, Margaret S. *Ezekiel*. Macon, GA: Smyth & Helwys, 2005. (B)

Zimmerli, Walther. *Ezekiel*. Vol. 1. Philadelphia: Fortress Press, 1979. (C)

Monographs and Other Studies

Davis, Ellen F. *Swallowing the Scroll: Textuality and the Dynamics of Discourse in Ezekiel's Prophecy*. Sheffield: Almond Press, 1989.

Launderville, Dale F. *Spirit and Reason: The Embodied Character of Ezekiel's Symbolic Thinking*. Waco: Baylor University Press, 2007.

Mayfield, Tyler D. *Literary Structure and Settings in Ezekiel*. Tübingen: Mohr-Siebeck, 2012.

Robson, James. *Word and Spirit in Ezekiel*. New York: T&T Clark, 2006.

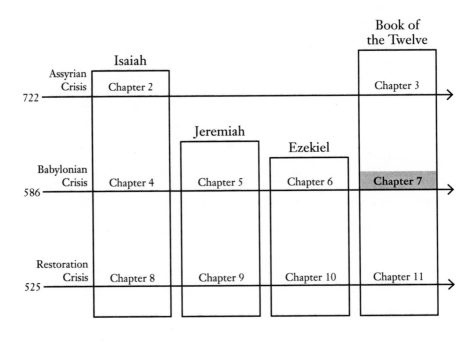

Book of
the Twelve

Isaiah

Assyrian
Crisis | Chapter 2 | Chapter 3

722

Jeremiah

Ezekiel

Babylonian
Crisis | Chapter 4 | Chapter 5 | Chapter 6 | **Chapter 7**

586

Restoration
Crisis | Chapter 8 | Chapter 9 | Chapter 10 | Chapter 11

525

7

The Scroll of the Twelve Continued

Response to the Babylonian Crisis

When the discussion of the Book of the Twelve paused at the end of chapter 3 of this book, the parts of the scroll that had received significant attention were Hosea, Joel, Amos, Nahum, Jonah, and Micah. Of these six components, four clearly set themselves against the backdrop of the Assyrian crisis of the eighth century. Two factors complicate the relationship of the first half of the Book of the Twelve to the Assyrian period, though. First, two of the components listed above, Joel and Jonah, are not overtly connected to the events of the Assyrian period. Joel has no distinct chronological markers, and only its placement between Hosea and Amos in the Masoretic tradition and all English versions of the Old Testament provides it an eighth-century context. Nothing in the book is in serious conflict with this placement, though, so it does not seem out of place in the second position. The chronological ambiguity of Joel has led to various proposals about why this component of the Book of the Twelve sits in such a prominent position in some canonical traditions. One of the most influential ideas is that the placement in the second position allows Joel to introduce two of the scroll's central themes, the day of YHWH and the fertility of the land, as major ideas for the entire Book of the Twelve, so these themes should be a persistent object of attention throughout our examination of the Twelve. Jonah, on the other hand, connects itself to the Assyrian period by identifying Nineveh as the setting for much of the book, but there is no historical connection between the story told by the book of Jonah and the story of Israel in the Old Testament, other than the name of the prophet, which is mentioned briefly in 2 Kings 14:25.

A second complication for the process of dividing the Book of the Twelve chronologically is that large components—such as Hosea, Amos, and Micah—show signs of continuing internal development beyond the Assyrian period and into the later crises of Israel's history. In the Book of the Twelve, these factors make it difficult to draw clear boundaries separating sections on the Assyrian, Babylonian, and Persian/Restoration periods; yet that differs little from the situation in the other prophetic scrolls, which do not always follow clear chronological lines. With all of this in mind, it is easiest and probably best to begin this chapter with the parts of the scroll most obviously connected to the Babylonian period, and such a choice leads to considering the books called Obadiah, Habakkuk, and Zephaniah.

Because of the nature of these three books, it will be difficult to gain a view of the prophet(s) as a narrative character in this section. Obadiah, Zephaniah, and Habakkuk all have little more than a minimal superscription in their first verses to introduce the prophets. In each case, the prophet fades out of view as the proclamation of prophetic oracles proceeds. The only exceptions are in two parts of Habakkuk. First, Habakkuk 2 opens with first-person references to the prophetic task; second, the prayer in Habakkuk 3 has its own superscription, naming the prophet as the speaker of the prayer, and uses some first-person language throughout its eighteen verses (2–19). An important question for this study will be whether it is possible and appropriate to keep characters like Hosea, Amos, and Jonah in view as we read the relatively faceless parts of the scroll, just as we might keep Isaiah son of Amoz in view as we read parts of the scroll of Isaiah in which he is not explicitly present as a narrative character.

Choosing an order in which to discuss these three components is challenging because their canonical placement and their chronological references are at odds. The discussion below will begin with Obadiah, which is placed fourth (Hebrew) or fifth (Greek) in the Book of the Twelve, though it assumes a perspective after the Babylonian invasion. Because Zephaniah is consistently located in ninth position in the scroll, it will be treated third, after Habakkuk, even though it places itself in the reign of Josiah, early in the Babylonian period. Following Zephaniah the discussion will conclude with a brief examination of the part of Micah that explicitly connects to the Babylonian period.

THE PROCLAMATION OF THE BOOK OF THE TWELVE CONCERNING THE BABYLONIAN PERIOD

It would be easy to assume that a "book" like **Obadiah**, with only twenty-one verses and no chapter divisions, could be dispensed with quickly in a discussion of the prophetic literature, but the web of connections between Obadiah and other parts of the prophetic literature, and its own surprising internal complexity, defeat such an assumption.[1] On the surface Obadiah is an oracle against Edom and therefore another portion of the oracles concerning foreign nations that find fuller expression in Amos and Nahum. This aspect of Obadiah may account for its placement in the Book of the Twelve, which seems too early in chronological terms. Edom (at Seir) is a common element of the Oracles against Foreign Nations (see Isa. 21:11–12; Jer. 49:7–22; Ezek. 25:12–14; Amos 1:11–12), and any reference to Edom within Israelite literature requires keeping the Jacob and Esau stories in view as part of its background.

The oracle against Edom in Jeremiah 49:7–22 has invited the most intense comparison with Obadiah because of a high frequency of verbal overlap between the two texts.[2] Nevertheless, there are striking differences between the two, the most notable difference being the lack of attention in the Jeremiah oracle to any sins against Judah by Edom. Obadiah, on the other hand, is consumed with a desire for revenge against Edom because of its complicity with Babylon in destroying Judah and the subsequent gloating (vv. 8–14). The accusations refer to Edom as Esau and Judah as Jacob, reminding readers of the closely connected origins of the two peoples, descended from twin brothers, according to Genesis. The narrative books of the Old Testament demonstrate no awareness of Edom's participation in the invasion of Jerusalem, and its inclusion here is one factor supporting the view that Obadiah is a later text than Jeremiah 49 and has added this element. On the other hand, Jeremiah's invective against Babylon is so fierce that one can imagine the writer avoiding any possibility of letting Edom carry some blame for the invasion of Judah.

Obadiah declares that Edom will be destroyed, like Judah, but Judah will be restored again, while "there shall be no survivor of the house of Esau" (v. 18). Furthermore, the survivors of Judah who reestablish themselves will also possess the territory of Edom (vv. 19–21), but the statements concerning Judah's restoration are not specific enough to require a postexilic date. The inclusion of the territory of the Edomites does not connect to any apparent geographical or political reality outside the text and seems purely polemical in force. The Babylonian king, Nabonidus, eventually defeated Edom about three decades after the fall of Jerusalem, so the book of Obadiah relates almost entirely to the sixth century, with (at most) vague glimpses of Judah's future beyond that time. The final verse of the book unites Mount Zion with "Mount Esau" in YHWH's kingdom. The latter almost certainly refers to Mount Seir, the mountain most often associated with Edom and Esau, and completes Jacob's displacement of his older twin, which began in Israel's distant past. The last look at Esau as a character in the book of Genesis (chap. 36) shows the development of his family and their settlement in the country of Seir, after Jacob and Esau reconciled in Genesis 32 and buried Isaac together in 35:29, so Obadiah presents a harsh reversal of that story.

The beginning of the book called **Habakkuk** is notable in at least two ways. First, the brief superscription, which provides no information about this prophet other than his name, uses the Hebrew word that literally means "burden," but which some translations, such as the New Revised Standard Version, render as "oracle." Isaiah, Jeremiah, and Ezekiel use this word from time to time, generally to introduce a negative pronouncement, so the sense of an oppressive weight is appropriate to this usage within the Book of the Twelve. The books called Nahum and Malachi use this word in their opening verses, and it helps open major sections of the book of Zechariah. So the idea of a prophetic speech as a burden appears throughout the prophetic literature and gains intensity toward the end of the Book of the Twelve. Second, the opening speech that begins in Habakkuk 1:2 is a complaint addressed to YHWH by the voice of the prophet. This relatively unusual phenomenon, in which the prophet talks to God, is most reminiscent of the Confessions of Jeremiah, which received significant discussion in chapter 5 of this book. Three prayers like this frame Habakkuk, one at the beginning (1:2–4), a second later in the first chapter (1:12–17), and a lengthy third prayer that fills all of Habakkuk 3. The first two prayers of Habakkuk address themes similar to some of those found in Jeremiah's Confessions, such as the prevalence of violence, the prosperity of the wicked, and God's inaction during a time of difficulty, but they do not delve into the effects of these circumstances on the prophet's personal life as the book of Jeremiah does.

YHWH responds to Habakkuk twice, in 1:5–11 and 2:2–5. The first response brings the Babylonian army into full view and expands the idea, prominent in Jeremiah and Ezekiel, that YHWH is using the Babylonians to punish not just Israel, but also "the breadth of the earth" (1:6). The first divine response is clear in its meaning, even if troubling because of its promotion of violence as a solution to violence, but the second response is puzzling in form and content. It has received a great deal of attention in Christian interpretation because of Paul's famous uses of 2:4b in his Epistles to the Romans (1:17) and the Galatians (3:11). The divine speech in 2:2–5 is beset by textual and grammatical difficulties, perhaps chief among them being the appearance of numerous pronouns whose antecedents are not clear.[3] In a brief first-person narrative in 2:1, Habakkuk indicates that he has not yet received a satisfactory response from YHWH, so he will continue to wait for one. The divine response in 2:2 is a command to write down a vision, which is confusing enough, but the precise content of what he should write is uncertain. This is a point at which readers' conclusions may depend upon whether they think the book depicts events outside of itself, or whether it develops its own literary world and presents ideas that function only within that world. Some interpreters argue for 2:4–5 as the content of the vision that is to be written and then to be proclaimed by the runner mentioned in verse 2, while others extend the content of the vision to include the woe oracles in verses 6–20.[4] Obviously, because of its length and complexity, the latter choice presents problems if this is a message proclaimed by an actual person, outside of the text, running through the land; but if the runner is a literary device, then a longer message is not so problematic, and it seems a better choice since otherwise the woe oracles have no introduction. The opening part of the vision in 2:4–5 is a collection of somewhat abstract statements. Given the clear identification of the Babylonians (Chaldeans) in the first divine response as those who "seize dwellings not their own" (1:6), they would seem the best fit for the description in 2:5 as those who "gather all nations for themselves, and collect all peoples as their own." They are also the ones about whom Habakkuk has complained in 1:17, asking: "Is he then to keep on emptying his net, and destroying nations without mercy?" The prophet needs reassurance that the imperial expansion of the Babylonians will not continue forever and that they will also eventually receive their due punishment, and this is what the entirety of the second divine response provides.

The second response of YWHW continues into a sequence of five woes, which fill the remainder of Habakkuk 2. In these woe statements, readers may find a condemnation of behaviors among the people of Judah, but the preceding understanding of 2:4–5 would seem to require them to include judgment against Babylon as well. It is easier to understand the fifth woe, which primarily addresses idolatry, as one directed internally at Judah, but the first oracle, which condemns those who "have plundered many nations" (v. 8) is more likely aimed at Babylon. So there is no need to identify a single target for all five of the woe statements. The runner can identify and condemn the sins of Judah and the sins of its Babylonian enemy, though this understanding of the text fits better as a literary presentation, after the Babylonian invasion, than as a depiction or a prophetic action before or during that event.

The final chapter of Habakkuk has received the most scholarly attention because of its mysterious character. The entire chapter, except for the opening superscription in 3:1 and closing statement in verse 19b, is a prayer uttered by Habakkuk. An intense dispute about the prayer's age and origins has divided interpreters into three groups. One group contends that the writer of Habakkuk 1–2 also wrote the third chapter. The stark stylistic differences could have been a deliberate choice of this writer, perhaps Habakkuk himself. Those who think the final prayer has a different author fall into two quite different groups: those who argue that it was composed as part of a postexilic revision of the book of Habakkuk, and those who contend that it is an ancient poem taken up and reused by the writer of the rest of the book.[5] Those arguing for a separate origin point to the introduction in 3:1, which sounds like some of the superscriptions in the book of Psalms, particularly Psalm 7, and the three appearances of "Selah" in the margins (Hab. 3:3, 9, 13), which also resembles a number of poems in the book of Psalms. Such stylistic features from the psalmic tradition could easily have been imitated, of course, but in recent decades the view that Habakkuk 3 is an ancient poem, reused here, has gained popularity. Perhaps the more significant indicators of age and external origin are the tone, contents, and many unusual geographical references in the body of the poem.[6] The overall grand theophanic nature of the poem invites comparisons to poems like Exodus 15, Judges 5, and Psalm 18. The depiction of YHWH as warrior, riding the clouds as his chariot, is perhaps most similar to the latter. These poems are often included among those that most interpreters consider to be the most ancient parts of the Old Testament. Along with the metaphors of warfare are also metaphors of nature, including the sunrise, storms, and earthquakes that emphasize the power of YHWH to vanquish Israel's enemies.[7] If this is the reuse of an ancient divine combat motif, then its placement in a sixth- or fifth-century prophetic work begins to invite comparisons to the later reuse of these mythological motifs in apocalyptic literature. The emergence of elements that eventually became part of the developments known as apocalyptic thought and apocalyptic literature takes place within some of the later prophetic literature. This type of return to ancient mythological motifs was one common element, and the presence of apocalyptic elements in the prophetic literature will be addressed more directly and thoroughly in chapter 11 of this book.

The placement of the book of **Zephaniah** in the Book of the Twelve is mysterious. On the one hand, it is consistent, always ninth, and always between Habakkuk and Haggai. This placement, which provides a context in the Babylonian crisis of the early sixth century, may create some tension with the chronological note in Zephaniah 1:1. The phrase "In the days of King Josiah son of Amon of Judah" has led some readers to assume an earlier date for the prophet called Zephaniah, placing his words in the context of the Josianic reforms, perhaps in the 620s.[8] The difference may not be as great as some interpreters make it appear, however, because the superscription in Zephaniah 1:1 does not specify when, in the thirty-one-year reign of Josiah, the prophet named Zephaniah received and proclaimed these words. The death of Josiah in 608, in a battle with the Egyptians, may be perceived as the beginning point of the Babylonian crisis, since it was this advance of the Egyptian army to which the Babylonian army responded, leading to the Babylonian assertion of control over the Levant. By 604 the Babylonians had established Jehoiakim as their vassal king over Judah, and the first deportation of Judahites to Babylon came only seven years after that. So there is little if any distinction between the latter parts of the reign of Josiah and the beginning of the Babylonian crisis.

What may be more important than the chronological issues concerning the prophet and the origins of the book is the degree to which Zephaniah was written, or at least heavily revised, after the exile. Some interpreters understand "the remnant of my people" in 2:9 as distinctively postexilic language, and the focus on a restored remnant in Zephaniah may have pushed the book to its late position in the Twelve.[9] The Hebrew and Greek versions of Zephaniah differ significantly, which is another factor that may inform questions about its formation. One difference arises in 2:1–3, which raises the possibility that at least one group, the "humble of the earth," might avoid punishment because of their obedience to YHWH. The Greek text in 2:1–3 sounds more open and hopeful about such a reprieve, referring to the audience in 2:1 as "uneducated," rather than "shameless."[10] If there were competing forms of Zephaniah, then they may have been part of a dispute about how to conduct the restoration of Judah.

Zephaniah falls into three main sections. The oracles in 1:1–2:3 speak primarily of the coming judgment on Judah, noticeably reviving the idea of "the day of YHWH," the full phrasing of which has not appeared since Obadiah. The oracles in 2:4–3:8 direct judgment toward the enemies of Israel, including the Philistines, the Moabites, the Ammonites, the Ethiopians, and the Assyrians. Chapter 3 of this book (above) observed that the Book of the Twelve has a section dedicating much of its attention to "Oracles against the Nations" (Amos, Obadiah, Jonah, and Nahum), as Isaiah 13–23 does, but that part of each scroll contains other material, and there are Oracles against Foreign Nations outside of those sections, as Zephaniah 2 illustrates. Zephaniah demonstrates additional internal complexity by weaving a reiteration of YHWH's judgment on Judah into the judgment of the nations in 2:4–15 and 3:6–8. The closing of Zephaniah in 3:9–20 makes a distinct positive turn toward restoration, so it will also be included in chapter 11 of this book, which will return to the parts of the Book of the Twelve that address the Restoration period. The position of Zephaniah in the Book of the Twelve plays an important transitional role. It contains the final declaration of YHWH's judgment against Judah in the Babylonian crisis, yet the book does not end there: in 2:3 it even raises the possibility that not all are guilty. The character named Zephaniah may play an important role by connecting the book's hope for the future back to King Josiah's reforms (1:1). The inability of the earlier effort to halt Judah's plunge toward destruction may create a struggle for other prophets as well, most notably Jeremiah.

One fascinating aspect of Zephaniah is the way it alludes to and reverses major emphases of Genesis 1–11. This feature begins in 1:2–3 with a divine statement of intent to reverse the elements of creation God performed in Genesis 1. Not only does the text reverse the making of all the living creatures and "sweep away everything," but it also highlights the reversal syntactically by reversing the order in Genesis 1, sweeping away first humans, then other land animals, birds, and fish.[11] This rhetorical move continues in 2:4–15 as Zephaniah takes a unique approach to presenting Oracles against Foreign Nations. Many of the usual suspects—Philistines, Moabites, Ammonites, and Assyrians—are present, but the absence of Edom and Babylon are likely indications that the collection comes from a time before the Babylonian invasion of Judah. A surprising inclusion is Ethiopia in 2:12, but this may provide a clue to what Zephaniah is doing here. Ethiopia, or "Cushites" (2:12; see discussion box 7.1 for ways of understanding how and why the Old Testament refers to this part of Africa), along with other unusual words, including "seacoasts" and "Canaan," connect 2:4–15 to the Table of Nations in Genesis 10, where these people are assigned their respective lands. The removal of people from their territories represents a second reversal of Genesis 1–11. The end product of YHWH's actions in Zephaniah 2:5–15 is the reversal of urbanization, as the greatest city in the world, Nineveh, becomes a wasteland overrun by wild animals.[12] This may be a confusing choice of reversals, since Genesis 1–11 has its own way of reversing the human tendency toward city building in the Babel story in 11:1–9, but this is exactly where Zephaniah is going. The final allusion to Genesis 1–11 is in Zephaniah 3:9–10, where both the confusion of speech and the scattering of people are reversed. The reversal results in the ability of all people to worship YHWH, and Zephaniah connects 3:9–10 to 2:5–15 by repeating Ethiopia, or Cush, in 3:10, a territory that represents the farthest extent of Israel's geographic awareness. Zephaniah uses the universal scope of God's creative activity in Genesis 1–11 to portray the universal scope of God's punishing and restoring work in the book's own time.

The Babylonians are not yet in full view in Zephaniah. Judah has survived the Assyrian Empire, and Nineveh is headed for defeat; yet there is corruption in Jerusalem that will result in divine punishment, according to 1:10–13, though the enemy approaching to inflict that punishment is nondescript. The final form of Zephaniah is able to see beyond the destruction, however, to a time of restoration, which makes it a good transition to the book of Haggai. The closing verses of Zephaniah and the elements of the Book of the Twelve that follow it will be treated in chapter 11 of this book.

Table 7.1 on page 146 demonstrates that references to the Babylonian Empire in the Book of the Twelve are few. Other texts may point toward them more vaguely, but the passages listed in table 7.1 are the only ones that

---

Discussion Box 7.1 Africa in the Old Testament

Usually the geographical context of the Old Testament is conveniently labeled the ancient Near East. Most readers probably equate this roughly with the contemporary area called the Middle East, which generally includes a cluster of nations with Iran farthest east, Yemen farthest south, Turkey farthest north, and Egypt farthest west. This means it comprises the Western end of Asia plus the northeast corner of Africa. The modern borders of Egypt were set in the 1950s with the establishment of the independent nations of Sudan and Libya, and it is difficult to know exactly what the writers of the Old Testament would have considered the extent of the land they called Egypt. The words "Libya" and "Libyans" appear in the Old Testament a handful of times, demonstrating an awareness of territory west of Egypt. The words "Ethiopia" and "Ethiopians" are more common in many English versions, though some have used the terms "Cush" and "Cushites" instead. Certainly this indicates an awareness of territory in Africa south of Egypt.[13] The more difficult question is whether this is a defined territory, perhaps similar to the modern nation of Ethiopia, or a general term meaning the rest of Africa, south of Egypt. A negative tone about this territory and its people is established early in the Old Testament by the connection of Noah's son, Ham, with Cush/Ethiopia in Genesis 10:6. The occasional inclusion of Ethiopia in Oracles against Foreign Nations (Isa. 20:4; Zeph. 2:12) or other negative comments (Ezek. 30:9) may be surprising because the narrative portions of the Old Testament do not contain extensive traditions of conflict with these people. The exception is the story of King Asa of Judah in 2 Chronicles 14–16, who fought a war with and defeated the Ethiopians, an account that is absent from the parallel material in 1 Kings. On other occasions, such as Zephaniah 3:10, Ethiopia seems to be used primarily as an example of a far-off place, perhaps because it was the most geographically distant area for which Israelites seem to have had a name.

---

name them. Micah 4:10 stands out as the single, specific reference to Babylon by name in any part of the Book of the Twelve that relates primarily to the Assyrian period. The discussion of Micah in chapter 3 of this book identified the problems created by the failure of Micah's predictions, counter to Isaiah's, that the Assyrians would destroy Judah and. In light of this, 4:9–13 looks like an insertion in the book of Micah that carries the threats of judgment and destruction forward to the Babylonian period.[14] A depiction of the invasion,

Table 7.1 References to Babylon in the Book of the Twelve

Text	Quotation
Mic. 4:10	O daughter Zion, . . . you shall go to Babylon. There you shall be rescued. . . .
Hab. 1:6	For I am rousing the Chaldeans, that fierce and impetuous nation. . . .
Hab. 1:15	The enemy[15] brings all of them up with a hook. . . .
Zech. 2:7	Escape to Zion, you that live with daughter Babylon.
Zech. 6:10	Collect silver and gold from the exiles . . . who have arrived from Babylon.

however, is not its primary purpose, because the reference becomes decidedly positive in verse 10:

> Writhe and groan, O daughter Zion,
>   like a woman in labor;
> for now you shall go forth from the city
>   and camp in the open country;
>   you shall go to Babylon.
> There you shall be rescued,
>   there the LORD will redeem you
>   from the hands of your enemies.

Micah 4:10 views the exile and captivity of Judah's people as a necessary part of their redemption. Though the text speaks of invasion and exile, it may seem unsuitable for an audience of that time because of the lack of sensitivity to the suffering and trauma such an event creates, so it might fit a context nearer the end of the captivity than the beginning.[16] Thus Micah 4:10 takes us at least to the verge of the restoration and signals the next pause in the discussion of the Book of the Twelve.

THE BOOK OF THE TWELVE INTERRUPTED AGAIN

We cannot completely leave behind the nine components of the Book of the Twelve treated so far at this point. A distinct block of books—Haggai, Zechariah, and Malachi—clearly address the portion of Israel's story during which it rebuilds the temple in Jerusalem and works to reestablish its life and worship of YHWH there while living under the political control of the Persian Empire. Yet the production of the Book of the Twelve as a complete prophetic scroll in the Persian period did not include merely attaching additional pieces. Like Isaiah, and perhaps to a lesser degree Jeremiah and Ezekiel, the entire work was revised and reshaped at this point, including internal revisions of some of the earlier components. The discussion of the Book of the Twelve will continue in chapter 11 of this book: along with a careful look at Haggai, Zechariah, and Malachi, certain parts of the earlier components will be revisited.

Resources for Further Research

Commentaries

The divisions used to publish commentaries that treat more than one portion of the Book of the Twelve are not the same as the divisions used to discuss the Twelve in this book, so some commentaries relevant to material in this chapter may be listed at the end of chapter 3 or 11.

Achtemeier, Elizabeth. *Nahum–Malachi*. Louisville, KY: Westminster/John Knox Press, 1988. (A)

Andersen, Francis I. *Habakkuk: A New Translation with Introduction and Commentary*. New York: Doubleday, 2001. (C)

Bennett, Robert A. "The Book of Zephaniah: Introduction, Commentary, and Reflections." In *The New Interpreter's Bible*, edited by Leander E. Keck et al., 7:657–704. Nashville: Abingdon Press, 1996. (B)

Berlin, Adele. *Zephaniah: A New Translation with Introduction and Commentary*. New York: Doubleday, 1996. (C)

Hiebert, Theodore. "The Book of Habakkuk: Introduction, Commentary, and Reflections." In *The New Interpreter's Bible*, edited by Leander E. Keck et al., 7:621–56. Nashville: Abingdon Press, 1996. (B)

Nogalski, James D. *The Book of the Twelve: Micah–Malachi*. Macon, GA: Smyth & Helwys, 2011. (B)

Pagán, Samuel. "The Book of Obadiah: Introduction, Commentary, and Reflections." In *The New Interpreter's Bible*, edited by Leander E. Keck et al., 7:433–60. Nashville: Abingdon Press, 1996. (B)

Rabbe, Paul R. *Obadiah: A New Translation with Introduction and Commentary*. New York: Doubleday, 1996. (C)

Sweeney, Marvin A. *Zephaniah: A Commentary*. Minneapolis: Fortress Press, 2003. (C)

Monographs and Other Special Studies

Brueggemann, Walter. *Hopeful Imagination: Prophetic Voices in Exile*. Philadelphia: Fortress Press, 1986.

Hiebert, Theodore. *God of My Victory: The Ancient Hymn in Habakkuk 3*. Atlanta: Scholars Press, 1986.

LeCureux, Jason T. *The Thematic Unity of the Book of the Twelve*. Sheffield: Sheffield Phoenix Press, 2012.

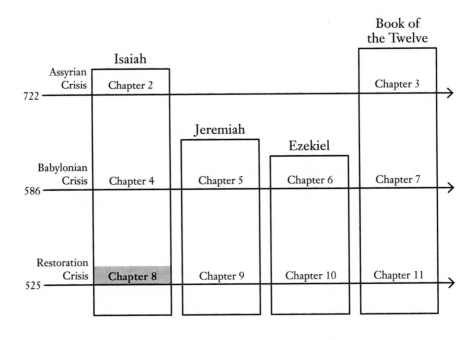

8

The Scroll of Isaiah Continued Again

Response to the Restoration Crisis

Two previous chapters of this book have examined Isaiah in various ways. The present chapter will explore the parts of Isaiah that primarily address the Persian period, during which Jerusalem and the temple were rebuilt and reestablished. The major sections of Isaiah that fall into this category are chapters 1–5, 24–27, and 56–66. The understanding of Isaiah with which this book operates is that it went through a series of reformulations in response to the continuing experiences of Israel. The reformulations included adding new material and reshaping the existing parts of the book. The three texts cited above reveal three aspects of such reshaping, placing new material onto the beginning, in the middle, and onto the end of an earlier version of the scroll, but it is also important to remember that smaller units may have been added, along with comparatively minor adjustments to existing material.

Some interpreters have vigorously opposed the division of Isaiah, arguing from two somewhat different perspectives. First, some insist that all of Isaiah must be directly connected to the prophet called Isaiah son of Amoz in the eighth century. This claim is not based upon evidence from the contents of Isaiah, but relies on a particular understanding of divine inspiration and canonization. It applies the introductory superscription in 1:1 literally to the whole book and makes the book's authority dependent upon a literal reading.[1] The assumption that Isaiah's name on the book identifies him as the author of the entire book also contributes to this view. Others argue, on a more strictly literary basis, that the final form of Isaiah is the form the Bible contains and the one to which we have the most certain access, so it should be the sole object of our reading.[2] These readers properly caution us against what is lost in reading practices that only divide and fragment a book like Isaiah into smaller pieces, without ever returning to an examination of the whole work. Most interpreters in this group would not deny that Isaiah is a composite work with a long developmental history, but contend that giving too much attention to the composition process distracts from careful reading of the final form.

Those who recognize Isaiah 56–66 as an addition to the book during the Persian period most often understand 56–66 itself as a composite work. Some have argued for the unity and single authorship of 56–66, even claiming that it was produced and used as a separate entity before being attached to the book of Isaiah; yet the general idea that 56–66 consists of incremental additions to the book of Isaiah is more commonly accepted.[3] Perhaps the most widely accepted part of the incremental view is that Isaiah 56–66 began with the composition of 60–62 as the core. Many interpreters also agree with the basic idea that the addition of 56:1–8 and 65–66 came late in the process, to form a frame around all of 56–66.[4] The discussion below will treat 56:1–8 and 65–66 in further detail. Nevertheless at the beginning it is important to notice in broad outline that the process created an overwhelmingly optimistic core, reflecting the new beginnings of Jerusalem's restoration, surrounded by a more realistic framework developed in the light of the struggles and conflicts that became a part of the restoration process.

The material added to Isaiah in the Persian period avoids distinct historical or chronological references to an even greater degree than the material added in response to the Babylonian crisis, which was treated in chapter 4 of this book. The avoidance of distinct historical references creates many difficulties for reading this part of Isaiah and understanding how it relates to other parts of the scroll. The dissipation of a human character in the book of Isaiah continues with the material added on the end. Isaiah of Jerusalem disappears after chapter 39, and the somewhat elusive Servant of YHWH has replaced him, appearing periodically in 40–55. In Isaiah 56–66 we have difficulty finding any identifiable character on to which we can hold. There is still a speaker who opens 56:1 with "Thus says YHWH . . . ," but the extent to which we can and should continue to imagine the speaker as Isaiah or the Servant is uncertain.

Dating Isaiah 24–27 has been a matter of some contention. Most who hold to an early date seem to do so based on a desire to connect it to Isaiah son of Amoz and the resulting assumptions about authorship.[5] Many others who have looked for specific dates have used the numerous references to an unnamed city that has been destroyed (e.g., 24:10; 25:2). By assuming that the city is Nineveh, Jerusalem, or Babylon, they have established a date for the writing of chapters 24–27 close to a date for that city's destruction.[6] This is a lot to hang on to one vague reference. Establishing a precise date is not possible, but the majority of interpreters conclude, for a variety of reasons, that 24–27 was composed and added to the book of Isaiah after the exile.

Identifying Babylon as the ruined city and setting the text in the early Restoration period solves the most problems. In the final form of the book, Isaiah 24–27 serves as a completion of the oracles against Babylon that are at the beginning of the Oracles against Foreign Nations in chapters 13–23.[7]

The discussion below will present Isaiah 1–5 as the opening framework of the book of Isaiah, as functioning along with 56–66 to enclose the earlier traditions of the book in a framework that revises the entire book to address the concerns of a Restoration audience. Some of the smaller components of 1–5, such as 2:5–22, could have an earlier origin.

THE PROCLAMATION OF ISAIAH CONCERNING THE RESTORATION PERIOD

The separation of Isaiah 56–66 from 40–55 relies on a number of factors, perhaps the most important of which is a shift in the text's primary concern, from defining the place of Judah in an international context, to focusing on the internal operation of a religious community.[8] The initial discussion in Isaiah 56 demonstrates concern for Sabbath observance, which has caused some interpreters to associate Isaiah 56–66 with a general decline of Judaism into legalistic concerns (see discussion box 8.1 on page 152). The Sabbath poem in Isaiah 56:1–8, however, offers a remarkably open invitation that includes eunuchs and foreigners, persons that earlier traditions may have excluded. Beginning a new subject does not require rejecting the previous one or the spirit inhabiting it.

This study operates with the conclusion that Isaiah 56–66 was written during the Persian period, and that it was deliberately shaped at some point to augment the Isaiah material, so there are deliberate points of connection to earlier parts of the scroll. Two important examples are the phrases "former things" and "new thing(s)." Table 8.1 on page 153 lists the occurrences of these phrases.

Table 8.1 demonstrates that the phrase "former things" is versatile, and Isaiah uses it both to designate traditions and memories from that past that should be retained and those that should be rejected and forgotten. In the climactic use of the phrase in 65:17, YHWH declares the intent to "create new heavens and a new earth." The book of Isaiah is consciously declaring to the audience that it is telling the story of Israel through periods of transition, during which they are to replace some things from earlier times.

Another important connection to other parts of Isaiah is the word "servants," specifically referring to some group of people as servants of YHWH. The plural word used this way appears ten times in Isaiah 56–66, after

---

*Discussion Box 8.1 Anti-Semitism and Christian
Interpretation of the Prophetic Literature*

Christian readings of the prophetic literature have long operated from an assumption of decline, including the additional assumption that the best Israelite prophecy occurred in the eighth century, with figures like Isaiah, Hosea, Amos, and Micah. Figures like Jeremiah and Ezekiel revived the great prophetic tradition during the Babylonian period, but prophetic literature after the exile became consumed with the legalism of Second Temple Judaism and eventually disappeared, leaving the great "intertestamental gap" that did not end until the writing of the New Testament. The "intertestamental period" was part of a large scheme that presumed the decline of Israelite religion into the rigid, Pharisaic Judaism that Jesus challenged in the New Testament Gospels. It is increasingly apparent that such an understanding is based on a bias against Judaism and misunderstandings about how the law functioned within it. The resulting dismissal of Judaism allowed Christianity to connect itself to "classical prophecy" and deny any connection to Second Temple Judaism. This view largely ignores the broad diversity of literature that Jewish writers produced during the Hellenistic era and fails to recognize that the composers of prophetic scrolls at the end of the process, in the Persian period, were the eloquent developers of the narrative characters we recognize as the early prophets, who were able to continue their work as textualized prophets because of the skill these writers displayed.

---

appearing only a single time up to this point, in 54:17 (see the list in table 8.2).[9] The simplest and most useful understanding of these characters is that they are the followers of the Servant figure who plays such a prominent role in chapters 40–55.[10] Just as the Servant figure in 40–55 need not be tied to a specific figure, neither do these servants nor their connection to the singular Servant need to be precisely identified in order for them to play a literary role in the scroll of Isaiah.

One important question to the "servants," given the development of the Servant figure in Isaiah 40–55, is if and how these plural servants identify with the suffering of the earlier servant. Many examples in table 8.2 appear to make a distinction between the servants and another group(s) of people. This, among other factors, has given rise to the influential idea that Isaiah 56–66 addresses a situation of internal conflict among the inhabitants of Judah during the Persian period.[11]

Table 8.1 "Former Things" and "New Thing(s)" in Isaiah

Isaiah	Quotation
41:22	Tell us the former things. . . .
42:9	See, the former things have come to pass. . . .
43:9	Who among them declared this, and foretold to us the former things?
43:18	Do not remember the former things, or consider the things of old.
46:9	Remember the former things of old, for I am God. . . .
48:3	The former things I declared long ago. . . .
65:17	The former things shall not be remembered or come to mind.
42:9	The former things have come to pass, and new things I now declare.
43:19	I am about to do a new thing.
48:6	From this time forward I make you hear new things.

Table 8.2 "Servants" of YHWH in Isaiah

Isaiah	Quotation
54:17	This is the heritage of the servants of the LORD. . . .
56:6	. . . to love the name of the LORD, and to be his servants . . .
63:17	Turn back for the sake of your servants. . . .
65:8	. . . so I will do for my servants' sake, and not destroy them all.
65:9	. . . and my servants shall settle there.
65:13a	My servants shall eat. . . .
65:13b	. . . my servants shall drink. . . .
65:13c	. . . my servants shall rejoice. . . .
65:14	. . . my servants shall sing. . . .
65:15	. . . but to his servants he will give a different name.
66:14	. . . the hand of the LORD is with his servants. . . .

To many interpreters, Isaiah 56–59 looks like a relatively cohesive unit. The introduction in 56:1–8 is framed by "Thus says the LORD . . ." statements that promote justice and promise the gathering of outcasts, prominent themes in Isaiah 40–55, so the passage is commonly understood as a deliberate link between the sections most often called Second Isaiah and Third Isaiah. The reference to YHWH's servants in 56:6, discussed above and listed in table 8.2, also connects this text to Isaiah 40–55. As the introduction to this chapter has indicated, 56–66 may delineate groups within the Restoration community that were parties to the conflicts defining the era, and 56–59 works along with 65–66 to define the group to which it speaks in various ways. While definitions cannot be precise, some clues may emerge about the divisions, such as in

56:9–12, which denounces persons designated as "sentinels" and "shepherds," metaphors that most often describe religious leaders like priests and prophets, so conflict over leadership roles seems likely. In addition, 57:1–13 lists several worship practices it considers corrupt and associated with idolatry, so ways of worshiping in the Second Temple were likely a point of contention. Though 58:13 refers to observing the Sabbath, it would seem impossible to imagine that any among the residents of a restored Judah would not have kept Sabbath. More likely, there were disagreements concerning how to observe the Sabbath. Several points within this passage sound as if the group to which it is speaking is at a disadvantage and needs encouragement to remain faithful to their understanding of important religious practices. This seems particularly true in Isaiah 59, which urges faith, persistence, and repentance from sin. The final poetic verse in 59:20 makes a promise to this apparently beleaguered group:

> And he will come to Zion as Redeemer,
>   to those in Jacob who turn from transgression, says the LORD.

The significance of Isaiah 60–62 for understanding the whole of 56–66 means that this section deserves some special attention. It would be difficult for a prophetic proclamation to sound more optimistic and exuberant in tone than these entire three chapters in the center of 56–66; the opening poem in 60:1–7 sets the tone for a vision of what Israel can be, with light as its dominant motif. Isaiah 60 sounds like a fulfillment of the promise YHWH made to Abraham in Genesis 12:1–3. The blessing of nations that bless Abraham/Israel is echoed in Isaiah 60:3, and the cursing of nations that curse Abraham/Israel resounds in 60:12. Having emerged from the brutal suffering of the Babylonian period, Judah and Jerusalem are ready for a new period of prosperity that will include relief for the suffering, most clearly expressed in 61:1:

> The spirit of the Lord GOD is upon me,
>   because the LORD has anointed me;
> he has sent me to bring good news to the oppressed,
>   to bind up the brokenhearted,
> to proclaim liberty to the captives,
>   and release to the prisoners.

The opening address to a beleaguered group transforms the audience and ends by bestowing four new names upon them in 62:12.

> They shall be called, "The Holy People,
>   The Redeemed of the LORD";

and you shall be called, "Sought Out,
    A City Not Forsaken."

These new names reverse the afflictions that opened the section in 61:1.

Many are abandoning the old label for Isaiah 24–27, the "Isaiah Apocalypse," as our use and understanding of the term "apocalypse" becomes more precise. Some part of the text may come close to assuming a temporal dualism, but the spatial dualism so characteristic of apocalyptic literature is absent. Nevertheless, the identification of chapters 24–27 as a unit and the awareness that it is doing something different plays an important role in understanding it. The Oracles against Foreign Nations in Isaiah 13–23 depend upon precise national boundaries and names, and the reframing of the collection that attached chapters 13 and 14 to an earlier collection brought the primary focus of YHWH's judgment of Israel's enemies onto Babylon. One of the effects of Isaiah 24–27, with its notorious lack of precise boundaries and identities, is the dissolution of the historical and geographical specificity of the first half of Isaiah. Divine judgment on evil cities becomes universal. According to 24:1, divine judgment will yield an earth that is laid waste and desolate, with a surface twisted so that previous forms and boundaries are unrecognizable. It is always possible for a people to survive the desolation, though, if they follow the advice of 26:16–21:

> Come, my people, enter your chambers,
>   and shut your doors behind you;
> hide yourselves for a little while
>   until the wrath is past.
>
>   (v. 20)

Of course, it is possible to understand such instruction to be directed specifically to the captives in Babylon, but the text has broken free from the limits of such a singular identification. The final verse of this section promises,

> On that day a great trumpet will be blown, and those who were lost in the land of Assyria and those who were driven out to the land of Egypt will come and worship the LORD on the holy mountain at Jerusalem. (27:13)

The great empires that used to be Israel's enemies and oppressors, Assyria and Egypt, have become ways of encompassing and naming the whole world from which the people of YHWH will be gathered.

One final step is necessary in presenting the proclamation of the scroll of Isaiah, and that is the opening chapters, which are best understood as a deliberate framework for the book, along with 65–66. Whether or not all of Isaiah 1–5 comes from the Restoration period and was added to the book as enclosure at about the same time as 56–66, it appears that the beginning of the book was significantly reshaped at or near the end of the formation process. The case is easier to make for a connection between Isaiah 1 and 65–66, but it is difficult to ignore two important aspects of 1–5 as a unit. First, except for the initial superscription in 1:1, there is almost no direct, concrete information contained within them about their historical context. This timelessness plays an important role at both the beginning and the end of the book. The army that invades at the command of YHWH in 5:24–30 can be the armies of the past, Assyria and Babylon, and the cosmic armies of the future, as portrayed in Isaiah 13 and 24.[12] Those punished for their rebellion against YHWH in 66:24 can also be the Assyrians (37:36), the Babylonians (14:22–23), or the opponents of the book's audience. The vagueness about time and place shifts abruptly at 6:1, which seems to be a natural continuation of 1:1. One of the questions this helps to answer is why the call narrative of Isaiah is in Isaiah 6 and not at the beginning of the scroll. The answer is that at some point what is now chapter 6 *was* the beginning, and the scroll of Isaiah grew around an earlier collection.

Second, chapters 1–5 as a unit seem to be most concerned with a corrupt leadership in Judah, a concern that is also prominent in 56–66.[13] These leaders are the opponents of the audience who is inheriting the book of Isaiah, as revealed in the initial use of first-person-plural language in 1:9–10:

> If the LORD of hosts
>   had not left us a few survivors,
> we would have been like Sodom,
>   and become like Gomorrah.
> Hear the word of the LORD,
>   you rulers of Sodom!
> Listen to the teaching of our God,
>   you people of Gomorrah!

The "we" who take up this proclamation are the righteous ones that Abraham urged YHWH to look for in Sodom and Gomorrah, as a reason to save the cities from destruction, but which YHWH did not find. Later in the book of Isaiah, Babylon will be destroyed "like Sodom and Gomorrah" (13:19). The "we" who see themselves as survivors appear from time to time in the book of Isaiah, but their presence does not become consistent until the end of the book. These survivors emerge more clearly in 59:9–15 and 63:7–64:12.[14] In the former passage this group cries out for justice:

> Therefore justice is far from us,
>   and righteousness does not reach us;
> we wait for light, and lo! there is darkness;
>   and for brightness, but we walk in gloom.
>   (59:9)

The latter passage begins with a recollection of "all that the LORD has done for us" (63:7) in the past, in hopes that such a recitation will stir YHWH into action in the present. The passage ends with a question that begs for this action:

> After all this, will you restrain yourself, O LORD?
>   Will you keep silent, and punish us so severely?
>   (64:12)

It is possible to understand Isaiah 65–66 as YHWH's response to this question. The promises in these chapters are abundant, both with blessing to the audience and divine judgment for their opponents. One of the more poignant images is the reversal of the Song of the Unfruitful Vineyard in Isaiah 5:1–10. Using the themes of restoration also found in Jeremiah, Israel's God promises:

> They shall build houses and inhabit them;
>   they shall plant vineyards and eat their fruit.
>   (65:21)

It is important to acknowledge the painful ending of the book of Isaiah. All of the promises that have come to the audience after their plea for help might seem to be abundant enough for the whole nation and all of its neighbors, but the fire of judgment (66:15–16, 24) accompanies restoration and remains a necessary component of it all the way to the end of the book. The scroll of Isaiah shows us a grand vision of another reality, but it will not let us detach that vision from the struggle to survive.

RETROSPECTIVE ON THE BOOK OF ISAIAH

In the finished book of Isaiah, it is now possible to understand a process in which a grand vision of Jerusalem is first attributed to an eighth-century prophet named Isaiah son of Amoz. This character takes the first small steps toward embodying the prophetic message he proclaims by having children, to whom he gives symbolic names in Isaiah 7–8, and performing an action that mimics being taken as a prisoner of war in 20:1–6. His degree of success as a prophet is uncertain, since his preaching does not increase understanding (6:10) and must be projected forward to a later generation (8:16). Nevertheless, through his interaction with two kings of Judah in the last decades of the eighth century (Ahaz and Hezekiah), he manages to broker a temporary reprieve for Judah and Jerusalem in his own time (39:5–8). As the book turns its attention to the terrible fate and suffering of Judah during the sixth century, the character named Isaiah gives way to a more ambiguous character called the Servant of YHWH, who embodies both Jerusalem's future hope for a just society and its present pain in the midst of defeat and captivity. This part of the book of Isaiah points to the emerging Persian Empire as God's way of providing a new context for the establishment of Jerusalem as a place for the people of YHWH to worship (45:1–3), and this is accomplished through the redemptive suffering of the Servant (53:10–12). The mathematical certainties of a theology of retribution that had been destabilized in the character named Isaiah are overturned by the Servant.

While one of the Servant Poems had hinted at a plural identity for the Servant (49:3), this plurality becomes fully visible in the transition from Isaiah 40–55 to 56–66. After the first occurrence of the plural form in 54:17 and the second in 56:6, this identification becomes abundant in the closing chapters, 65–66, which form a framework for the book with Isaiah 1–5. These servants, to whom the book is speaking at its end, have inherited the vision of Isaiah:

> You shall see, and your heart shall rejoice;
>   your bodies shall flourish like the grass;
> and it shall be known that the hand of the LORD is with his servants,
>   and his indignation is against his enemies.
>
>   (66:14)

So all readers are invited to identify as servants of YHWH and to see, with Isaiah, the vision of God's redemption of Israel, through the struggles and triumphs of Jerusalem's long story. The opening superscription in 1:1, which may have initially introduced Isaiah's temple vision in 6:1, now introduces a larger vision that has grown around it, and the group to which the finished scroll is addressed is invited to see that larger vision with Isaiah son of Amoz.

This description of the book of Isaiah (above) contends that the predisaster preaching of Isaiah son of Amoz has become part of a larger vision, which does not operate with all of the assumptions of divine retribution that are present within some of the judgment oracles when they are read in isolation, as predisaster announcements of judgment. The scroll of Isaiah has thus freed its readers from the brutal accusation that all who suffer are wicked and are receiving the divine punishment they deserve. Like all such theological developments, however, this move raises new difficulties while it resolves old ones, so the process of theological development is never finished. In this particular case, at least two problematic new ways of addressing suffering emerge. One of these is the trivialization or even denial of suffering. This understanding claims that if such struggle and pain are part of a divine process that is leading to redemption and triumph, then it should not be viewed as suffering at all. This too easily becomes a tool for the powerful to use against the marginalized, encouraging them not to resist their plight because there will be some future reward that is much greater.

A second problematic result is the near reversal of retribution theology that takes place in the glorification of martyrdom. This is a development that eventually took place within both Judaism and Christianity. A central expression in Judaism is the dramatic collection of stories about Greek persecution of Jews in 2 Maccabees 6–7. These narratives follow a pattern very similar to the persecution stories in the book of Daniel. Faithful Jews refuse to comply with a foreign law requiring false worship, and they are sentenced to death. Of course, the striking difference in 2 Maccabees 6–7 is that the scribe, Eleazar, and the unnamed mother and her seven sons are all killed in brutal, agonizing fashion, and no divine intervention saves them. Stories of other martyrs in the Apocrypha and Pseudepigrapha seem to compete with one another in presenting graphic and horrifying details.[15] There is a standard pattern of elements in these martyrdom stories, and in similar ones found in other literature, that typically include an emphasis on the refusal of the martyrs to relent, even under the most extreme conditions, and they include the dying utterances of the martyrs.[16]

The emphasis on suffering and martyrdom as a sign of faithfulness eventually intersected with Isaiah's own life in a fascinating piece of literature known as the *Ascension of Isaiah*, which emerged in the first century CE, probably from a mixture of Jewish and Christian sources. A portion of that text that sometimes goes by the independent title *Martyrdom of Isaiah* (5.1–16) tells the story of Isaiah being sawed in two at the command of King Manasseh for refusing to relent from his claim to have seen YHWH (Isa. 6:1), a claim that brought a charge of heresy. A similar, though far less elaborate, account of Isaiah's death is provided in another later document called *Lives of the Prophets*, which the last chapter of this book will incorporate into the discussion of the reading of prophetic literature. The proliferation of martyrdom stories may indicate the success of the Isaiah scroll and other prophetic books in transforming suffering from a sign of divine disfavor and punishment into a task of the faithful.

The finished book of Isaiah carries three centuries of Israel's experience forward into the conflicted lives of its audience in the Persian period. The ancient prophet and his extension in the Servant offer a continuation of their work to this audience. In the grand vision encompassing the entire scroll, the redemptive work of all these faithful Israelites is a complete whole, bringing the salvation of YHWH to the Jerusalem of the present and future. In the final form of the Isaiah scroll, suffering is a complex phenomenon. Some in the past have suffered because of their disobedience to YHWH, and this will happen to some in the future as well, as the final verse of the book makes brutally clear. Some have suffered as a part of their faithful service to YHWH, and their suffering has become part of the process of redemption that will bring about a new Israel defined by justice and proper worship. Others have suffered or are still suffering innocently, and these people are invited to understand themselves as servants of YHWH and to see their suffering as part of the redemptive process embodied in Isaiah son of Amoz and the Servant who continued his work and now passes it on to them. In the final chapter of this book, this understanding of the book of Isaiah will be joined to the readings of the other scrolls of the prophetic literature, so that it may participate in the larger presentation of these ideas, both adding to and receiving from the other voices.

Resources for Further Research

Commentaries

Blenkinsopp, Joseph. *Isaiah 56–66: A New Translation with Introduction and Commentary*. New York: Doubleday, 2003. (C)
Miscall, Peter D. *Isaiah*. Sheffield: JSOT Press, 1993. (A)

Monographs and Special Studies

Hanson, Paul D. *The Dawn of Apocalyptic*. Rev. ed. Philadelphia: Fortress Press, 1979.
Hibbard, James Todd. *Intertextuality in Isaiah 24–27*. Tübingen: Mohr Siebeck, 2006.
Schramm, Brooks. *The Opponents of Third Isaiah: Reconstructing the Cultic History of the Restoration*. Sheffield: Sheffield Academic Press, 1995.
Stromberg, Jacob. *Isaiah after Exile: The Author of Third Isaiah as the Reader and Redactor of the Book*. Oxford: Oxford University Press, 2011.

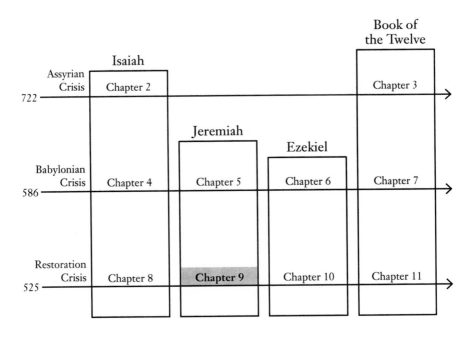

9

The Scroll of Jeremiah Continued

Response to the Restoration Crisis

The fifth chapter of this book moved through the scroll of Jeremiah all the way to the final chapter, which reports the Babylonian invasion of Jerusalem in the early sixth century BCE. The presence of destruction at the end of the book means that if Jeremiah speaks about the Restoration period, then it is elsewhere in the book. Without sharp boundaries, discerning such texts may prove somewhat difficult and controversial. In addition to individual texts, this book functions with the conclusion that the final form of the book of Jeremiah is a product of the Persian period, during or after what may be defined as the Restoration. Therefore the whole book addresses the Restoration period as well. The most significant text in this chapter will be Jeremiah 30–33, often called the Book of Consolation, which is best known for its language about a "new covenant" (31:31–37). Given the central location of 30–33 in Jeremiah, it will also be important to consider its role in the final form of the book and its relationships to other texts. Because Jeremiah 30–33 is filled with ideas that reverse those in other parts of the book, continued awareness of the rest of Jeremiah is essential to understanding what 30–33 is doing.[1] Perhaps the most visible reversal is the use of the themes of building and planting, which first appeared alongside the list of negative verbs in 1:10, but now appear in an exclusively positive manner in Jeremiah 30–33.

THE PROCLAMATION OF JEREMIAH CONCERNING THE RESTORATION PERIOD

The opening verses of Jeremiah 30–33 set it apart from texts immediately surrounding it. Jeremiah receives many divine commands, but only three of them tell him to write something. In 30:2, God tells Jeremiah, "Write in a book all the words that I have spoken to you." On only two other occasions (36:2, 28) is Jeremiah told, "Take a scroll and write on it all the words that I have spoken to you. . . ." The writing in Jeremiah 36 requires repetition because Jehoiakim burns the first copy of the scroll. There are some small but important differences between the commands to write that require some attention here, in part because they highlight some of the ways 30–33 stands out in its literary context. First, 30:4 tells the reader specifically that the following words are those that Jeremiah has been commanded to write down, but there is no narrative setting for the writing event, and it is not certain where the writing ends. It seems most logical to assume that it continues through the end of chapter 31, where the narrative accounts of Jeremiah being imprisoned and buying the field interrupt it. The command to write is just an introduction for presenting the word of YHWH. In Jeremiah 36, on the other hand, the writing of the scroll is a narrative event in the flow of the plot, to which other characters in the story respond. The text of Jeremiah 36 never presents the actual contents of the scroll but merely says that Jeremiah dictates them to Baruch, who writes them down and reads them in public, and that Jehoiakim responds by burning the scroll. Second, the translation of chapters 30 and 36—in most English versions, including the NRSV—describes the writing material differently on the two occasions. In 30:2, God commands Jeremiah to write in "a book," while in 36:2 and 28 it is "a scroll." The word translated "book" in 30:2 is problematic because the kind of physical object we think of as a book, a codex, did not exist at that time, so "book" should not be taken literally. The description in chapter 36:2 uses the same word, but the specific word for scroll precedes it, literally, "a scroll of a book." The specificity of the writing material is necessary in the later account to make sense of the episode in 36:23, in which the king cuts off pieces of the scroll as they are read to him and puts them in the fire. The description of writing in Jeremiah 30 presents no such drama.

The poetic contents of Jeremiah 30–31 break the pattern of prose narrative that has dominated since chapter 26. The poetic form, the unusual introduction discussed above, and the unmistakably positive tone of both chapters are the primary reasons most interpreters identify it as a distinct section of the book. The idea of restoration appears in straightforward terms in 30:3:

> For the days are surely coming, says the LORD, when I will restore the fortunes of my people, Israel and Judah, says the LORD, and I will bring them back to the land that I gave their ancestors and they shall take possession of it.

After the first poetic unit in 30:5–7, which recalls so much of the terror of Jeremiah 1–25, one more brief section of prose in 30:8–9 recalls the image of the yoke, which was the central symbol of the conflict between Jeremiah and Hananiah in Jeremiah 27–28. The image is reversed when YHWH promises to break the yoke from the neck of the audience (30:8). A remarkably revealing statement comes from YHWH in 30:14:

> For I have dealt you the blow of an enemy,
>   the punishment of a merciless foe,
> because your guilt is great,
>   because your sins are so numerous.

The idea of deserved punishment is here, but there is a hint from the divine voice that the impact has been too great, comparing it not to a parent punishing a wayward child, but to the actions of a brutal enemy. At this point, however, it is important that YHWH accept responsibility for the "incurable" pain and hurt (30:12, 15), because the one who inflicted it can also heal it, and YHWH promises healing in verse 17. The words of comfort and healing and the joy they will bring back to Judah continue to intensify in Jeremiah 31 yet are abruptly interrupted in 31:15, a sign that restoration does not simply cover up all the pain of the trauma that has gone before it.

The ensuing discussion after the interruption of "Rachel weeping" addresses the difficult issues of sin, guilt, and punishment. The proverb about inherited guilt and punishment, which also appears in Ezekiel 18:2, brings the debate into clear focus. In this instance, after YHWH promises in Jeremiah 31:28 to reverse the negative verbs from 1:10 and accentuate the positive ones, the promise extends to reversing the proverb:

> In those days they shall no longer say:
> "The parents have eaten sour grapes,
>   and the children's teeth are set on edge."

The meaning of the proverb has generated some disagreement. The translation above, from the NRSV, points to the immediate reaction of the mouth to eating sour fruit, but a different rendering of the verb in the second colon, describing the "blunting" of the teeth, points toward long-term damage caused by a repeated behavior. The behavior might be passed from one generation to the next, along with the negative consequences, rather than just the negative consequences being passed on.[2] The change here may be more about a move from collective to individual responsibility, rather than just a repudiation of inherited guilt and punishment. The disruption of community that took place with the exile led to a situation in which individuals had to make their own choices about religion in a world with many options, so a move toward individuality might be fitting.[3]

Is this promise of reversal in the proverb, whatever the principle behind it, a divine admission that such a principle has been in effect in the past? Many texts in the Old Testament have no difficulty in saying that subsequent generations are punished for the sins of the past. Such an idea is explicitly connected to Jeremiah in 2 Chronicles 36:21, which attributes to him the idea of the exile as seventy years of enforced land Sabbath for all the years that Israel did not keep such a Sabbath. Twice in the book of Jeremiah, at 25:11–12 and 29:10, the exile is defined as a seventy-year period, but the connection to land Sabbath from Leviticus 25 is not present in these texts as it is in 2 Chronicles. It is difficult to escape the conclusion that Jeremiah 31:29–30 establishes a new divine policy, and the idea is particularly important when YHWH proposes a "new covenant" with Israel in 31:31. The description of the new covenant in 31:31–37 is difficult to follow because of its metaphorical nature and will need further clarification in chapters 32–33, but for now, it is not like the covenant with the ancestors at the time of the exodus (31:32), and it will involve writing the law on the hearts of the people (v. 33). This idea and the following one, that teaching will no longer be necessary (v. 34), may be an attack on the role of the priesthood.

The failure of the priests as leaders is a major issue in the book of Jeremiah. The establishment and definition of the priesthood was part of the covenant made with the ancestors, so Jeremiah may envision an Israel with no priests. Other texts in Jeremiah, such as 33:18, however, contend for a continuing and perpetual role for the priesthood. As the discussion above about the proverb in 31:29 has indicated, the exile had served its purpose, from a Babylonian perspective, by breaking down the social cohesion of Judah and making old ways of religious practice impossible. The new covenant of Jeremiah responds to questions about how Israelites might worship YHWH without access to written law and a temple structure. The point is not rejection of the old covenant, but in practice the old covenant may no longer be possible for the audience of the book of Jeremiah, so the reliability of Israel's God makes a new way of faithfulness possible.[4]

Jeremiah 32–33 is typically treated as a unit because 32:2 and 33:1 provide the two chapters with the same setting, the period of Jeremiah's confinement in the "court of the guard" in the palace. Chapter 32 is a complex narrative, with many prophetic formulas that at times make it difficult to determine who is speaking. For example, 32:1 introduces a "word that came to Jeremiah from the LORD," but it is followed by a long parenthetic statement explaining why Jeremiah came to be confined. In 32:6, Jeremiah begins speaking, "The word of the LORD came to me," but then proceeds by telling the story about buying a field. The prophetic word from YHWH does come until verse 27, after being introduced by another prophetic formula.[5] The result of the delay is that by time the word of YHWH finally comes to the reader, the behavior of Jeremiah, who has made an investment in a (future) restored land of Judah, has already reinforced the verbal message. Moreover, Jeremiah's captivity reflects the Babylonian captivity of the ancestors of the apparent audience.

One problem chapter 5 of this book (above) identified is that Jeremiah struggles with the punishment of all the people of Judah because of the disobedience of some among them. One way the book has dealt with undeserved suffering is by highlighting the prophet himself as the recipient of such undeserved pain, particularly in the Confessions in chapters 11–20. The earlier discussion of Jeremiah identified some individuals and groups that seem to be separated out for salvation or blessing because of their faithfulness, including the Rechabites (35:1–19) and Baruch (45:1–5). As the period of the Restoration dawned, the book of Jeremiah needed to identify another group that had benefited from divine blessing and protection: the exiles themselves. Such a case may have been difficult to make about a group of people that had been invaded, taken captive, and carried off to a foreign land, but Jeremiah tries it on several fronts. First, the description of Jeremiah's prophetic task in 1:10 contains six verbs in infinitive forms, four negative and two positive. The final two positive verbs, "to build and to plant," become the themes of Jeremiah's Letter to the Exiles in Babylon in 29:4–23.[6] While the restoration of Judah would ultimately require them to build houses and plant gardens in their own land, Jeremiah urges engagement in building and planting activities while the captives are still in Babylon. Jeremiah's message counteracts the messages of other prophets in the midst of the exiles, those who are saying that the captivity will be brief and that the Judahites should already begin making preparations to return. On the contrary, Jeremiah's message is that the captivity will last several more decades, and the exiles should go ahead and begin practicing acts of restoration while they are still in Babylon. Eventually YHWH will make it possible for them to return to Judah, but the full realization of restoration will take a long time and a lot of work. Here it is important to emphasize the distinction between the recipients of the letter in the book and the audience of the book itself. The former, whom Jeremiah encourages to engage in acts of restoration while in captivity in Babylon, are the ancestors of the latter, who are living under Persian rule in Judah, struggling to engage in the same tasks of building and planting.

A second crucial piece of Jeremiah's argument originates in the passage describing the two baskets of figs in Jeremiah 24 and finds completion in chapters 32–33. The text opens with some of the language characteristic of visions, but like other things that Jeremiah reports seeing, the basket of ripe figs and the basket of rotten figs sitting in front of the temple are relatively ordinary objects.[7] Like the almond branch and boiling pot in Jeremiah 1:11–12, the baskets are signs of things to come, most significantly that the rotten figs are the disobedient of Judah who will be destroyed, and the exiles are the good figs that will be saved. The exiles may be in captivity, but they will survive. They will have descendants and can begin rebuilding their lives, even if they have to do it in Babylon for a considerable time. This interpretation of the events of the early sixth century in Judah is not without its problems. Perhaps most significantly, it is difficult to accept that the swords of the Babylonians were such discriminating tools of divine judgment. Jeremiah's claims here need to work together, and innocent suffering in the past cannot be denied. This is why the new covenant, which includes the rejection of inherited guilt, must be included.

Discussion Box 9.1 Postcolonialism and Prophetic Literature

The period typically described as "colonial" has a somewhat shifty definition. The colonization of one group and their land by another group has been happening throughout human history. This includes the activities of the Assyrian, Babylonian, and Persian Empires in relation to Israel in the first millennium BCE. But the intense level of colonization brought about by the rather sudden ability of the Western European countries to explore the entire globe in the sixteenth and seventeenth centuries was unique. During these two centuries, the British, French, Dutch, Portuguese, Spanish, German, and Belgian kingdoms divided up much of the world, controlling lands in Africa, Asia, and the Americas and plundering them for their resources, including human resources taken as slaves. We tend to think of colonialism in terms of military conquest and economic oppression, but it is also a practice that makes use of ideas that perpetuate dominance, and these ideas can become embedded in texts and our habits of reading them. Therefore it becomes necessary to interrogate texts and traditional ways of reading that emerge from colonial settings with careful questions about how they are influenced by and participate in the colonial enterprise.[8] Jeremiah's Letter to the Exiles in chapter 29 urges its audience to play along with their Babylonian colonizers and captors, just as Isaiah 45 urges complicity with a Persian colonial power. It is possible that in these narrow, temporary situations, such complicity is the wisest course of action, but interpreters must be careful not to allow such advice to become a general rule, while colonizers might like it to be so. A postcolonial perspective must always ask, Whose political and economic interests are served by a particular text or by a particular interpretation of a text?

The character named Baruch of Neriah plays a significant role in the second half of Jeremiah, and he has an interesting life in traditions outside of the book. Table 9.1 contains a list of Baruch's appearances in the Old Testament and the role he plays within the texts. The list includes his appearances in the book called Baruch that appears in the Greek Old Testament and some other canonical traditions, but not in the Tanak.[9] One way to look at the Baruch character is as an extension of Jeremiah himself. In Jeremiah 32, Baruch assists Jeremiah in a transaction that he cannot fully carry out on his own because he is imprisoned in the palace. In Jeremiah 36, Baruch writes a scroll for Jeremiah, then takes it to the temple and reads it aloud, because Jeremiah has apparently been banned from the temple.

Table 9.1 Appearances of Baruch, Son of Neriah

Text	Name Appears	Narrative Role
Jer. 32	3× (vv. 12, 13, 16)	Receives deed for Jeremiah's field
36:4–8	3× (vv. 4, 5, 8)	Writes scroll as dictated by Jeremiah
36:9–19	9× (vv. 10, 13, 14 [2×], 15, 16, 17, 18, 19)	Reads scroll to the people and officials before king burns it piece by piece
36:20–32	3× (vv. 26, 27, 32)	Rewrites scroll after the king burns it
43:1–7	2× (vv. 3, 6)	Accused of manipulating Jeremiah; taken captive with Jeremiah to Egypt
45:1–5	2× (vv. 1, 2)	Receives a blessing from Jeremiah
Bar. 1:1–3	2× (vv. 1, 3)	Writes a book in Babylon; reads it to the captives
Bar. 1:5–9	1× (v. 8)[10]	Takes possession of temple vessels in Babylon

The blessing that Baruch receives from Jeremiah, with a promise of survival, is likely the source of Baruch's persistence in tradition (see discussion box 9.2). A second way to view Baruch is in association with the audience of the book of Jeremiah. When Baruch transmits the Jeremiah tradition forward and is promised survival of captivity, he offers a narrative identity to which readers might attach themselves. Thus the scroll of Jeremiah may function in a manner similar to the scroll of Isaiah, which transforms the prophet himself into an anonymous identity, the Servant of YHWH, who in turn becomes pluralized into an identity that readers may claim for themselves. Readers of Jeremiah may receive for themselves the statement he makes to Baruch in 45:5b: "But I will give you your life as a prize of war in every place to which you may go."

Discussion Box 9.2 Baruch, Son of Neriah,
and the "Baruch" Literature

The character named Baruch plays a limited, but important, role in Jeremiah, and his function as a scribe seems to have captured the imagination of later tradition. Like Enoch and Ezra, Baruch apparently became a favorite assumed identity for Jewish writers of later eras who continued to write books in his name. The books known as *2 Baruch* and *3 Baruch* are both apocalyptic in nature and depict him as a powerful seer who has divine revelations and even ascends to heaven for a tour. Baruch's status as a prophet in his own right was a matter long debated within Judaism.[11] Some have assumed he was the writer of the full scroll of Jeremiah, but there is no evidence for such claims.

In the 1970s a clay object called a bulla appeared with writing meaning "Belonging to Berekyahy son of Neriyahy, the scribe." A scribe of the period might have used such an object to seal a document and mark it as his writing. Because the object appeared on the antiquities market in Israel without evidence of when and where it was found, it is difficult to authenticate it. Another similar object appeared in the 1990s, again with no clear origin. The potential value of objects like these creates a strong motive for forgeries. Nevertheless, the appearance of the Baruch Bulla created new, modern interest in the character named Baruch.

RETROSPECTIVE ON THE BOOK OF JEREMIAH

If Jeremiah has any chance of offering hope to the community in a restored Judah, then the book must outlive the prophet himself. It may be disappointing to think that groups within the restored community might have been competing to see which was the proper owner of the Jeremiah tradition; yet such a situation demonstrates an ongoing vitality for both the community and this particular prophetic tradition, steeped in pain and suffering. The book of Jeremiah does not move as far into the Restoration period as any of the other three scrolls, and the recovery it does accomplish is still hidden amid defeat and destruction. In 30:2, the unusual command for Jeremiah to write down his prophetic message allows the prophet's tradition a life beyond his own physical presence, which fades at the end of the book's narrative. Two groups seem to be struggling to possess the legacy of Jeremiah: (1) the returned exiles and (2) those who stayed in Judah during the exilic period.[12] The group of exiles, the *golah*, seems to have won this competition for much, if not all, of the Old Testament.

Significant dispute exists concerning the percentage of Judah's population that was exiled in comparison to the percentage that remained in the land after the Babylonian invasion. Statements like the ones in Jeremiah 33:10, about Judah and Jerusalem being "a waste without human beings or animals," seem largely metaphorical. The Old Testament does not provide enough demographic information to answer this question, but the *golah* story became the dominant narrative of the Restoration period.[13] The verb from which *golah* derives means "uncovered" or "exposed," so it need not mean, by definition, only those who were taken into captivity. The story of exile and return is the better story, though, and its resemblance to the exodus may be why it won the competition. The exile story is imprinted all over the Old Testament. The older exodus story begins in Canaan when Jacob's family departs for Egypt to escape the famine. One member of the family, Joseph, leaves Canaan and goes to Egypt as a captive, and the remainder leave when the famine becomes too severe. Exile is also present in the story of Abram and Sarai in Egypt the first time (Gen. 12), Jacob in Paddan-aram, Moses in Midian, Jephthah in Tob, Naomi in Moab, and David in the wilderness. Some texts in the Old Testament seem to open a way for the people who remained in Judah, but they must accept the exile and return as their story too (e.g., Ezra 6:21). Such acts of inclusion have a precedent within the biblical story in Joshua's apparent joining of outside groups to those who came from Egypt, as long as the former groups choose to make the exodus story their story (Josh. 24:14–18). Similarly, the many voices included in the book of Jeremiah may indicate openness to all hearers who will accept its story of the exile and restoration of Judah.

The treatment of Jeremiah in this book has demonstrated that the character named Jeremiah becomes so entangled with the prophetic message the book is communicating that the two become practically indistinguishable. In the first half of the book, he descends into despair and, through his voice in the poems called the Confessions of Jeremiah, readers get to hear from all who suffer the pain of failure and rejection. The extent to which the second half of Jeremiah represents an upward turn in the story of the prophet and the nation is uncertain, but it undoubtedly offers a portrait of survival.[14] The second half begins in Jeremiah 26 with the story of the prophet being put on trial but escaping a death sentence. On several occasions in the book, Jeremiah goes on to suffer captivity, but the story never gets to the point of his death. Depending on which version of the book of Jeremiah one reads, the last narrative act of Jeremiah may be the promise of such survival to Baruch. It is not always easy to find optimism in the second half of the book of Jeremiah:

the prophet's life continues to be a painful struggle. Nevertheless, some small acts like writing the Letter to the Exiles in chapter 29, purchasing the field in 32, and writing or dictating scrolls in 30 and 36—all these are claims that there is a future beyond the destruction and suffering. The scattered presence of these texts means that the book of Jeremiah is not as distinctly polar as the other prophetic scrolls, but the movement back and forth between judgment and salvation is more frequent in the second half of the book.

The presence of the Oracles against Foreign Nations near the end of the Hebrew version of Jeremiah raises a final question about the overall shape of the book. In the Greek version of the book, with these oracles beginning in Jeremiah 25, it is much more clear that the judgment of Judah is attached to the judgment of the nations. In the Hebrew version of the book, the placement of these texts at the end of the book and their internal rearrangement make it possible to see them as revenge and as a part of the restoration of Judah.[15] The one thing that still comes after them in this version of the book is the account of the actual invasion by the Babylonians, but Jeremiah has described this approaching event so many times, and made it so inevitable, that the invasion is anticlimactic. Jeremiah has made the case that this invasion is actually part of the process of restoring Judah. Like the rest of chapter 52, the final four verses are inherited from the end of 2 Kings yet offer the first step in the release of Judah from captivity: the release of King Jehoiachin from prison. To continue the story, readers must go back to texts in the center of the book, which is built around restoration rather than moving toward it.

Resources for Further Research

Commentaries

Because of how the book of Jeremiah is organized, there are no commentaries that deal only or primarily with the texts treated in this chapter. Each of the commentaries listed at the end of chapter 5 of this book will still be useful for doing research on these Jeremiah texts.

Lundbom, Jack R. *Jeremiah 21–36: A New Translation with Introduction and Commentary*. New York: Doubleday, 2004. (C)

Monographs and Special Studies

Becking, Bob. *Between Fear and Freedom: Essays on the Interpretation of Jeremiah 30–31*. Leiden: E. J. Brill, 2004.

Davidson, Steed Vernyl. *Empire and Exile: Postcolonial Readings of the Book of Jeremiah*. New York: T&T Clark, 2011.

Diamond, A. R. Pete, and Louis Stulman, eds. *Jeremiah (Dis)placed: New Directions in Writing/Reading Jeremiah*. New York: T&T Clark, 2011.

Plant, Robin J. R. *Good Figs, Bad Figs: Judicial Differentiation in the Book of Jeremiah*. London: T&T Clark, 2008.

Sharp, Carolyn J. *Prophecy and Ideology in Jeremiah: Struggles for Authority in the Deutero-Jeremianic Prose*. London: T&T Clark, 2003.

Shead, Andrew G. *The Open Book and the Sealed Book: Jeremiah 32 in Its Hebrew and Greek Recensions*. Sheffield: Sheffield Academic Press, 2002.

Stulman, Louis. *Order amid Chaos: Jeremiah as Symbolic Tapestry*. Sheffield: Sheffield Academic Press, 1998.

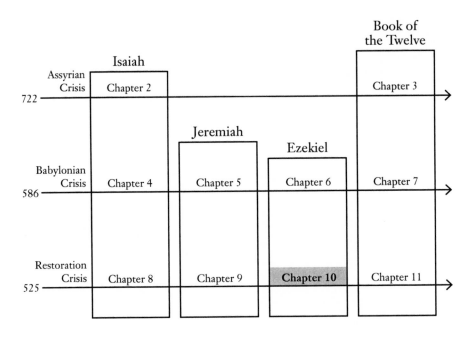

10

The Scroll of Ezekiel Continued

Response to the Restoration Crisis

Chapter 6 of this book introduced Ezekiel and examined how the book speaks about the Babylonian crisis. As demonstrated there, interpreters commonly divide Ezekiel into two halves, chapters 1–24 and 25–48, but the division is based more on the literary structure of the book than on the parts of Israel's experience the two halves address. Chapter 6 (above) went beyond the midpoint because the Oracles against Foreign Nations in Ezekiel 25–32 bring closure to the first half of the book, which focuses on YHWH's judgment of Judah and Jerusalem. At the same time, Ezekiel 25–32 may be a transitional element in the scroll, opening possibilities for Judah's restoration in the Persian period, which is the subject of the remainder of the book, chapters 33–48. In chapter 9 (above) the discussion of the Oracles against Foreign Nations in Jeremiah raised questions about whether these texts make YHWH's judgment of Israel part of the judgment of the whole world, or offer vengeance against Israel's enemies as an early step in the restoration process. The answer to the question in Ezekiel could be that it does both.

The purpose of several ideas that seem odd in the first half of Ezekiel becomes clearer during the second half. First, Ezekiel's priestly identity, which seems at odds with his behavior in 1–24, becomes essential to the tasks he performs in 33–48. Second, the concern for holiness or purity, which seemed strange or even trivial in the face of a pending military invasion by the Babylonians, may find a better fit in the story of Judah's restoration. Finally, the fantastical elements of Ezekiel, which looked like denial as a response to real tragedy, suffering, and death in the Babylonian period, help develop the framework for an imaginative vision that offers a new future for Judah.

The relative lack of an audience in Ezekiel will continue to be a challenge, since it makes the prophet appear detached. In addition, we do not see the effect of the actual events of the Babylonian invasion on the character named Ezekiel or anyone in his audience, but only the symbolic effects as he becomes captive to his prophetic role. Isaiah presents the suffering of the Servant after the fact, when the Babylonian invasion and captivity have already happened, and interprets the Servant's work as redemptive. Jeremiah's suffering, prior to the Babylonian invasion, is inflicted by his own people, as a response to his words of judgment against them, but it is not a necessary response. The audiences might have chosen other responses. Ezekiel's suffering differs because even if it is mimicked suffering, at his own hands, YHWH commands him to do it to himself. Suffering seems a necessary part of Ezekiel's prophetic work in the period leading up to the Babylonian invasion, so it sets up the portrayal of the Restoration in a different way. Ezekiel's suffering represents Israel's suffering, so what remains to be seen in the second half of the book is whether his life and work can embody Israel's future recovery and restoration.

THE PROCLAMATION OF EZEKIEL CONCERNING THE RESTORATION PERIOD

The oracle that begins a long sequence in Ezekiel 33–39 has the prophetic formula "The word of the LORD came to me . . ." at its beginning in 33:1, but it is missing the chronological marker that occurs so frequently in Ezekiel 25–32. Table 10.1 lists the occurrences of the oracular introduction "The word of YHWH came to me . . ." in a way that demonstrates two important patterns in the book. First, undated oracles are concentrated in chapters 11–24 and 28–38. Second, dated oracles are concentrated in 29–32, after which they stop completely. The sudden cessation of chronological markers raises the possibility that time is no longer the primary issue and 33:1–9 should be read closely with the preceding text, the lament over Egypt in 32:17–32, which begins with a date in 585, the year after the destruction of Jerusalem. Such a possibility fits the idea that oracles against foreign nations function as a transitional element in Ezekiel.

The description of Egypt's destruction (29:1–12) goes beyond a simple announcement of judgment and defeat and becomes part of the mythic imagination of the book of Ezekiel (see "Myth and the Prophetic Literature" in discussion box 10.1). The text compares Egypt to Assyria, which had begun its mythic existence as a great tree in the garden of Eden (31:8–9), and this existence now finds its end in the shadowy world of Sheol, where the only comfort Pharaoh finds is the company of all the armies he defeated (32:31–32). Following the king of Egypt to this place allows for the portrayal of many of Israel's enemies as dead in Sheol (vv. 22–30), and connecting this picture to

Table 10.1 "The word of YHWH came to me . . ." in Ezekiel

Time	Location in Ezekiel
No marker	In 1–24—3:16; 6:1; 7:1; 11:14; 12:1, 8, 17, 21, 26; 13:1; 14:2, 12; 15:1; 16:1; 17:1, 11; 18:1; 20:45; 21:1, 8, 18; 22:1, 17, 23; 23:1; 24:15, 20
Marker	In 20:1–2; 24:1; 26:1; 29:1, 17; 30:20; 31:1; 32:1, 17
No marker	In 25–48—25:1; 27:1; 28:1, 11, 20; 30:1; 33:1, 23; 34:1; 35:1; 36:16; 37:15; 38:1

the role of Ezekiel as a "sentinel" or watchman in 33:1–20 opens the way for new possibilities in the life of Israel.[1]

Ezekiel watches as the death of Israel is coupled with the death of all of these other nations in 33:1–10, but this is not the end of the story for Israel. The divine purpose turns in 33:11 as YHWH declares, "I have no pleasure in the death of the wicked, but that the wicked turn from their ways and live." Like other parts of Ezekiel, it is not difficult to imagine such a divine declaration as a response to a complaint not explicitly present in the text. The text goes on to present a destabilizing view of the simple equations about suffering and its relationship to righteousness and wickedness, as the two groups that the dichotomy creates become impossible to distinguish by verses 17–20, where "the righteous turn from their righteousness, and commit iniquity," while "the wicked turn from their wickedness, and do what is lawful and right." Such a claim counters, or at least makes an adjustment to, Jeremiah's simplistic description of "good figs and bad figs" (Jeremiah 24:1–10).

Immediately after the watchman oracle (33:1–20), Ezekiel receives the news from a fugitive that Jerusalem has fallen in the previous year. The arrival of the news in 33:21–22 releases Ezekiel from the inability to speak and makes possible the unleashing of a long sequence of oracles focused on the purification and restoration of the survivors of Judah. These oracles describe past impurity and condemn false leaders, replacing them with YHWH as the shepherd for the people of Israel.[3] Purity and holiness often appear as significant themes in the book of Ezekiel, but they can seem out of place, particularly in the first half of the book. Ezekiel's objection to the divine command concerning food preparation in 4:14 is based upon a sense of impurity that does not sit easily in its context. Ezekiel's actions in 4:4–14 mimic being held captive, a situation in which people have little or no control over what they eat.[4] If, however, the understanding of purity in the book of Ezekiel includes a source of distinction and identification of a group of people, then impurity is a loss of identity, and reestablishing it is a necessary part of restoration. The

---

Discussion Box 10.1 Myth and the Prophetic Literature

"Myth" is a challenging word to define and understand in biblical studies. First, it is a technical term that suffers from popular usage having
little to do with its technical meaning in the academic discipline of
religious studies. One understanding of myth relates primarily to stories
about gods, beings that live outside the normal boundaries of time and
space, where humans live, though such stories often involve these gods
entering into the arena of human life. The story of the "sons of God"
in Genesis 6:1–4 is a good example in the Bible, as is the garden of
Eden story in Genesis 3. Another understanding of myth describes what
might be called the "foundational stories" of a culture, stories that are
much more important than a singular event on a historical time line.
A culture often continues to act out such stories in ritual performance.
The escape of the Israelites from Egypt in Exodus 12 is a good example,
because it is foundational in the sense that it explains the origins of a
group of people, and it is reenacted annually in the festival of Passover.
There may not be any full stories in the prophetic literature that fit easily
into these categories, but some elements in these texts seem to come
from such stories, and the writers assume that readers are aware of
them, so they are being used as "backstories."[2] One element Ezekiel
uses is the image of a god riding on storm clouds like a chariot, which
is part of many stories from the ancient Near East. The image of nations
like Assyria and Egypt beginning their existence as trees in a great garden in Ezekiel 31 may assume a backstory we do not know, though
Ezekiel's first readers may have known it. The image may reappear in
the portrayal of the restoration of Israel in Ezekiel 47:12.

---

bound and motionless prophet may be giving voice to the community's grief
over the loss of identity.

The conditions in which the restoration of Judah would take place make
leadership a critical issue for the book of Ezekiel when it addresses this part of
Israel's story. Ezekiel 34:1–10 raises the issue by narrating the failure of past
leaders, and 34:11–31 begins to look ahead to future possibilities, using the
shepherd metaphor to portray leadership. One of the challenges faced by all
the parts of the prophetic literature addressing the Persian period is the question of Israel's national identity and the possibility of reestablishing the monarchy. Other prophetic texts, particularly Haggai and Zechariah, seem to hold
out hope for such a possibility, and they will be examined in the next chapter.
The hope of reestablishing the monarchy rests with the Davidic heir named

Zerubbabel, who also appears prominently in the book of Ezra (e.g., 3:2). The metaphorical nature of Ezekiel 34:11–31 makes it difficult to identify a concrete political position on a new monarchy in Ezekiel, but the idea of reasserting divine kingship over Israel is consistent with texts like the "YHWH is king!" declarations in Psalms 93–99. Divine kingship immediately elicits some practical questions: How does divine kingship work in practice? Does it eventually need to grant power to other human individuals? Do human possibilities include a reestablished priesthood, of which Ezekiel is a potential part? Or a foreign ruler like Cyrus, whom the book of Isaiah portrays as YHWH's anointed one? The visionary nature of Ezekiel makes the concrete resolution of such questions unlikely.

The sequence of oracles in Ezekiel 33–39 surrounds the most famous text in the book, the vision of the valley of bones in 37:1–14. It is easy to lift such a powerful text from the book and ignore its context, but the vision plays a vital role in the sequence of surrounding texts. The dead armies of Egypt and many of Israel's enemies appear in Sheol in 32:17–32, but when Ezekiel arrives in the unnamed valley in 37:1, he finds the dead bodies of Israel's army still lying on the ground in the bottom of the valley. If purity is an important aspect of the book of Ezekiel, then the corpses represent a problem beyond the representation of defeat, because they have not been properly buried. The larger metaphorical question may be how a new nation can be built upon the death of an old one, a question that takes on practical tones at the end of the vision in 37:11, when the Israelites in exile complain that they are dying in a foreign land, with no hope. Understanding the possible connections between this vision and the baffling material in Ezekiel 38–39 requires recognizing how the vision uses the elements of Israel's creation traditions. The movement of the wind through the valley uses the imagery of Genesis 1, where the word (*ruach*) that can mean "wind, breath, or spirit" is the animating power of God that moves across the face of the waters in Genesis 1:2. Restoring the army is a two-step process, like the creation of the first human in Genesis 2:7, that involves forming the bodies and then breathing life into them. When the second step occurs in Ezekiel 37:10, the word for "live," which is prominent in Genesis 2:7, appears.[5] This is not merely a resuscitation of Israel's army but a re-creation that looks back to YHWH's initial triumph over the forces of chaos at the beginning of the world. The issue of a restored monarchy arises again in 37:24–28, which describes David occupying the throne. In Ezekiel 37:22, YHWH proclaims that all of Israel will be reunited as one nation and that "one king shall be king over them all." In the midst of so much language that operates within the prophetic imagination, in the worlds of visions and mythic traditions, it is difficult to know whether the book of Ezekiel portrays a literal reestablishment of the Israelite monarchy here.

Interpreting Ezekiel 38–39 presents specific challenges because of the sudden and mysterious appearance of an entity called "Gog."[6] This character appears by name ten times in these two chapters and nowhere else in the Old Testament.[7] Here is another case where the book of Ezekiel appears to be using a mythical element (see discussion box 10.1) from the ancient Near East and assuming a backstory of which its first audience may have been more aware than are modern readers. In Ezekiel 38–39 the writer likely assumed some form of what is often called "the Combat Myth," in which a divine being defeats the forces of evil and chaos.[8] If so, then it is probably important that Gog and Magog not be identifiable with any one particular ethnic or national entity. The text contains connections to Egypt, Tyre, Babylon, and other nations that were enemies of Israel. The declarations against Gog that YHWH commands Ezekiel to deliver, such as 39:1–6, are much like the Oracles against Foreign Nations earlier in the book in both form and tone, except for the difficulty in identifying the villain.[9] So Gog is probably best understood as a placeholder, a blank for which the reader might imagine any of a number of nations or kings.

This understanding of chapters 38–39 leads to questions about why such a text appears here in Ezekiel. The oracles against foreign nations appear in 25–32, and YHWH's defeat of the nations serves as a transitional element for Ezekiel to begin looking toward the restoration of Judah. Ezekiel's vision in chapter 37 restores Judah's army and offers hope for restoration to the captives in Babylon. The vision of a rebuilt temple, reoccupied by YHWH in Ezekiel 40–48, seems to be the final piece of the story, and 38–39 is an interruption or a delay. If Ezekiel is a coherent and unified work of literature, however, regardless of the details of its formation process, then the Gog and Magog text requires a better explanation. Perhaps it is too little for Israel's God to declare victory over all the nations that may be enemies of Israel, and there is a larger victory to be won. For a restored Israel and a new temple to have meaning, YHWH must defeat all of Israel's future enemies too. Stepping outside time is what mythical portrayals can do, and that is why Ezekiel needs to make such a move before envisioning the new temple.[10] Therefore, the account of the defeat of Gog and Magog in Ezekiel 38–39 can end with YHWH declaring,

> Then they shall know that I am the LORD their God because I sent them into exile among the nations, and then gathered them into their own land. I will leave none of them behind; and I will never again hide my face from them, when I pour out my spirit upon the house of Israel, says the Lord GOD. (39:28–29)

The mythic defeat of Israel's enemies for all time allows such an eternal promise.

The doctrine of the inviolability of Zion, which many interpreters find in Isaiah 31:4–5 and confirmed in Isaiah 37:36–38, is refuted by Jeremiah in 7:4. The issue is more complex than the apparent disagreement might seem, however, as Micah proclaims the destruction of Jerusalem in the same time period as Isaiah, and Jeremiah seems to be responding to a more developed idea than the one found on one occasion in Isaiah. The end of the Gog and Magog text in Ezekiel raises the idea to a different level by making YHWH's perpetual protection of Zion a claim existing outside the historical movements of armies and nations.[11] The Zion receiving the promise of eternal protection is an idea of the imagination. What such a promise does not fully address, and what is left for readers of the book of Ezekiel to continue to work out, is how it relates to the concrete Zion in any particular time.

Interpretations of Ezekiel's new-temple vision in chapters 40–48 have encountered numerous difficulties through the years. First, the passage interacts with many important texts in the Old Testament that describe and define Israel's worship space. The first overt example is description and production of the tabernacle or tent of meeting in Exodus 25–31 and 35–40.[12] Other important examples include the accounts of Solomon building the temple in Jerusalem in 1 Kings 5–7 and 2 Chronicles 3–4. It would likely be a mistake to read any of these texts as a set of instructions that an architect could follow to produce drawings for building an actual structure resembling the one in the text. The passages are all parts of biblical books that tell a story, and they were written to play a role in the story, not to provide specifications for construction. This statement may be most true of Ezekiel 40–48, but the vision's preoccupation with measuring, which fills the first three chapters (40–42), may initially cause readers to assume otherwise.[13] The chapters following the measuring, however, reveal a portrait that moves far beyond reality into the imaginative world of Ezekiel.

There has been significant disagreement in assumptions about the unity of Ezekiel 40–48 and whether the text was a unified composition from the beginning. Some interpreters assume 40–48 is a unified vision experienced by the prophet Ezekiel and written by or for him. Others see an accretion of fragments, leading to the present text during a long process, and they work to separate the fragments out in order to determine the intent of all the layers. The argument ignores the possibility that the text consists of a core of material, perhaps closely connected to Ezekiel himself, which others revised and reshaped in the Restoration period to produce a coherent piece of literature that plays a vital role in the final form of the book of Ezekiel.[14] Readers may identify later editorial layers, but the layers are always best understood in terms of how they function in the final form of the vision.

The "glory of YHWH" Ezekiel first described by the river Chebar in Ezekiel 1 occupies the new temple structure in 43:1–9, an event that punctuates
the measurement of the structure by the man with the stick in his hand. For
Ezekiel, YHWH's return completes a long process in which YHWH aban-
dons his own house, in part to be gone when the Babylonian army invades
and destroys it, but also in order to be present with the exilic community in
Babylon, and finally returns to inhabit a new house. The return of the glory
of YHWH introduces a long section (43:10–46:24) describing the operation
of the temple, including some of its internal construction and the roles of
various priestly groups. The text connects the ritual instructions to the earlier
measurement section by including the altar measurements in 43:13–17. The
instructions that Ezekiel is commanded to write down in 43:11 receive the
designation "law of the temple" in verse 12,[15] and they include the consecra-
tion of the altar and various admission requirements for the new temple. The
instructions concerning priestly duties in Ezekiel 44 reveal significant conflict
concerning religious leadership in restored Judah, a subject that comes up
at other places in the prophetic literature.[16] It is difficult to discern a coherent resolution since some places exclude the Levites (44:10, 13) and others
include them (40:46; 45:5). Again, it is important to remember that this is an
imaginative vision of a restored temple, so tensions like that can exist within
the vision. The resolution of priestly conflict portrayed here need not precisely match whatever resolution may have actually happened outside the text.
After addressing the priestly conflict, the "law of the temple" can proceed to
other issues, such as offerings and festivals, but not before pointing ahead to
an issue that will conclude the entire vision: the allotment of land. In 45:1–8
the summary of land allotment sets aside land for the temple, the priests, the
Levites, the city, and the prince; a sequence for the more complete allotment
in 47:13–48:29 will follow.[17]

Ezekiel's involvement in the vision is a matter of significance because it
may highlight a significant shift that takes place in the second half of the
book. In Ezekiel's earlier visions in chapters 1 and 8–10, the extent to which
the prophet acts within the vision is difficult to determine, and this decision
may depend on where we establish the boundaries of the first two visions.
The glory of YHWH, which Ezekiel describes in 1:4–28, departs in 3:12–15,
so these can be established as the textual boundaries.[18] The spatial boundaries of the vision—that is, where Ezekiel is located in relation to it—are more
difficult to determine. Between 1:4–28 and 3:12–15, Ezekiel interacts with a
voice and a hand that accompany the vision, but it is not clear that he is inside
the vision, interacting with its components. Similar difficulties are present in
chapters 8–11. The temple to which the spirit takes Ezekiel in 8:3 is in his
vision, and he interacts by digging a hole through the wall in 8:8, but it is

unclear who speaks to him at 8:5. The NRSV tries to clarify the speaker by replacing the third-person pronoun "he" with "God," but it could be the fiery figure from 8:2 who speaks. On the other hand, this figure may actually be YHWH.[19] In the vision, Ezekiel also acts when he prophesies in 11:13, but his interaction here is with characters that seem like regular human beings, one of whom dies while he is prophesying. Ezekiel's role is clearer in 37:1–14, because the vision depends upon his prophecy and could not continue without him. While the first two visions are connected to real geographical places, whether Ezekiel was in those places at the time or not, the third one happens in an unnamed valley. The final vision in chapters 40–48 is, correspondingly, on an unnamed mountain. In one sense it is fine to say that this is Mount Zion, because the vision depicts the restored temple there, but the text does not make the identification too precise: neither Jerusalem nor Zion ever appear by name in 40–48. In the vision the mode of interaction changes when the man with the measuring stick speaks directly to Ezekiel on five occasions (40:4, 45–46; 41:4, 22; 42:13–14). In this case, though the man has a supernatural appearance (40:3), he is not YHWH.[20] He addresses Ezekiel the first time using the "Son of man" (RSV; NRSV, "Mortal") designation that YHWH uses for Ezekiel throughout the book, but the man does not use that address on the remaining occasions. Ezekiel the prophet could not be physically present in the Restoration with the Judean community whom the book addresses, so his distinct presence inside the vision is very important. He does not fully disappear from the picture until the last first-person pronoun for him appears in 47:7, and in 47:12 he finishes describing what he sees and hears from the man. The flowing river emerging from the restored temple (47:1) carries the readers into an undefined land the text must now apportion in Ezekiel 48. Though 47:13 opens with "Thus says the LORD . . . ," the characteristic connections to the prophet are gone.[21] There is no command to him to speak the words. While it is fine to understand that the authority of the literary voice of Ezekiel continues to the end of the book, it speaks in an entirely different tone beginning at 47:13. As a character, Ezekiel's task is finished, and he fades away. The book, like all others in the prophetic literature, does not present the literal death of Ezekiel in any overt fashion. A perception of Ezekiel's death, or at least of his disposal, may be present in 47:13, but the scroll continues to speak beyond his existence.

RETROSPECTIVE ON THE BOOK OF EZEKIEL

Ezekiel begins in more spectacular style than any other prophetic scroll. The opening vision and those that follow take command of the prophet named

Ezekiel. "The hand of the LORD was on him" (1:3), and the book uses the character as an eyepiece for the reader to see the visions. The seizing of the prophet continues in the elaborate symbolic actions that fill Ezekiel 4–5, as the text uses Ezekiel's body to dramatize the coming fate of Judah, which he will describe in the judgment oracles he delivers. The first-person nature of the book allows readers to experience Ezekiel's message in visions, symbolic actions, and verbal oracles in almost all cases as YHWH presents them to the prophet. Only on rare occasions do we see the assumed interaction between the prophet and an audience. Perhaps the most important exception is the question the people pose to Ezekiel in 24:19, when they observe the lack of mourning after the death of his wife. Again, the faithful prophet's behavior mimics the future behavior of the guilty in Israel whom God will punish for their sins of idolatry and injustice. Thus, while he is proclaiming the sins of Israel and the threatened punishment of YHWH, Ezekiel himself becomes the afflicted one: the experience of the prophet destabilizes the strict link between sin and punishment, and the grammar of the book invites the reader to participate in Ezekiel's experience. YHWH addresses the problem directly in Ezekiel 18:1–2 by accusing Ezekiel, and perhaps his audience as well, of misusing the proverb about sour grapes and commands him not to say it anymore. On the contrary, YHWH states directly:

> The person who sins shall die. A child shall not suffer for the iniquity of a parent, nor a parent suffer for the iniquity of a child; the righteousness of the righteous shall be his own, and the wickedness of the wicked shall be his own. (18:20)

The need for such a divine pronouncement indicates such a rule is not what is currently in operation. According to 18:25 someone, perhaps Ezekiel himself, is saying that the ways of Israel's God are unfair. We have observed this difficulty in other prophetic scrolls, and Jeremiah has used this same proverb about eating sour fruit to address the issue. Chapter 9 of this book raised the possibility that Jeremiah acknowledges a shift in the way divine retribution operates. Ezekiel may be doing this as well, but we should not assume that the issues are identical. Is YHWH declaring that the proverb was never valid, despite its apparent consistency with texts like Exodus 34:6–7, or that it has been valid in the past but now it is not? In Jeremiah 31:29 this looks like part of a movement toward a more individualized religion, instead of a communal understanding, and suggests a way of making faithfulness possible in a situation of dispersal. Ezekiel may be addressing the same point, but the problem of differential guilt and differential punishment that do not match precisely is also in view. A differentiation between the character named Ezekiel and the book of Ezekiel is essential on this point. The belief of the prophet seems to be that the punishment of Judah and Jerusalem, no matter how harsh, is just divine retribution for their behavior.[22] The book of Ezekiel, however, is addressing the aftermath of the destruction, in which not all individuals suffer to the same degree, and allows a complaint like this one to retain its voice. Furthermore, in promising that the future will be different, it offers at least a tacit agreement that the mechanisms of sin and punishment in the past have not operated fairly.

As Ezekiel moves into its second half and begins to address the Restoration period, it is not possible for the prophet himself to be present as a narrative character in all of the same ways as in the first half, but he is far from absent. One significant shift is that Ezekiel performs more clearly as a character inside of his visions in the second half of the book, allowing him to participate in the restoration, even if in a more imaginative way. Ezekiel's role as a priest and his concerns for purity are reborn in the second half of the book, which also imagines a space in which they can operate. Like Jeremiah, Ezekiel also receives a command to write down something (43:11). Ezekiel writes a set of instructions establishing an environment in which a person precisely like him can operate as YHWH intends, no longer bound or held down.

Resources for Further Research

Commentaries

Some of the commentaries listed at the end of chapter 6 of this book treat the entire book of Ezekiel, including the parts examined in this chapter.

Greenberg, Moshe. *Ezekiel 21–37: A New Translation with Introduction and Commentary.* New York: Doubleday, 1995. (C)
Zimmerli, Walther. *Ezekiel.* Vol. 2. Philadelphia: Fortress Press, 1983. (C)

Monographs and Special Studies

Fitzpatrick, Paul E. *The Disarmament of God: Ezekiel 38–39 in Mythic Context.* Washington, DC: Catholic Biblical Association of America, 2004.
Levenson, Jon Douglas. *Theology of the Program of Restoration of Ezekiel 40–48.* Missoula, MT: Scholars Press, 1976.
Stevenson, Kalinda Rose. *The Vision of Transformation: The Territorial Rhetoric of Ezekiel 40–48.* Atlanta: Scholars Press, 1996.
Tuell, Steven Shawn. *The Law of the Temple in Ezekiel 40–48.* Atlanta: Scholars Press, 1992.

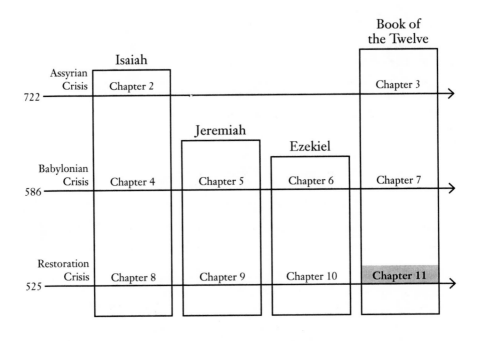

11

The Scroll of the Twelve
Continued Again

Response to the Restoration Crisis

Chapter 3 of this book introduced the Scroll of the Twelve and examined the parts of the scroll that address the Assyrian crisis of the eighth century. Chapter 7 continued the discussion by looking at the parts of the Book of the Twelve that address the Babylonian crisis of the late seventh and early sixth centuries. Moving into the Restoration period, the Book of the Twelve offers a tremendous opportunity because some portions of the scroll address the restoration of Judah in the Persian period in the most direct language found within the prophetic literature. The other three prophetic scrolls all address the Restoration crisis, but they do so in a way that does not put clear names and faces on the response to this set of events. One reason this may be true is because the books called Isaiah, Jeremiah, and Ezekiel wish to retain close connections to the characters for whom the books were named, so they speak furtively of the Restoration period. The Book of the Twelve has a unique advantage because its parts are developed under twelve different names, allowing prophets like Haggai, Zechariah, and Malachi to live and work more openly in the Persian period; that gives them an opportunity to clarify the proclamation of the prophetic literature about the restoration of Judah. Many interpreters find affinities between Haggai and Zechariah 1–8, and between Zechariah 9–14 and Malachi—affinities at least as strong as the connection between the two halves of the book of Zechariah, so the internal divisions of the Book of the Twelve will require some attention here. Some of the large portions of the Book of the Twelve—like Hosea, Amos, and Micah—probably received some revision in this period, so the final forms of these "books" will need to be reopened in this chapter.

187

In working with the other two eras in Israel's story that produced a dramatic prophetic response, the Assyrian and Babylonian periods, the prophetic literature obviously presumed a certain awareness of the narrative background against which it spoke. Both the books of Isaiah and Jeremiah contain parallel passages from 2 Kings. While the precise pattern of literary dependence in these cases may not be entirely clear, the need to read Isaiah and Jeremiah alongside the narrative account of Israel's past known as the Deuteronomistic History is apparent. The case is less clear when asking the same question about the relationship between the prophetic literature of the restoration on one hand, and the restoration narrative in the book(s) of Ezra–Nehemiah on the other hand. The prophets whose names are attached to the books of Haggai and Zechariah appear as characters, though not well-developed ones, in Ezra–Nehemiah, but whether these parts of the Book of the Twelve presume the book of Ezra–Nehemiah as their narrative background is hard to say. Making sense of the book called Malachi without assuming some kind of narrative backdrop seems nearly impossible. The appropriate historical setting for Malachi is universally understood to be the Persian Empire, but the Restoration period was evidently a time of significant internal conflict within Second Temple Judaism, and the points of view of Zechariah 9–14 and Malachi are difficult to determine.

THE PROCLAMATION OF THE BOOK OF THE TWELVE CONCERNING THE RESTORATION PERIOD

The little book called **Haggai** is the first portion of the Twelve that addresses only the Persian period, and it does so overtly, using a narrative character named Haggai. These characteristics of the book of Haggai make it the most obvious starting point for the discussion. Perhaps it is still not yet clear why the Restoration period can be characterized as a crisis. Certainly, the Persian Empire, as portrayed in the Old Testament, does not present a threat to Israel's existence as the Assyrians or Babylonians did. Isaiah and Ezra–Nehemiah portray Persia's king Cyrus as a liberator of Israel rather than an enemy or a destroyer, so the problems faced by Judah in the Restoration period are more subtle than the threat of a military invasion. Two issues identified in the parts of other prophetic books dealing with this murky part of Israel's story are clarified in Haggai, and the first is internal conflict in Judah. The Babylonian period fractured Judah into at least three major pieces: (1) those who remained in the land, (2) those who were taken captive to Babylon, and (3) those who fled to Egypt. The release of the Babylonian captives, and the policy of Persia to sponsor the redevelopment of areas like Judah conquered by the Babylonians, caused an additional reshuffling of the fractured situation. Not all who were in Babylon decided to return, and those who did go back found a community in Judah that had operated without them for two or three generations. Conflicts concerning who represents the true Israel and who has the authority to lead the restored community appear in the books of Isaiah, Jeremiah, and Ezekiel, but the identities of the groups and the issues dividing them are often covert. It may not be possible to line up events and characters precisely, yet the picture of internal conflict is generally consistent with the narratives in Ezra 4–6 and Nehemiah 4–5 and 10–13.[1] The second problem, as indicated in the books of Haggai and Ezra–Nehemiah, is the slow and disappointing progress of the restoration. Apparently the returnees assumed that their project had the favor of Israel's God and that progress would be quicker and easier than they were experiencing. The slow progress becomes a theological problem that the character named Haggai and the book named for him seek to resolve.

The book of Haggai is unique in the prophetic literature because it is entirely narrative in form. The oracles that the prophet named Haggai delivers are provided with dates, narrative contexts, and audiences (see the outline in table 11.1).[2] The dates indicate that the events of the narrative all happen within less than four months.

Table 11.1 An Outline of the Book of Haggai

Haggai	Description
1:1–15	Haggai encounters Zerubbabel, Joshua, the people (2nd year, 6th month, 1st day)[3]
2:1–9	Haggai encounters Zerubbabel, Joshua, the people (2nd year, 7th month, 21st day)
2:10–19	Haggai encounters the priests (2nd year, 9th month, 24th day)
2:20–23	Haggai encounters Zerubbabel (2nd year, 9th month, 24th day)

The primary issue Haggai's speeches address is the lack of prosperity within the restored community and the relationship between material success and rebuilding the temple. The conflict this creates reaches a climax in the third oracle, in Haggai 2:10–19, a text carefully set up by the preceding parts of the book so it can include interaction between the prophet Haggai and various parts of his audience.[4] The situation develops into a dialogue with multiple contributors, including YHWH, and purity becomes the primary issue. Most interpreters have concluded that Haggai's saying in 2:14 is the interpretive crux of the book, and there has been significant disagreement concerning whether the references to "this people" and "this nation" represent the same group or two different groups of people. The argument that both terms refer to the restored community in Israel has prevailed in recent years, which means the impurity to which Haggai refers is not the result of some second group of people who should not be involved, but because of the behavior of the one group to whom the text refers with both terms: the Juhahites.[5] The disadvantage of such a conclusion is the lack of a clear understanding of the impurity issue or Haggai's solution to the problem, beyond saying that the text supports an ongoing role for the priesthood and a concern for ritual purity. The final, brief oracle in Haggai 2:20–23 assumes the resolution of the problem and looks forward to a successful reign for Zerubbabel, but the oracle and its introduction are in a different form than others in Haggai. The introductory formula in 2:20 says, "The word of YHWH came unto Haggai . . ." (AT), and the wording of the oracle indicates that it is what Haggai heard from God. The text does not report the delivery of the oracle to Zerubbabel. The narrative thus leaves readers wondering if the message arrived, and our awareness of the failure of the returnees to reestablish the monarchy highlights the missing delivery.

At a point when the size and scope of the components of the Book of the Twelve may seem to wane, the part called **Zechariah** emerges with surprising size and complexity. Interpreters commonly divide Zechariah into two parts, chapters 1–8 and 9–14, but this is because of literary style and perspective rather than a difference in historical context, like the parts of Isaiah. All of Zechariah addresses the Restoration period. Those who divide the book more distinctly into two parts often recognize an affinity between Zechariah 1–8 and Haggai, and between Zechariah 9–14 and Malachi. The latter connection is apparent in the use of the Hebrew word for "burden," often translated as "oracle" at Zechariah 9:1 and 12:1 and Malachi 1:1. This distinct pattern indicates a possibility that Malachi was originally attached to the book of Zechariah and that the two were later separated, perhaps to create twelve named units in the Book of the Twelve. The link between Zechariah 1–8 and Haggai has two primary indicators. One is the association of the two prophets the books are named for, both of whom Ezra 5:1 identifies as leaders among the initial group of exiles returning from captivity in Babylon to Jerusalem. The second connection is the similarity of the chronological superscriptions in Haggai 1:1, 15 and 2:10, and Zechariah 1:1, 7 and 7:1, all of which refer to the Persian emperor Darius.

The character named "Zechariah son of Berechiah son of Iddo" in 1:1 is almost certainly the same character who appears as Zechariah son of Iddo in Ezra 5:1 and 6:14 and Nehemiah 12:16. The insertion of Berechiah has various explanations;[6] the most intriguing is that the insertion attempts to link this Zechariah with the character called "Zechariah son of Jeberechiah" in Isaiah 8:2.[7] The two halves of the book, and even some subunits within each, appear to have separate origins, but the final form is all under the name of this Zechariah, so interpretations of the book move in two quite different directions. Some readers separate the two halves of the book and search for an appropriate social and historical context in which to read each, while others are more interested in how the two parts work together in the present form of the book of Zechariah.

Zechariah 1–8 presents a sequence of eight visions in 1:7–6:15, with oracles on either side of the vision collection, introduced by the date formulas using the pattern found in Haggai. The boundaries of each vision and a description of the contents are in table 11.2. The characteristic verbs of looking and seeing introduce the visions.[8]

Table 11.2 The Visions of Zechariah 1–8

Zechariah	Description
1:8–17	Men on horses patrolling the earth and declaring it at peace
1:18–21	Four horns representing Judah's scatterers; four blacksmiths striking them down
2:1–13	A man measuring a new Jerusalem without walls, surrounded by YHWH
3:1–10	The high priest Joshua and the Adversary standing before YHWH
4:1–14	A golden lampstand with seven lamps and the work of Zerubbabel
5:1–4	The flying scroll of judgment
5:5–11	A flying basket (ephah) containing a wicked woman
6:1–8	Four chariots sent to patrol the earth

The visions of Zechariah typically arrive with an angel who shows and interprets them to Zechariah. The "angel" appears about twenty times in Zechariah 1–6, which uses the common Hebrew word to describe the character, a word that is part of Malachi's name. A spatial dualism that requires angelic representation for a far-removed deity is one common characteristic of apocalyptic literature. Spatial dualism and the symbolic nature of Zechariah's visions are the major reasons why some interpreters identify Zechariah as apocalyptic literature or a precursor to it. The other characteristic of apocalyptic, temporal dualism, is not clearly present in Zechariah 1–6 (see discussion box 11.1), but may be present in parts of Zechariah 9–14 and will be discussed below. Much of the attention in the first half of Zechariah is on promises to make Judah a prosperous nation again, with a rebuilt temple at its center. The opening oracle in 1:3–6 reviews Israel's past and reasserts YHWH's faithfulness. The closing oracles in 7:1–8:23 encourage justice and promise prosperity in return, not only for Judah and Jerusalem, but also for those who visit from other places. The promise leads to the grand conclusion of the first half in 8:23:

> In those days ten men from nations of every language shall take hold of a Jew, grasping his garment and saying, "Let us go with you, for we have heard that God is with you."

Zechariah 1–8 utilizes many traditions from earlier prophetic books. It participates in a conversation with Ezekiel 40–48, Jeremiah 30–33, Isaiah 40–55, and additional texts about YHWH's return to dwell in the midst of the people of Israel.[9] There are many connections between Zechariah and Isaiah 7–8. Though correspondence between the historical contexts of the two passages is not possible, it is understandable why the author of Zechariah might want to look toward that part of Isaiah for traditions to support the reestablishment of the Davidic monarchy. The book of Zechariah does not agree with the parts of Isaiah addressing the situation after the exile, but quite the opposite. Along with Haggai, Zechariah promotes the idea of a reestablished Davidic kingship in restored Judah, specifically in the person called Zerubbabel, who plays a prominent role in Zechariah 4. The portrait of a new Judean king riding into Jerusalem in Zechariah 9:9 stands in stark contrast to the characterization of King Cyrus of Persia as YHWH's anointed one, in Isaiah 45:1.[10]

Chapter 8 of this book examined the proclamation of Isaiah concerning the Restoration period. The discussion highlighted an important, developing tension among the books of the Old Testament, including the prophetic literature, concerning the resumption of the Davidic monarchy after the exile. A return to that issue is necessary now because Haggai and Zechariah (specifically chaps. 1–8) presume such a resumption.[11] The idea that YHWH promised David an eternal dynasty is a powerful force in Israelite tradition, portrayed directly in 2 Samuel 7. Psalm 89 recognizes the promise to David and complains powerfully that YHWH has broken the promise. The book of Psalms resolves the difficulty by proposing the idea of YHWH as king of Israel in Psalms 93–99, while Isaiah 40–55 denies the resumption of the Davidic monarchy by portraying Cyrus of Persia as YHWH's anointed one. The position of Ezra–Nehemiah on resuming the monarchy is difficult to clarify. Zerubbabel is present in the book and acts in an ambiguous position of leadership, but there is never any move to make him king. Haggai 1:1 labels Zerubbabel the "governor," but Ezra–Nehemiah names him nine times without ever using a title. The narratives of Ezra–Nehemiah seem resolved to accept the imposition of Persian-appointed governors over Judah and the

---

Discussion Box 11.1 Apocalyptic in the Prophetic Literature

The use of the term "apocalyptic" is common and often imprecise, leading to potential confusion for some readers. It is always important to distinguish between two different uses of the word in biblical scholarship: (1) an apocalyptic way of thinking about the world, and (2) apocalyptic literature as a genre. Two types of dualistic thinking, spatial and temporal, characterize apocalyptic thought. On the spatial axis, apocalyptic thinking makes a sharp separation between heaven, the abode of God, and earth, the place where humans live and where evil enjoys a temporary reign. Therefore apocalyptic thinking emphasizes God's transcendent nature and angelic beings who represent God on earth. The temporal axis of apocalyptic thinking pushes God's victory over evil forces into the distant future. When the two dualisms combine, they produce a present, evil world in which humans reside with limited divine assistance through emissaries, and a coming cosmic battle that will collapse the special dualism at the end of time. Writers of apocalyptic literature likely had an apocalyptic view of the world, but they also had a particular style of writing, one characterized by cryptic language, complex symbolism, and claims to know and reveal divine secrets. The only clear example of apocalyptic literature in the Old Testament is in Daniel 7–12, but many scholars have pointed to early developments of apocalyptic writing in texts like Isaiah 24–27 and 56–66 and Zechariah 9–14. These texts present ideas like the laying waste of the entire earth (Isa. 24:1), the creation of new heavens and a new earth to replace the destroyed ones (Isa. 66:22), and a great future battle between God and the nations of the world (Zech. 14:1–5), but the stylized manner of writing—characteristic of Daniel 7–12; *1 Enoch* 1–36; and the Revelation of John in the New Testament—is not yet present in them. Because of the partially developed style, some scholars refer to such parts of Isaiah and Zechariah, and even Joel and Ezekiel, as "proto-apocalyptic."

---

continued need to court the Persian Empire's favor. Ezra (e.g., 5:3) portrays a Persian named Tattenai as the governor of the region; the book of Nehemiah (5:14) reports that Nehemiah himself became governor of Judah. So the Book of the Twelve in its final form—including Haggai and Zechariah, along with additions to earlier sections, such as Micah 4:1–5:8 and Amos 9:11–15—is the most powerful advocate for resuming the Davidic monarchy as a core element of Judah's restoration after the exile.

Zechariah 1–8 has many elements in common with Ezekiel, perhaps the most significant of which is the first-person presentation of the visions by the prophetic character, who also reports conversations with the angel that presents the visions to him. When Zechariah 9–14 opens with the striking phrase "An Oracle, the word of YHWH . . . ," the prophetic character and his first-person language are nowhere in sight, which is one of the most significant reasons most interpreters divide the book in half at this point. This is a situation reminiscent of Isaiah 40–66, where the prophetic character also disappears and is replaced by a largely disembodied voice. Further, as in Isaiah 56–66, there are no identifiable characters in Zechariah 9–14.[12] In one sense, we might say that Zechariah 9–14 needs 1–8 in order to provide it with a framework, so we can imagine we continue to hear the voice of Zechariah in the latter parts of the book.

Zechariah 9 operates outside of a normal chronological framework. It opens with pronouncements against Israel's enemies, some of them ancient, who continue to appear through the end of chapter 10, where Assyria and Egypt are in view. The collapse of chronology is another feature of Zechariah 9–14 that sometimes invites identification with apocalyptic literature. In the midst of the timeless enemies lies the promise of YHWH to restore Judah. If this section does demonstrate a temporal dualism, with divine intervention to save Israel pushed to a time after the end of history, this would qualify as the second major feature of apocalyptic, along with the spatial dualism that may be found in Zechariah 1–8. The possible appearance of an early form of apocalyptic literature is another feature that often links the interpretation of Zechariah with Isaiah 56–66 (see discussion box 11.1). In the second half of the twentieth century, the academic study of the Old Testament went through a period during which it associated a growing body of texts with the category called apocalyptic literature, as a phenomenon of Second Temple Judaism, but more recent developments have resulted in narrower and more precise definitions, reducing the scope of apocalyptic in the Old Testament. It may be helpful to examine why parts of Zechariah have sometimes been labeled apocalyptic, even if such an identification has become less common. Some interpreters understand apocalyptic as derived from prophecy, resulting primarily from adapting hopes of divine deliverance in the near future to a distant eschatological fulfillment. The shift may have resulted from disappointment in the pace and scope of the restoration. A developmental scheme like this may find confirmation in Zechariah, particularly when such promises are accompanied by symbolic messages delivered by heavenly messengers in a text like Zechariah 1:7–2:5. Among Christian readers in particular, the abundance of imagery—such as horses, horns, and lampstands—that Zechariah shares with the New Testament apocalyptic book called Revelation also motivates some to put Zechariah in the apocalyptic category.

The frequent reference to shepherds, in both singular and plural form, is a mysterious element of Zechariah 9–14. The initial reference to a shepherd in 10:2 calls attention to a lack of leadership.[13] The image of a leader as a shepherd is common in the Old Testament, so it is not surprising to find it in Zechariah, but two aspects of the use in Zechariah 9–14 are challenging. The first is the apparent identification of the prophet as a shepherd in 11:4. The shepherd metaphor is not commonly attached to prophets and, because the identity of the prophetic voice has become vague in 9–14, it is difficult to understand what is happening at this point.[14] The one who accepts the role as shepherd dismisses other shepherds who are apparently unfaithful to the task (11:8), but then abdicates his own position as shepherd (11:9–11). The second problem becomes more apparent after this, when the references to the shepherd in 11:15–17 become quite negative. It may be impossible to connect references in the text of Zechariah 9–14 with specific persons or groups outside of the text, but it is reasonable to conclude that difficulties and conflicts concerning leadership in a restored Israel are a significant issue, which points ahead to the closely related book called Malachi.[15]

The discussion of Zechariah (above) has already indicated the connections between the second half of that book and the book called **Malachi**. While many printed Bibles present the opening words of Malachi 1:1, "An oracle," in a format that looks different, in the Hebrew text they look the same as the headings at Zechariah 9:1 and 12:1. The NRSV mentions in a footnote that the designation *malachi* may mean "my messenger" instead of a proper noun. The word has that meaning, but most other names in the Old Testament have meaning that could also be translated into English words rather than transliterated into what looks like a name. The two differences here are the unusual nature of the pronoun as part of a name and the way the translation as a regular noun fits into the grammatical flow of the opening sentence.

The most common interpretive observation about the book of Malachi is its use of a series of disputations. Interpreters disagree about the precise boundaries of each disputation and how the book as a whole is organized, yet a characteristic speech pattern appears throughout the book. Table 11.3 lists the texts that present a saying of YHWH, followed by a contradictory question from the audience. Other texts in Malachi, besides those listed in the table, are similar to this pattern and add to the sense of disputation as a defining feature.

Table 11.3 Disputation Sayings in Malachi

Malachi	Saying
1:2	I have loved you, says the LORD. But you say, "How have you loved us?"
2:17	You have wearied the LORD with your words. Yet you say, "How have we wearied him?"
3:7	Return to me, and I will return to you, says the LORD of hosts. But you say, "How shall we return?"
3:8	Will anyone rob God? Yet you are robbing me! But you say, "How are we robbing you?"
3:13	You have spoken harsh words against me, says the LORD. Yet you say, "How have we spoken against you?"

The behavior for which 1:6–14 condemns the priests is in stark contrast to YHWH's favor for Israel, depicted in 1:2–5. The appearance of Esau and Edom in the opening verses may be incidental, but it seems more likely that Edom is deliberately chosen as the example of a foreign nation that YHWH does not care for the way YHWH cares for Israel, through the covenant that originated with Israel's ancestors, like Jacob. The context of the disputations is the legal framework of the covenant between YHWH and Israel. The word *covenant* does not appear in Haggai and is present only twice in Zechariah, but it reasserts itself in Malachi, appearing seven times in Malachi 1–3. The attempt to reestablish a covenant amid the struggles of the restoration connects Malachi with the story in Ezra–Nehemiah. The same general context fits, but attempts to draw precise connections between the two books encounter problems.[16] Conflicts concerning religious leadership in a restored Jerusalem have already arisen in Isaiah 56–66; Ezekiel 40–48; and Zechariah 9–14, so it should not be surprising to find them in Malachi also. These texts and others provide more than ample evidence that great conflict existed in restored Judah during the Persian period. Given this situation, the texts in Malachi likely present multiple points of view, perhaps some that are in conflict with each other. Attempts to reconstruct the social situation, however, have proved too hypothetical, so reading such texts against a general background of community conflict is probably the best choice.

Here it is not possible to list and describe all of the texts from earlier parts of the Book of the Twelve that have been proposed as editorial additions in response to the events of the Restoration period, so a few examples need to suffice. Hosea, which begins the Book of the Twelve, focuses primarily on the judgment of northern Israel in the Assyrian period and also addresses the sins of Judah, but it ends on a decidedly positive note. In Hosea 14:1–9, YHWH calls on Israel to return, and promises to heal it in response:

> I will heal their disloyalty;
>   I will love them freely,
>   for my anger has turned from them.
>   (14:4)

The book of Amos also primarily addresses the Assyrian crisis, but it ends with a text focused on Israel's restoration in 9:11–15. In the final form of Amos, restoring Israel also includes restoring the Davidic monarchy (9:11). The final verse of the book makes an eternal promise, in language reminiscent of Jeremiah:

> I will plant them upon their land,
>   and they shall never again be plucked up
>   out of the land I have given them,
>   says the Lord your God.
>   (9:15)

Because the proclamations of judgment in Micah during the Assyrian period focus on Judah and Jerusalem, it is not surprising that its words about restoration in 4:1–5:8 have the same focus. Like Amos 9:11, Micah 5:2–4 also presents the reestablishment of the Davidic monarchy. The restoration is so complete that Judah will rule over Assyria, "the land of Nimrod" (5:6), a reference that goes all the way back to the great-grandson of Noah, depicted in Genesis 10:8–12 as the great builder of cities and empires. In reference to both the past and the future, the promises go beyond the scope of ordinary human experience:

> Then the remnant of Jacob,
>   surrounded by many peoples,
> shall be like dew from the Lord,
>   like showers on the grass,
> which do not depend upon people
>   or wait for any mortal.
>   (Mic. 5:7)

The texts of restoration, along with others at the end of the Book of the Twelve, such as Malachi 3:12 and 4:6, emphasize the theme of the blessing and fertility of the land, a reversal of the images of drought and desolation frequently used in the book, beginning in Joel, to portray divine judgment.

RETROSPECTIVE ON THE BOOK OF THE TWELVE

The discussion of the Book of the Twelve has taken place in three install-
ments in this book, because parts of the collection address all three major
crises in the life of Israel during the eighth through fifth centuries. A sense of
overall organization has been present all along, but following a line of development is more difficult because of the continuous beginnings of new books
and the appearance of new prophetic names, only a few of which are significantly developed as characters within the literature attributed to them. Some
persistent themes, like the "day of YHWH" and the fertility of the land, have
helped add a greater sense of coherence. The Book of the Twelve began with
one of its most important narrative characters, Hosea, whose own life carried
the marks of the message that YHWH commanded him to deliver to Israel.
Moreover, Hosea's own children carried the divine message of judgment and
suffering in the names that YHWH, through Hosea, placed upon them. The
roles that the children and their mother, Gomer, play may be even more
important because Hosea's identity as a betrayed husband aligns him more
with God than with the people of Israel. Gomer and her children bear the
weight of accusation and rejection, such as the people of the northern kingdom, Israel, will experience in their destruction at the hands of the Assyrians.
Though the narrative portrayal of Amos is brief in Amos 7, it presents a situation in which his prophetic role brings him into conflict with his own people,
a theme developed far more extensively in the book of Jeremiah.

With these two thin narrative portrayals in mind, it may be important to
reexamine and reevaluate the narrative character of Jonah, the most highly
developed character in all the Book of the Twelve. Perhaps it is too easy
to dismiss him as a recalcitrant prophet or a vengeful despiser of YHWH's
mercy. The similarities of Jonah to some of the great narrative prophetic
characters of Israel's past, like Elijah and Elisha,[17] and his inclusion among
the Twelve urge us to take a more careful look at his role. We may find Jonah
to be lacking strong credentials as a prophet, because of the lack of oracular
material assigned to him. Even his one brief prophetic statement is addressed
to foreigners, not to Israel,[18] but this may be where the bargain of the Book
of the Twelve as a unified document becomes most visible: Jonah receives
his credentials as a prophet from the other prophets that the book places
around him, and he supplies the fascinating character development that the
middle of the collection badly needs. If there is one message demonstrated by
Jonah's character and the book in which he appears, it is that YHWH wishes
to be compassionate, even when that compassion is entirely perplexing to
an observer. Can what Jonah has learned be passed on to and carried by the
prophetic characters who appear later in the Book of the Twelve, specifically

by Haggai and Zechariah, who must speak to Israel at a time that YHWH's compassion seems far away and is most desperately needed?

Before the restoration happens, however, the Book of the Twelve must acknowledge the Babylonian invasion and captivity, which it does in the rather faceless books called Habakkuk and Zephaniah, creating a pattern of presentation not entirely unlike Isaiah. With the massive voices of Jeremiah and Ezekiel addressing that part of the Israelite story, any grand addition to the prophetic message about it may be neither possible nor necessary. On the other hand, the portrait of the restoration in Isaiah, Jeremiah, and Ezekiel is far from complete and coherent, but this is a task which the Book of the Twelve is uniquely equipped to perform. Having introduced and used multiple narrative prophetic characters already, it is able to place new ones directly in the restoration story of Judah during the Persian period. In a more overt and direct manner, the prophets Haggai and Zechariah are able to address the issues of the restoration, such as the struggles to build the temple, the lack of material prosperity, the need for political leadership, and conflict within the community and the priesthood. The final element of the Book of the Twelve, the Haggai-Zechariah-Malachi complex, is unable to move beyond this situation with anything more than a vague, general promise of YHWH's deliverance and perpetual care, a move that causes some interpreters to begin to identify some of the characteristics of apocalyptic literature in these books. The Book of the Twelve ends in a place similar to its beginning, portraying the struggles of covenant loyalty by using terms of familial and household fidelity. In its beginning, Hosea as spurned husband represents YHWH; and near its end at Malachi 1:6, YHWH speaks directly as a parent experiencing rejection. Even amid this rejection, there is the possibility of renewed loyalty. The ancient covenant, preserved in the teachings of Moses (Mal. 4:4), provides a path toward a restored family through the work of a prophetic figure like Elijah (4:5–6).

Christian interpreters have made a habit of talking about the end of prophecy after Malachi, creating an interim period before the time of Jesus and the New Testament. What this view misses is the ongoing process of textualization of prophecy and its results. The promise of a new Elijah at the end of Malachi makes little sense if it is not intimately connected to the written work that presents him at its end. In the finished forms of the four great scrolls, the presentation of the prophetic characters during the great crises in Israel's past allowed for an ongoing process of interpreting these characters and their words in new situations, which has continued until today. The final chapter of this book will take up the task of hearing these scrolls speak together as the way in which the work of the prophets has continued, rather than fading away.

Resources for Further Research

Commentaries

Conrad, Edgar W. *Zechariah*. Sheffield: Sheffield Academic Press, 1999. (B)

March, W. Eugene. "The Book of Haggai: Introduction, Commentary, and Reflections." In *The New Interpreter's Bible*, edited by Leander E. Keck et al., 7:705–32. Nashville: Abingdon Press, 1994. (B)

Meadowcraft, Tim. *Haggai*. Sheffield: Sheffield Phoenix Press, 2006. (B)

Meyers, Carol L., and Eric M. Meyers. *Haggai and Zechariah 1–8*. Garden City, NY: Doubleday, 1987. (C)

Ollenburger, Ben C. "The Book of Zechariah: Introduction, Commentary, and Reflections." In *The New Interpreter's Bible*, edited by Leander E. Keck et al., 7:733–840. Nashville: Abingdon Press, 1994. (B)

Petersen, David L. *Haggai and Zechariah 1–8: A Commentary*. Philadelphia: Westminster Press, 1984. (B)

———. *Zechariah 9–14 and Malachi: A Commentary*. Louisville, KY: Westminster John Knox Press, 1995. (B)

Redditt, Paul L. *Haggai, Zechariah, and Malachi*. Grand Rapids: Wm. B. Eerdmans Publishing Co., 1995. (A)

———. *Zechariah 9–14*. Stuttgart: W. Kohlhammer, 2012. (B)

Schuller, Eileen M. "The Book of Malachi: Introduction, Commentary, and Reflections." In *The New Interpreter's Bible*, edited by Leander E. Keck et al., 7:841–77. Nashville: Abingdon Press, 1994. (B)

Stuhlmueller, Carroll. *Rebuilding with Hope: A Commentary on the Books of Haggai and Zechariah*. Grand Rapids: Wm. B. Eerdmans Publishing Co., 1988. (A)

Monographs and Special Studies

Boda, Mark, and Michael Floyd, eds. *Tradition in Transition: Haggai and Zechariah 1–8 in the Trajectory of Hebrew Theology*. New York: T&T Clark, 2008.

Petterson, Anthony R. *Behold Your King: The Hope for the House of David in the Book of Zechariah*. New York: T&T Clark, 2009.

Stead, Michael R. *The Intertextuality of Zechariah 1–8*. New York: T&T Clark, 2009.

12

Hearing the Scrolls Together

A discussion of listening to or reading the various parts of the prophetic literature together requires some initial attention to the difficult concept called "intertextuality." This problematic and controversial term originated in general literary theory and was brought into the academic study of the Bible overtly during the 1990s, though it describes ideas interpreters have used for a long time.[1] The simplest sense in which two texts can interact with each other is when one text overtly refers to another by naming it or using a quotation from it so precise that the borrowing is obvious. Such cases require some conclusion about which text came first in order to know who is quoting whom. Common quotations may also be the result of two sets of writings having a third, shared source, which may or may not be available. In some cases the shared source might be a common tradition that is not a fixed, written text.

One interesting case of a shared quotation or tradition begins with Isaiah 2:4, which famously says:

> They shall beat their swords into plowshares,
> and their spears into pruning hooks.

This line seems to be about turning weapons into agricultural tools and is a frequent favorite of persons using the Bible to advocate for peace. The saying appears in identical form in Micah 4:3, but the relationship between the two uses of the quotation is difficult to determine. The persons named Isaiah and Micah were roughly contemporaries, but many interpreters argue that the writing of Isaiah 2 took place at a much later time than the life of the prophetic figure himself, so the Micah text may be earlier. On the other hand, the book of Micah also exhibits signs of editing and revision long after the prophet's life. Isaiah 2:4 and Micah 4:3 both appear to be additions to existing prophetic collections during the Persian period. One can easily imagine that writers of the two books could have had independent knowledge of a memorable saying like this. What makes the questions even more interesting is the appearance of the saying in Joel 3:10 with the elements reversed, so farming tools are transformed into weapons.[2] A broader understanding of intertextuality would contend that proving literary dependence and the direction of the borrowing is not necessary for texts to interact with each other, because they interact in the formation of the canon and the reading process. Either way in which the quotation is used indicates that the prosperity of the land, represented by agriculture, cannot coexist with a state of violent conflict.

The use of a common source outside the prophetic literature is most apparent in the many references to Exodus 34:6–7 in the prophetic literature. The full saying that YHWH pronounced to Moses on Mount Sinai is this:

> The LORD, the LORD,
>   a God merciful and gracious,
>   slow to anger,
> and abounding in steadfast love and faithfulness,
>   keeping steadfast love for the thousandth generation,
> forgiving iniquity and transgression and sin,
>   yet by no means clearing the guilty,
> but visiting the iniquity of the parents upon the children
>   and the children's children,
>   to the third and the fourth generation.

Various parts of this saying appear in Jeremiah 32:18; Joel 2:13; Jonah 4:2; and Nahum 1:3, as well as other books of the Old Testament besides Exodus.[3] Apparently the tradition became a focal point in the prophetic discussion of sin, responsibility, and punishment.[4] On this matter, it is helpful to quote Michael Fishbane at some length:

> The considerable weight of the notion of vicarious punishment as a theological factor, is powerfully reflected in the contestations of the matter in the late prophecies of Jeremiah and Ezekiel. In them decisive attempts were made to qualify ambiguities and injustices which were felt to obtain in the juridical notion of transgenerational or deferred punishment—ambiguities and injustices latent in the formulation of Exod. 34:6–7 as well. Indeed, in the context of exile, the matter became one of pressing concern.[5]

It is not possible to trace the development and use of the saying in order to determine who got it from whom. We cannot even say for certain that it originates in Exodus and that all the prophets who use it got it directly or indirectly from there. What we can say is that these prophetic texts participate together in the difficult discussion of the balance between divine mercy and divine justice, and they make use of this set of words to do so, perhaps adding something, perhaps omitting something, and perhaps rearranging the saying.[6]

An important issue emerging from this discussion is whether intertextuality depends upon something the author does, a deliberate quotation from or allusion to another text, or is something readers do, bringing two texts together in an attempt to understand each and apply both to the reader's context. If intertextuality lies in the reading process, then the broadest sense might be what happens any time the reading of two texts together helps inform our understanding of each, but such a definition may threaten to expand the concept of intertextuality beyond any attempt to define it. The formation of the canon within Judaism was an intertextual process because it used common features to put texts together.[7] The forming of the Latter Prophets was part of that process, which leaves us no choice but to read them together, so it is important how we decide to do that. The central claim of this book is that we should read prophetic scrolls together in a way that also recognizes and gives attention to the individual voices within the scrolls. Such reading becomes a task with multiple layers when we recognize that each scroll also has multiple voices within it, so that the "chorus of prophetic voices" is a chorus of choruses. This observation is most evident in the Book of the Twelve because the individual components received different names, but it should help us listen more carefully for multiple voices in the other scrolls, which the preceding chapters of this book have attempted to do.

As we have worked to listen to the prophetic voices together, whether the connections between them lie in their production or only in our act of reading, we have discovered the voices are not always in harmony with one another. Still, we may identify some core questions that all of the prophetic voices address, even if their answers to the questions are dissonant. These questions are all attached to the story of Israel as it unfolds in the Old Testament. The nation of Israel was able to establish itself as a small kingdom in the Levant during the tenth, ninth, and eighth centuries. Despite a split that led to the separate development of two nations with separate monarchies, they enjoyed an era of relative peace and prosperity. There are geopolitical ways of understanding this story. The growth of Israel as a nation took place in an era when no great empire was expanding to encroach upon its territory, and military concerns primarily involved regional conflicts with neighboring nations of similar size and power, such as Moab, Ammon, and Syria. The story of Israel in the Old Testament also acknowledges the making of alliances to help avoid conflict during this period, but the prophetic literature generally takes a dim view of such arrangements because they often involved some accommodation to the religions and cultures of the allies. The middle of the eighth century brought drastic changes in the situation, as larger empires began to expand and Israel and Judah came under increasing threats of conflict and destruction. If one understands the era of growth and prosperity in theological as well as geopolitical terms (which is exactly how the narrative books of the Old Testament did understand that era), then the threats against Israel that arose at the end of that era also need a theological explanation, which brings into the picture the prophets whose names appear on the scrolls of the prophetic literature. They had to answer questions like these:

1. Why did the expanding Assyrian Empire threaten the nations of Israel and Judah if they were YHWH's chosen people, living in the Promised Land?
2. Why did the Assyrian expansion destroy the northern nation, Israel, yet leave Judah damaged but still in existence?
3. If YHWH saved Judah from destruction by the Assyrians, then why were they threatened again a century or so later by the expansion of the Babylonian Empire?
4. Was everybody who suffered in the events that destroyed Israel and Judah guilty? Or was there some innocent suffering?
5. If all were guilty, then why did some survive? Does that survival present any hope for the rebirth of the nation?

The list of questions above is not exhaustive, and there are no final answers in the prophetic literature. Every provisional answer produces new problems and questions, which is also why the prophetic scrolls required continued growth beyond the originating personalities behind them. As these scrolls grew and developed, the originating personalities became the primary narrative characters in the books, and their lives became potential answers to some of the difficult questions. This book has followed a convoluted path in order to pay attention to that development process. The attempt to summarize the prophetic literature below will need to return repeatedly to the crucial question created by the nature of the literature: how do we read predisaster prophetic oracles of judgment and condemnation as part of postdisaster works of literature, which are trying to provide a way forward for a restored community? Answering such a question requires understanding that the prophetic scrolls had a long process of composition and that they achieved finished forms that have been transmitted through time as the sacred literature of multiple faith traditions. Addressing the questions requires recognizing that the prophets were both persons living in particular contexts in the past and also narrative characters in works of literature that continue to develop after their lifetimes. Finding ways to allow these dichotomies to speak productively to each other, rather than dividing our reading and sending it along two diverging paths, is the process this book seeks to begin, but will not bring to an end.

Discussion Box 12.1 Female Prophets in the Old Testament

In the midst of discussing questions that arise from the prophetic literature, some other questions may emerge from the collision of our own culture with the ancient texts. One important one might be why the fifteen individuals named in the titles of the prophetic books are all male. Was prophecy an exclusively male role, or was there some reason why only male names could be attached to written prophetic literature? There are four named women the Old Testament designated as prophetesses: Miriam (Exod. 15:20 NASB), Deborah (Judg. 4:4), Huldah (2 Kings 22:14), and Noadiah (Neh. 6:14). To these we can add the woman Isaiah specifically called a prophetess in Isaiah 8:3, without providing a name. Other texts, such as Ezekiel 13:17 and Joel 2:28, refer generally to women prophesying, without identifying any specific individuals.[8] While such texts indicate that there was no prohibition against women acting in the prophetic role, it is still one dominated by men, and in terms of generating prophetic literature, exclusively so. Perhaps male exclusivity is to be expected in an ancient culture in which men dominated all areas of public life. So some might argue that even the minimal presence of women in the prophetic role is a liberating phenomenon; after all, female priests were not allowed in Israel at all. At the same time, we must remain aware of the maleness of prophecy and of prophetic literature in our reading. One set of places where male orientation becomes obvious is where marriage texts are used as a metaphor to talk about the relationship between YHWH and Israel, in Jeremiah, Ezekiel, and Hosea. In every case, the text depicts Israel as an unfaithful wife and YHWH as an offended husband, who inflicts brutal punishment and shame to resolve feelings of betrayal and jealousy. Only during the last few decades, as female voices have become prominent in biblical scholarship, have serious questions been raised about these texts and the effects they have on readers.

THE PROPHETIC LITERATURE
AND THE ASSYRIAN PERIOD

The prophetic voices addressing the story of Israel in the second half of the eighth century and much of the seventh century, a period dominated by Israel's interaction with the Assyrian Empire, are in the book of Isaiah and in the parts of the Book of the Twelve called Hosea, Joel, Amos, Jonah, Micah, and Nahum. The prophetic texts participating in this conversation now help comprise large prophetic scrolls that later writers revised, perhaps multiple times, in light of subsequent events. The prophetic characters of the Assyrian period and their message, in both words and actions, are the products of the final writers working two or three centuries later.

Collectively, the Assyrian-period prophets speak to five important ideas or issues, and it will be helpful to list these briefly before examining each one in greater detail:

1. The situations in Israel and Judah that the prophets understand to be disobedience or disloyalty to YHWH, requiring radical social change
2. The divine punishment the prophets claim will come as a result of the violations
3. The execution of the divine punishment, particularly the differing fates of the northern kingdom, Israel, and the southern kingdom, Judah
4. The divine attitude toward Israel's enemies, particularly the ones YHWH uses as instruments of punishment
5. The future of Israel and Judah beyond the Assyrian crisis

The behaviors that the prophets of the eighth century condemn fall into two broad categories: improper worship, sometimes of gods other than YHWH; and the construction of unjust systems that oppress powerless members of the society. The former is the primary concern of Hosea, which is one reason why the problematic marriage metaphor is central to the beginning of the book. Isaiah and Amos express greater concern about the second category. The differing concern may be because the prophetic characters named Isaiah and Amos are southerners, and Amos directs his words of judgment primarily to a northern audience, while Hosea appears to be a northerner, speaking to his own community. If these conclusions are correct then the views of northern Israelite society come from a mixture of insiders and outsiders. Scholars generally agree, based on biblical texts and archaeological evidence, that at the beginning of the Assyrian period northern Israel enjoyed a period of relative economic prosperity. Although precise data is not available to make such determinations, we can reasonably conclude that Judah was less prosperous. The northern kingdom certainly had much greater access to natural resources in terms of fertile land, productive bodies of water, and trade routes, including coastlines with ports.[9] The economic disparity might explain why the southern perspectives were more concerned with unjust economics than with idolatrous worship. At the same time, Amos connects the two categories of disobedience in texts like 4:1–5, where corrupt worship appears to be part of the cover-up of, or justification for, economic injustice.

The condemnations of Isaiah sometimes take direct aim at the northern kingdom, Israel, such as in 7:9; 8:4; 9:9; and 28:1, but at other times the target is less precise. The more direct proclamation about the sins of Judah, however, comes from Isaiah's Jerusalem contemporary, Micah. The juxtaposition of these two characters is important because they represent two different modes of prophetic activity. Chapter 1 of this book (above) presented the two models as central versus peripheral (Wilson), cult versus radical (Gotttwald),[10] or establishment versus antiestablishment (my own more general terms). Isaiah typifies the former mode in each of these schemes, as a prophet who advises kings; but Micah looks like the ultimate outsider, and hearing their voices together is challenging. The book of Micah opens with a judgment oracle that includes the northern nation, Israel, but eventually Judah becomes the primary focus. Like Amos, Micah blends condemnation of corrupt worship and economic oppression in 3:9–11a:

> Hear this, you rulers of the house of Jacob
>   and chiefs of the house of Israel,
> who abhor justice
>   and pervert all equity,
> who build Zion with blood
>   and Jerusalem with wrong!
> Its rulers give judgment for a bribe,
>   its priests teach for a price,
>   its prophets give oracles for money. . . .

It is possible to imagine that Micah saying this on the day when Isaiah was having his call experience inside the temple (Isa. 6) or advising Hezekiah inside the palace (Isa. 37–39). Worse yet, would Micah have identified Isaiah as one of the paid prophets he was denouncing? Such a possibility might unnerve some contemporary readers, but others may find comfort in knowing that the Bible codifies criticism of institutions from both insiders and outsiders.

The potential conflict between Isaiah and Micah provides a useful point of transition to the second and third concerns listed above (on divine punishment), which are difficult to treat separately. Micah continues condemning Judah in 3:11b–12 with this declaration:

> Yet they lean upon the LORD and say,
>   "Surely the LORD is with us!
>   No harm shall come upon us."
> Therefore because of you
>   Zion shall be plowed as a field;
> Jerusalem shall become a heap of ruins,
>   and the mountain of the house a wooded height.

In the context of the Assyrian crisis, Micah appears to have been wrong; meanwhile the promise of Isaiah that YHWH would rescue Jerusalem comes true with the miraculous defeat of the Assyrian army in Isaiah 37, keeping alive the even greater possibility of eternal protection of the city. The prophetic work of Isaiah son of Amoz during the Assyrian period ends, however, with the recognition that Judah receives only a temporary reprieve (Isa. 39:5–8). Still, the connections between disobedience and punishment, plus the timing and severity of punishments, are an unresolved theological problem in the layer of prophetic literature related to the Assyrian crisis—a problem that all the scrolls addressing the Babylonian crisis take up vigorously.

Israel's enemies are a major subject of both Isaiah and the Book of the Twelve. Although Assyria is understood to be an instrument of YHWH's wrath used to punish Israel, numerous texts—such as Isaiah 10:5–19 and 14:24–27, the entire book of Nahum, and Zephaniah 2:13—promise that God's wrath will ultimately turn on Assyria. The book of Jonah may mitigate this sense of divine anger, yet long after Assyria's days are over, the prophets of the Old Testament continue to heap divine judgment on it in texts like Ezekiel 31–32 and Zechariah 10:11. The problem this creates, however, is that if YHWH is the ultimate attacker of Israel, then this vengeance seems misplaced. If the foreign nations are doing YHWH's work by destroying Israel then why do they deserve punishment? These kinds of questions await later developments in the prophetic literature.

It is difficult to determine the extent to which the prophetic traditions of the eighth century address a recovery for Israel beyond the Assyrian period in their own time. Later writers felt a need for these scrolls to do so, and they continued to develop them to perform that task. One could imagine a scenario in which, following the Assyrian crisis, the traditions that arose to address it just stopped. New centers of prophetic tradition, forming around Jeremiah and Ezekiel, arose during the Babylonian period to address the next crisis. So why did Isaiah and the earliest components of the Book of the Twelve continue to develop? The most apparent reason arose from their initial claim that YHWH had destroyed the northern kingdom and had almost allowed the Assyrians to destroy Judah as punishment for national disobedience; but this claim made an unsatisfying story and raised too many theological problems. There were survivors, and the scrolls from the eighth-century prophets had to have something to say to them.

THE PROPHETIC LITERATURE
AND THE BABYLONIAN PERIOD

The movement forward to a new time in Israel's story first takes us back to Isaiah, which addresses the Babylonian period in productive but incomplete ways. This time the voices of Isaiah and representatives of the Twelve are joined by a greater variety of voices because the large scrolls called Jeremiah and Ezekiel enter the discussion. Isaiah is limited in its response to the Babylonian crisis for at least two reasons. First, the manner in which it presents YHWH's miraculous rescue of Judah from the Assyrian crisis makes an explanation of the cause of the Babylonian invasion difficult. Isaiah is reduced to portraying the invasion as a tour by Babylonian envoys and a brief prophecy by Isaiah concerning a distant future defeat, both in the very brief Isaiah 39. These are the last words Isaiah son of Amoz explicitly speaks in the book and the last time his name appears. The need to be evasive about the events of the early sixth century points to the second reason for the limitations of the book of Isaiah in its response to the Babylonian period. Although from the very first verse the book has portrayed itself as a vision, it seems to touch the ground of reality on occasion in the person of Isaiah; yet the scroll is unable to disrupt the Isaiah tradition by introducing a new, concrete prophetic figure in the Babylonian period. Therefore the voice that cries out in 40:3 is anonymous, and its proclamation remains somewhat vague. The appearance of the Servant figure in 42:1, however, suddenly brings to life new possibilities. This figure is also anonymous, for the most part, but this anonymity allows for the presentation of ideas that may be larger than any one specific character could carry. The Servant connects the task of proclaiming justice with enduring suffering, and the suffering of a faithful and innocent one generates the possibility that such suffering may have a redemptive, rather than a punitive purpose. Here was the beginning of a message to the survivors of trauma: their suffering could play a role in making a future possible and not just be a result of something in the past.

The missing concrete personality in the Babylonian portions of Isaiah is filled to overflowing by the emergence of the characters named Jeremiah and Ezekiel. These two powerful figures both take on the sins of Judah with full force, but with surprising results. While both announce the infliction of punishment on Judah, it is these two prophets themselves who become afflicted. Jeremiah is arrested, put on trial, thrown in a cistern, and kidnapped to Egypt. He is commanded by YHWH to neither marry nor have children, in an odd reversal of the commands given to prophets like Isaiah and Hosea, and that compounds Jeremiah's loneliness. All of these external afflictions find their agonizing internal parallel in the poems known as the Confessions of Jeremiah, in which the prophet reaches such a point of despair that he wishes he had not been born (20:14).

Ezekiel finds himself tied up and immobilized for more than a year in a pantomime of captivity, and when his wife dies he is forbidden to mourn her death. Though in their speeches these two prophets frequently present a case in which the pending destruction of Judah and Jerusalem is a punishment more than deserved by their inhabitants, in the full scrolls of Jeremiah and Ezekiel, the two prophets frequently agonize over these events, weighing degrees of responsibility and punishment, while portraying the horror of the invasion in graphic ways that Isaiah never approaches. In this way, Jeremiah and Ezekiel embody Israel's suffering, but the survival of their voices beyond the Babylonian period, joined with that of the Servant in Isaiah, points to a future beyond the pain.

Isaiah and Jeremiah agree that YHWH will judge Babylon for its role in Judah's destruction. The Babylonian portions of Isaiah, centered in chapters 40–55, reach back into earlier parts of the book, reshaping the oracles against foreign nations in 13–23 and giving them a strong anti-Babylonian emphasis. Likewise, Jeremiah's oracles against foreign nations include the destruction of Babylon as revenge for the destruction of Judah. The Hebrew version of Jeremiah accentuates this, placing the whole oracle sequence near the end of the book and putting the oracle against Babylon at the end of the sequence. It is an argument from silence, but Ezekiel appears skeptical of the vengeance idea as part of Judah's way of surviving defeat and destruction. Ezekiel contains a long section of oracles against foreign nations, but the only part Babylon plays is in inflicting a similar punishment on some other nations as they inflicted on Judah. Divine revenge against Babylon is not part of Ezekiel's program, and the Israelite army he helps bring back to life in Ezekiel 37 stands but does not go anywhere. The Book of the Twelve contains no oracle against Babylon, but the entirety of Obadiah spews vengeance at Edom for its complicity in the Babylonian attack on Judah. The Oracles against Foreign Nations throughout the prophetic scrolls vary in terms of understanding God's destruction of the other nations. Sometimes the oracles announce divine punishment of the nations alongside Israel because they are also unjust or disobedient, but at other times the destruction of the nations is divine vengeance on Judah's behalf.

The most difficult question emerging from the Babylonian period is where the future hope of Israel lies among the fragmented survivors. Jeremiah and Ezekiel are most explicit in their answer: both address those held captive in Babylon, denounce those who have escaped to Egypt to survive, and virtually ignore those who remain in the land of Judah. Isaiah's position is not as direct, but the depiction of a return across the desert in Isaiah 40–41 and the celebration of Cyrus of Persia as God's anointed, the one who frees Israel from captivity—these elements draw attention to the captives returning to Judah as the remnant that will reestablish the nation. Finding a definition of the survivors in the portions of the Book of the Twelve that address the Babylonian period is more difficult. The clearest statement may be Zephaniah 3:20:

> At that time I will bring you home,
>   at the time when I gather you;
> for I will make you renowned and praised
>   among all the peoples of the earth,
> when I restore your fortunes
>   before your eyes, says the LORD.

Following this verse, the Book of the Twelve directly addresses the Restoration period in the voices of two prophets, Haggai and Zechariah, who are closely associated with the group returning from Babylon.

THE PROPHETIC LITERATURE AND THE PERSIAN/RESTORATION PERIOD

The preceding section demonstrates that the prophetic literature primarily aligns itself with other parts of the Old Testament in choosing to make exile, return, and restoration the dominant narrative of Israel's experience in the sixth and fifth centuries. In different ways this decision finds support in all four prophetic scrolls, and all four offer some sense of a portrait of the Restoration. The question for each scroll is how to do this, and the three organized and developed under the name of a single prophet are limited in their ability to perform the task. Isaiah 56–66 speaks from and about the restoration, along with much of Isaiah 1–5, forming a restoration framework for the book, but the book still presents these sections as part of the "vision of Isaiah son of Amoz." The real actors in the Restoration period remain cloaked and unidentified to keep the literary drama within the vision of the eighth-century prophet.

Jeremiah and Ezekiel are in a somewhat better position to speak to the restoration community, because the prophetic characters have some connection to it, though neither of them can be physically present. Jeremiah and Ezekiel give significant attention to establishing a new theological framework for the restoration, and both must renegotiate the ideas of inherited and communal guilt and punishment in order to make a new beginning possible. For Jeremiah, the new framework is a "new covenant," defined in 31:27–34. YHWH takes the initiative in announcing the new covenant, using the images of plucking up, breaking down, overthrowing, destroying, building, and planting, first given to Jeremiah in 1:10. The oracle denounces the idea of inherited guilt and rejects the idea YHWH is just wiping the slate clean to start again with the Sinai covenant. Such an offer would surely have been discouraging for Jeremiah's listeners, who would have had no reason to believe they could keep the Sinai covenant any better than their ancestors did: "It will not be like the covenant that I made with their ancestors when I took them . . . out of the land of Egypt—a covenant that they broke" (31:32). Jeremiah can then move on to describe the rebuilding of the city of Jerusalem in verses 38–40. Ezekiel's declarations on this issue reveal that the ideas of inherited and communal punishment for sin were deeply entrenched within Israelite tradition, and that the developers of the Ezekiel tradition understood how essential it was to overcome this tradition if the restoration was to become a possibility, and they seem to have found their basis for doing this in Deuteronomy 24:16. Beyond just rejecting these notions, the book of Ezekiel, in 18:18–32 and 33:12–20, contends that repentance is possible even within the life of an individual. Thus the Ezekiel tradition seeks both to remove the weight of inherited guilt from its audience, so that they can move forward, and to convince them that future success is possible.[11]

The most concrete portrait of the restoration is drawn in the last three portions of the Book of the Twelve, the Haggai-Zechariah-Malachi complex. Evidence of struggles within the restoration community can be found in Isaiah and Ezekiel, if the reader knows to look for them, but the book of Haggai is able to open in the midst of these struggles and address their concrete realities because of the strong presence of the character named Haggai among the returnees. The abstract notion of building and planting in Jeremiah becomes actual building and planting in Haggai, and the imaginative vision of a new temple in Ezekiel becomes an actual structure, built by named characters. The book of Haggai connects the prosperity of the land with the completion of the temple in a narrative that pays attention to the challenges of life in restored Judah.

The multiple meanings of the Hebrew word that means "return" play an important role in Zechariah and Malachi. This word can mean a spatial return to a place, which is what both the Israelites and YHWH do when they reinhabit a rebuilt Jerusalem and a rebuilt temple, and it can denote the restoring of a relationship. The same word is also frequently used to mean "repent," in both the senses of ceasing to sin and of abandoning previous actions. Perhaps all these meanings are on display in Zechariah 1:1–6, the brief oracle or sermon introducing the vision sequence that dominates the first half of the book, and the various meanings of "return" play a role in numerous texts in the remainder of Zechariah.[12] Haggai does not use this word but does demonstrate in concrete examples how changes in behavior can lead to divine blessings. Both Haggai and Zechariah extend the ideas about sin and responsibility developed in Jeremiah and Ezekiel into the real lives of the returnees. Regardless of the behavior of their ancestors and even their own past behavior, the citizens of a restored Judah are able to make the right choices to ensure divine favor. This idea must be continuously negotiated, amid the hard realities of life in a Persian province, as the disputations in Malachi make apparent, but it opens a way forward for the returned community.

There is significant agreement that the Persian period in Judah was a time of intense internal conflict within the Judean community. The later sectarian divisions that characterized Judaism at the turn of the eras find their origins in the Persian period, even if they are murky. Differences of opinion exist concerning precisely where the lines of division were drawn and what issues created the lines. In such a context, it should not be surprising to find conflict among the pieces of prophetic literature generated by that period, even to an extent that one could call debate. One important issue in such a debate would have been how the restored community should relate to the Persian Empire. Some prophetic texts suggest a high degree of cooperation, understanding that Judah could best operate as part of the empire and should seek Persian authority in the restoration process. This seems to be Isaiah's position in a text like 2:1–4, which promotes a picture of international peace and cooperation in which a restored Judah may play a part. On the other hand, the nearly identical passage in Micah 4:1–4 seems to be part of a portrait of a restored Judah that has its own king and operates independently from Persia and other nations. The view presented by Isaiah matches the narrative in Ezra–Nehemiah, in which political leaders, priests, and prophets cooperate with the Persian Empire and see its willingness to help restore Judah as part of a divine plan. Micah's more independent perspective finds connections in the books of Haggai and Zechariah, which specifically promote the Davidic heir Zerubbabel as the new king of Judah.[13] The hopes for a renewal of the monarchy generate many of the texts that later readers would connect to the idea of a "messiah," a reading practice that can obscure the genuine struggle of Jews in the Restoration period to determine how they should govern themselves and express their political identity. Discussion box 12.2 presents additional problems with this mode of reading. The other primary point of conflict seems to have been the rights and responsibilities of competing groups of priests. This subject has arisen in previous chapters a number of times. It is apparent such conflict existed, but from our perspective it is difficult to identify the players in the drama and the issues dividing them. Interpreters have developed some elaborate proposals to explain this, but none has anything close to a consensus of opinion.[14]

Discussion Box 12.2 Messianism and the Prophetic Literature

Christian readings of the prophetic literature are often preoccupied with finding predictions of a "messiah," specifically Jesus. Three ideas are central to careful thinking about this issue. First, the explicit notion of a divine messiah, as expressed in Christian traditions, arose within Judaism after all of the prophetic literature was written. The word *messiah* derives from the verb meaning "anoint," and within the Old Testament almost all references are still connected to kingship within their own time frames. The clearest expressions of a future messiah figure appear in Daniel 12, *1 Enoch* 37–71 (the Parables of Enoch), the *Psalms of Solomon*, and the Qumran writings known as the *Community Rule* and the *Damascus Document*, but individually and collectively they do not provide a clear, coherent portrait of the developing tradition of messianism. Texts in the prophetic literature only look "messianic" when this later idea is superimposed onto them.

Second, the New Testament writers knew the prophetic literature very well and deliberately used its words, images, and ideas to write about Jesus. Interpreters who insist that these descriptions are then fulfillments of specific predictions about Jesus in the prophetic literature are being disingenuous. Early Christians, and Christian readers today, find language and ideas in the prophetic literature that help them think about the meaning of Jesus' life and death, and this is a legitimate way to read and use the Bible, but it does not mean that the writers of the prophetic literature were making predictions about the distant future.

Third, turning the prophets into prognosticators who predicted the distant future removes them from their own time and the concerns of their original audiences. Worst of all, it misappropriates them for a purely Christian task and leaves them with nothing to say to Jewish audiences, either ancient or modern.

THE CONTINUING LIVES OF THE PROPHETS OF ISRAEL

A large gap stands between the finished forms of the prophetic scrolls and modern readers. Examining some of what happened to the prophetic tradition within that gap may help clarify our modern approach to the literature. This book has given extensive attention to the role of prophetic characters in

the books and the way the composers of the scrolls made use of such characters, but this feature may have some unintended consequences. Apparently
the makers of tradition were dissatisfied that the prophetic literature of the
Old Testament says so little about the personal lives of most of these individuals and nothing at all about the deaths of the fifteen persons whose names
are attached to its books, and we might share such a feeling after looking at
the lives of Isaiah, Hosea, Jeremiah, and others. The lack of death notices
is an important feature of the prophetic scrolls themselves because it allows
them to live beyond the biological lives of their namesakes. One response to
this dissatisfaction is a collection of traditions that appears in a puzzling little
work called *Lives of the Prophets*. Some explanation of the background of the
document and its contents related to the deaths of the prophets is necessary
here, because it is a piece of literature with which few are familiar.

The document commonly known as *Lives of the Prophets* contains biographical notices of widely varying length concerning twenty-three characters. It
begins with Isaiah and continues through the characters whose names match
the biblical prophetic books, including Daniel in his position in the Christian
canon between Ezekiel and Hosea. Following these sixteen figures are seven
others who appear in various places in the Hebrew canon: Nathan, Ahijah,
Joed, Azariah, Zechariah ben Jehoiada, Elijah, and Elisha.[15] There appears to
be some relationship between *Lives of the Prophets* and another document from
about the same time called *Martyrdom and Ascension of Isaiah*, which includes
a more elaborate story of Isaiah's death as a martyr at the hands of King
Manasseh. The dates and origins of documents like *Lives of the Prophets* and
Martyrdom and Ascension of Isaiah are matters of difficulty and dispute. Perhaps
the central question is whether their origin is Second Temple Judaism or
early Christianity. Some scholars have argued for a Christian origin for *Lives
of the Prophets*, as late as the year 300 CE.[16] One of the primary reasons for
this conclusion is that only Christian communities appear to have transmitted
this work, and all available manuscripts are Christian in origin.[17] The *Ascension of Isaiah* and many other documents once assumed to have a Jewish origin
now appear more likely to have been the products of early Christianity.[18]
Nevertheless, others take a different position, arguing that early Christian
communities preserved these traditions and probably expanded them into
their current forms, but the origin of the traditions, perhaps in oral form, lies
within Judaism.[19] There seems to be a reasonable, middle position, identifying both Jewish and Christian elements in such writings, elements that origi-
nate from a time when the two religious traditions were more closely related.
Within each tradition, stories of martyrdom eventually became more significant and more elaborate, but that does not seem to be the primary interest in

Lives of the Prophets.[20] Instead, the primary question seems to be about what happened to these figures whose words fill up so much of Scripture and whose lives are sometimes entangled with those words. It seems safe to conclude that there are both Jewish and Christian elements in *Lives of the Prophets* and that they cannot be reliably separated, yet this may merely mean that both religious traditions had a desire to know what happened to these characters.

The most significant feature in *Lives of the Prophets* is probably the common inclusion of death notices for the prophetic figures, and six of the twenty-three prophetic figures die violently. The account of Isaiah's death is brief but matches the story of him being sawn in two by Manasseh, found in *Martyrdom and Ascension of Isaiah* (5.1–16), and it is difficult to imagine that the two accounts are not related. The stoning of Jeremiah by "Jews" in Egypt is a well-known extrabiblical tradition, an example of a tradition more likely Christian in origin.[21] Ezekiel is murdered by an unnamed "leader" of the exilic community, whom he has accused of idol worship. In the Old Testament, Amos has significant yet nonlethal conflict with Amaziah in the book of Amos; in *Lives of the Prophets*, Amaziah's son kills Amos by striking him on the head. Ahab's son Joram kills Micah by throwing him from a cliff. The only account of a violent death parallel to a biblical account involves Zechariah ben Jehoiada and closely matches 2 Chronicles 24:21–22. The *Lives of the Prophets* describes the remaining seventeen prophets as having peaceful deaths and honorable burials. The six violent deaths are reported with such remarkable brevity that it is difficult to identify the narrative purpose of the account: is it to emphasize the executioners' resistance to the divine message, or the faith of the dying prophet? Yet none of the texts glorify the deaths of prophets with elaborate detail.[22] The lack of elaboration helps keep attention on the prophets' lives and their task of proclaiming the word of YHWH. At most, *Lives of the Prophets* supports the idea that living faithfully in this way will sometimes lead to suffering and death at the hands of those who refuse to listen, but it does not portray martyrdom as a goal or ideal.

Another significant effect of *Lives of the Prophets* is bringing all the prophets together, in this case to talk about some biographical details of their lives, even if they are only legendary. The interest in their deaths, however, also points to how they were received and how they were heard or read at the time these traditions were produced. The work of the prophets of Israel had not ceased at all: readers continued to find in their textualized work a way of understanding the world to which they wanted to connect on a more human level. The reading of the prophetic scrolls in this book has attempted to strike a delicate balance, one that takes seriously the development of the prophets as narrative characters, yet also understands why and how the prophetic scrolls extended themselves beyond the ordinary lives of these figures.

THE PROPHETIC LITERATURE
IN THE MODERN WORLD

The approach to the prophetic literature practiced throughout this book should demonstrate not only the possibility, but also the responsibility of continuing to read these books in new contexts. The ongoing growth of the four great prophetic scrolls, throughout three centuries of extreme turmoil in Israel's story, demonstrates how the process might work. The use of the prophetic characters in the scrolls also demonstrates the way others can continue to use their voices beyond their physical lives. The production of the scrolls did not mark an end for the prophetic role or a pause in its presence, but rather a shift toward a textualized presence for these great characters. Too many interpreters have portrayed the shift as a decline, but we might better understand it as the building of tradition that resulted in literary achievements. The characters whom the literature presents, the words that the characters proclaim, and the imaginative world that the written scrolls construct for readers—all provide a place for modern readers not only to survive the traumas of their own worlds but also to envision new ways of existence that address those traumas and their causes.

As we seek to make use of the prophetic literature in responsible ways, a few guiding principles emerge from the literature itself and may be helpful. In many discussions and debates that invoke the Bible, one of the most common charges is that a text is "taken out of context." Unless someone quotes the entire Bible, such an accusation is always true, but empty of meaning. To give it meaning, the accuser would need to demonstrate that the way a biblical text is used is inconsistent with the meaning of the text when considered in its proper historical and literary context. Whose obligation is it to be certain that a biblical text is used appropriately in such circumstances? Throughout this book the discussion of the prophetic literature has demonstrated, among other things, that biblical texts are intimately connected to human situations, particularly to the period of about three centuries in Israel's story, characterized by crisis, turmoil, and disaster. The prophetic literature is not a container full of detached, independent sayings to be pulled out for our easy use. Our response to such a realization should be to make certain we understand and acknowledge the situations that generated these texts as best we can and to understand our own human situation in which we are making use of them.

It is also apparent that the four scrolls of the prophetic literature are carefully crafted works of art, formed over long periods of time by persons struggling to find a way to address their communities, a realization requiring us to honor their complexity, which we can only do by applying all the tools we can develop to study them. The divide between diachronic approaches, seeking to look at the development of the writings through time, and synchronic approaches, examining only their final forms, is no longer tenable. An understanding of the prophetic characters present at the origins of these traditions and the circumstances in which they lived must combine with the work of following these traditions through time, examining how they adapted to meet new circumstances, and this includes the stage when they reached the form in which we now have them. Even this is not the end of the process, however, as tradition continued to accrue to these texts, even if it did not change their written form. There is no line separating the production of a text from the interpretation of it: the growth of the scrolls and their interaction with each other demonstrates how the interpretive process had begun before they were fully written. This understanding of the scrolls' development leads to questions about how we make use of the prophetic literature, an issue that has not been the primary aim of this book. Nevertheless, the way the scrolls have been presented here may point in some helpful directions that require brief expression as a matter of conclusion.

The use of prophetic literature should not be limited only to helping us think about the questions and issues confronting the people who produced them; yet our use should be guided by knowing the kinds of questions that were still unsettled and being negotiated by the prophetic literature when it reached the form in which we have it. It is not possible to produce a complete and definitive list of such questions, but I propose some of the following:

1. How do we think and talk about the differing fates of human beings in terms of faithfulness and unfaithfulness, and divine blessing and curse?
2. How can survivors of disaster understand their experience in a way leading to constructive living in the present and the future?
3. How do we understand and evaluate competing claims of leadership within religious communities?
4. What should be the relationship between religious and political leadership, and what should religious communities do when they have no control over this decision?
5. How can religious communities understand their relationship to God in times and circumstances that shift and change so radically and sometimes threaten their own existence?

Not only are there no final answers to such questions, but even the provisional ones offered by the prophetic literature are not always in agreement. Readers of the literature may be inclined to have a favorite among the many voices, and this is fine as long as we remember that our favorite is likely to be the one whose sound pleases us most, and listening to voices that startle or disturb us is equally important. The chorus of voices created by the canonical collection of the prophetic literature in the Latter Prophets is the fullest expression of the human drama that lies behind them and a powerful resource for surviving, understanding, and proclaiming our own experience.

Resources for Further Research

Brenner, Athalya. *Prophets and Daniel: A Feminist Companion to the Bible (Second Series)*. Sheffield: Sheffield Academic Press, 2001.

Day, John, ed. *Prophecy and Prophets in Ancient Israel: Proceedings of the Oxford Old Testament Seminar*. New York: T&T Clark International, 2010.

Fishbane, Michael. *Biblical Interpretation in Ancient Israel*. Oxford: Clarendon Press, 1985.

Schultz, Richard L. *The Search for Quotation: Verbal Parallels in the Prophets*. Sheffield: Sheffield Academic Press, 1999.

Sharp, Carolyn J. *Old Testament Prophets for Today*. Louisville, KY: Westminster John Knox Press, 2009.

Sweeney, Marvin A. *Form and Intertextuality in Prophetic and Apocalyptic Literature*. Tübingen: Mohr Siebeck, 2005.

Notes

Chapter 1: Defining Prophetic Literature

1. For some explanation of the process, see Gerhard von Rad, *The Message of the Prophets*, trans. D. G. M. Stalker (New York: Harper & Row, 1967), 8.
2. Ibid., 107–9.
3. Abraham Joshua Heschel, *The Prophets: An Introduction*, 2 vols. (New York: Harper & Row, 1962), 1:vii–viii. Perhaps of greater lasting value is Heschel's second volume, offering a series of philosophical essays on prophets and prophecy, with the idea of pathos as something of a common thread. See ibid., 2:263–64.
4. For a superb analysis of these developments in Isaiah scholarship, see Rainer Albertz, *Israel in Exile: The History and Literature of the Sixth Century B.C.E.*, trans. David Green (Atlanta: Society of Biblical Literature, 2003), 376–93.
5. This tendency of interpreters was sometimes motivated by anti-Semitism, a factor in Christian reading of the prophetic literature examined more fully in discussion box 8.1 in chap. 8.
6. Von Rad, *Message of the Prophets*, 19.
7. Walter Brueggemann, *The Prophetic Imagination*, 2nd ed. (Minneapolis: Fortress Press, 2002), 3.
8. Walter Eichrodt, *Theology of the Old Testament*, trans. J. A. Baker (Philadelphia: Westminster Press, 1961), 1:342.
9. The work of Wilson and Gottwald will receive fuller attention in a section below, "The Prophets as Figures in Ancient Israel."
10. Edgar W. Conrad, *Reading Isaiah* (Minneapolis: Fortress Press, 1991), 6–10.
11. Ibid., 27–33.
12. David L. Petersen, *The Prophetic Literature: An Introduction* (Louisville, KY: Westminster John Knox Press, 2002), 132–34. The introduction by Marvin Sweeney published three years later is another excellent example of this approach: *The Prophetic Literature* (Nashville: Abingdon Press, 2005).
13. Christopher R. Seitz, *Prophecy and Hermeneutics: Toward a New Introduction to the Prophets* (Grand Rapids: Baker Academic, 2007), 9–10.
14. Ibid., 16–18.
15. Louis Stulman and Hyun Chul Paul Kim, *You Are My People: An Introduction to Prophetic Literature* (Nashville: Abingdon Press, 2010), 9.

16. Ibid., 10.
17. Ibid., 147–48.
18. Ibid., 147.
19. Edgar W. Conrad, *Reading the Latter Prophets: Toward a New Canonical Criticism* (New York: T&T Clark, 2004), 92.
20. Ibid., 78–86.
21. Ibid., 69–78.
22. The idea of multiple prophetic voices and lives functioning together in a narrative context within one prophetic book was one that I first explored about a decade ago: see Mark McEntire, "A Prophetic Chorus of Others: Helping Jeremiah Survive in Jeremiah 26," *Review & Expositor* 101 (2004): 301–14.
23. These variations will be demonstrated and discussed in the appropriate chapters below.
24. Keith Bodner has effectively argued that the Deuteronomistic History presents the idea of prophets as a check on royal power from a very early point in its portrayal of the monarchy. See Bodner, *Jeroboam's Royal Drama* (Oxford: Oxford University Press, 2012), 18–29.
25. For an expression of this view, see Hans Barstad, *The Myth of the Empty Land: A Study in the History and Archaeology of Judah during the "Exilic" Period* (Oslo: Scandinavian University Press, 1996).
26. For a much more thorough presentation and discussion of the prophetic characters in these texts, see Thomas L. LeClerc, *Introduction to the Prophets: Their Stories, Sayings, and Scrolls* (New York: Paulist Press, 2007), 61–97.
27. See the discussion of this feature, particularly concerning what it means for the development of the divine character, in Mark McEntire, *Portraits of a Mature God* (Minneapolis: Fortress Press, 2013), 139–40.
28. Walter Brueggemann, *Theology of the Old Testament: Testimony, Advocacy, Dispute* (Minneapolis: Fortress Press, 1996), 624–25.
29. For a thorough discussion of the Mari texts, see Brian E. Keck, "Mari (Texts)," in *The Anchor Bible Dictionary*, ed. David N. Freedman (New York: Doubleday, 1993), 4:529–38.
30. Petersen, *Prophetic Literature*, 16–17.
31. Robert R. Wilson, *Prophecy and Society in Ancient Israel* (Philadelphia: Fortress Press, 1980), 135–294.
32. Ibid., 62–88.
33. Ibid., 306–8.
34. Norman K. Gottwald, *The Hebrew Bible in Its Social World and Ours* (Atlanta: Society of Biblical Literature, 1993), 117.
35. James C. Scott, *Domination and the Arts of Resistance: Hidden Transcripts* (New Haven: Yale University Press, 1992), 19.
36. Daniel L. Smith-Christopher, *A Biblical Theology of Exile* (Minneapolis: Fortress Press, 2002), 21–26.
37. This is not to say that the book of Jeremiah is a straightforward biography of its title figure. There are significant nonchronological features of the book. On this, see the discussion in Albertz, *Israel in Exile*, 339–45.
38. See the discussion of these features in Conrad, *Reading Isaiah*, 34–35.
39. Mary E. Mills, *Alterity, Pain, and Suffering in Isaiah, Jeremiah, and Ezekiel* (New York: T&T Clark, 2007), 6–7.
40. Ibid., 7.
41. Ibid.

42. Daniel Berrigan, *Jeremiah: The World, the Wound of God* (Minneapolis: Fortress Press, 1999), 1.

43. See esp. the groundbreaking work in Walter Brueggemann, *The Prophetic Imagination* (Philadelphia: Fortress Press, 1978).

44. See Kathleen M. O'Connor, *Jeremiah: Pain and Promise* (Minneapolis: Fortress Press, 2011), 1–6. This kind of approach is part of the work of Stulman and Kim, discussed above. See esp. their work *You Are My People*, 6–8.

Chapter 2: The Scroll of Isaiah:
Introduction and Response to the Assyrian Crisis

1. The exception to this is a collection of three Christian Bibles written in Greek and from the fourth and fifth centuries known as Codex Sinaiticus, Codex Vaticanus, and Codex Alexandrinus, all of which place the Book of the Twelve in the first position, followed by Isaiah, Jeremiah, and Ezekiel.

2. There is no such thing as a perfect or even a "correct" outline of the book of Isaiah. The nature of the book resists an outline. All outlines are pedagogical tools, allowing for a broad but limited view of the whole book at one time, so they beckon us to look past and through them. For some helpful alternatives to the attempt above, see Marvin A. Sweeney, *The Prophetic Literature* (Nashville: Abingdon Press, 2005), 51–52; Walter Brueggemann, *Isaiah 1–39* (Louisville, KY: Westminster John Knox Press, 1998), v–viii; and Walter Brueggemann, *Isaiah 40–66* (Louisville, KY: Westminster John Knox Press, 1998), v–vii. Both of these outlines are longer and more detailed than the one presented above.

3. The only way to avoid this conclusion is to adopt a view of divine inspiration that is magical in its effect, allowing an eighth-century writer, perhaps Isaiah himself, to write an entire book that looks like it was completed in the fifth or fourth century. This kind of argument does itself in, though, because if one believes that God went to all that trouble to make the book look like the composite product of three centuries of work, then surely one ought to read it that way.

4. Joseph Blenkinsopp, *Isaiah 1–39: A New Translation with Introduction and Commentary* (New York: Doubleday, 2000), 171. Blenkinsopp has presented a definitive argument for the need to combine "diachronic" and "synchronic" approaches to reading the book of Isaiah. The finished scroll is the result of a "complex of successive restructurings," whose "interconnections and continuities belong not just to the history of the book but [also] to its total meaning."

5. The term "successive restructurings" comes from Blenkinsopp (ibid.). The value of this term is that it indicates a change in the nature of the full book on multiple occasions, not merely adding new material onto the end.

6. Bernhard Duhm, *Das Buch Jesaja* (Göttingen: Vandenhoeck & Ruprecht, 1914), ix–xxii.

7. Edgar Conrad has made observations similar to these about the role of the "royal narratives" in the book's structure. See Conrad, *Reading Isaiah* (Minneapolis: Fortress Press, 1991), 34–36.

8. Ronald E. Clements has cautioned against placing too much weight on this single reference. See Clements, *Jerusalem and the Nations: Studies in the Book of Isaiah* (Sheffield: Sheffield Phoenix, 2011), 11–16. The discussion of these disciples here will focus more on their literary presence and purpose in the book of Isaiah than on their presence outside of the text.

9. On the details of what the adding of 40–55 might have looked like, see the reconstruction in Rainer Albertz, *Israel in Exile: The History and Literature of the Sixth Century B.C.E.* (Atlanta: Society of Biblical Literature, 2003), 393–404.

Albertz's reconstruction of stages of development within Deutero-Isaiah reaches levels that are too detailed and speculative for use here, yet many of his broader observations seem reasonable and helpful.

10. A similar understanding of Isa. 56–66 is part of Paul Hanson's understanding of the early development of apocalyptic literature. See Paul D. Hanson, *The Dawn of Apocalyptic: The Historical and Sociological Roots of Jewish Apocalyptic Eschatology*, rev. ed. (Philadelphia: Fortress Press, 1979), 32–45. This is another example of a study that has pressed details to the level of extreme speculation, but nevertheless it offers many useful observations at more general levels.

11. H. G. M. Williamson, *A Critical and Exegetical Commentary on Isaiah 1–27* (New York: T&T Clark, 2006), 1:15. Williamson has also offered a thorough review of scholarship on the function and meaning of 1:1 (ibid., 1:12–21).

12. Brueggemann, *Isaiah 1–39*, 2.

13. Marvin A. Sweeney, *Reading the Hebrew Bible after the Shoah: Engaging Holocaust Theology* (Minneapolis: Fortress Press, 2008), 86–91.

14. Ibid., 89.

15. Ibid., 91.

16. See Rebecca Raphael, "The Bible and Disability Studies: An Editorial Introduction," *Perspectives in Religious Studies* 34 (2007): 3–4.

17. See the discussion in Saul M. Olyan, *Disability in the Hebrew Bible: Interpreting Mental and Physical Differences* (Cambridge: Cambridge University Press, 2008), 2–10.

18. Peter D. Quinn-Miscall, *Reading Isaiah: Poetry and Vision* (Louisville, KY: Westminster John Knox Press, 2001), 19. As Quinn-Miscall has stated, the vision "reaches in time from God's original creation to the creation of a new heaven and a new earth," and it "encompasses past, present, and future." He has also observed that these qualities of the book of Isaiah have led to English translations of the book that vary widely in their uses of verbal tense (19–20).

19. These total counts include references to the people of these places, such as "Babylonians" or "Egyptians" or "the king of Assyria," which are sometimes indistinguishable in meaning from references to the place.

20. Mary E. Mills, *Alterity, Pain, and Suffering in Isaiah, Jeremiah, and Ezekiel* (New York: T&T Clark, 2007), 60.

21. Ibid., 47.

22. I have borrowed this line from the musical artist Bruce Springsteen, who has said in interviews that the purpose of his music is "to measure the distance between the American dream and the American reality."

23. The naming of children is an element of even greater emphasis in the prophetic work of Hosea in Hosea 1–3. Blenkinsopp has proposed that these elements of the books of Isaiah and Hosea may even be "alternative versions of one and the same episode." See Blenkinsopp, *Isaiah 1–39*, 173. This issue will receive further treatment in the next chapter. Blenkinsopp also points to significant parallels between the birth of the child in Isa. 7:10–17 and the one in 8:1–4 (238–39).

24. Naomi Steinberg, *The World of the Child in the Hebrew Bible* (Sheffield: Sheffield Phoenix Press, 2013), 11–25.

25. Ibid., 98–105.

26. Walter Brueggemann, *Theology of the Old Testament: Testimony, Advocacy, Dispute* (Minneapolis: Fortress Press, 1996), 567–70.

27. See the account of past scholarship on this question in Christopher R. Seitz, *Zion's Final Destiny: The Development of the Book of Isaiah* (Minneapolis: Fortress Press, 1991), 37–39.

28. Patricia K. Tull, *Isaiah 1–39* (Macon, GA: Mercer University Press, 2010), 524–25.

29. Ronald E. Clements, *Jerusalem and the Nations: Studies in the Book of Isaiah* (Sheffield: Sheffield Phoenix Press, 2011), 101–3.

30. This phrase to describe Isa. 12 comes from Blenkinsopp, *Isaiah 1–39*, 270.

31. Ibid.

32. See the discussion of this idea and other related texts in John Barton, *Isaiah 1–39* (New York: T&T Clark, 2004), 69–70.

33. Many interpreters have understood the beginning of Jeremiah's Temple Sermon in Jer. 7:4 as a direct refutation of this idea. See Walter Brueggemann, *Jeremiah 1–25: To Pluck Up, to Tear Down* (Grand Rapids: Wm. B. Eerdmans Publishing Co., 1988), 74–75.

34. Gene M. Tucker, "The Book of Isaiah 1–39," in *The New Interpreter's Bible*, ed. Leander E. Keck et al. (Nashville: Abingdon Press, 2001), 6:230–31.

35. Blenkinsopp, *Isaiah 1–39*, 380–82.

36. Peter D. Miscall, *Isaiah 34–35: A Nightmare / A Dream* (Sheffield: Sheffield Academic Press, 1999), 16.

37. This is another example of a way of reading prophetic literature that flows out of Brueggemann's initial articulation of the prophetic imagination.

Chapter 3: The Scroll of the Twelve:
Introduction and Response to the Assyrian Crisis

1. See, e.g., Ehud Ben Zvi, "Twelve Prophetic Books or 'The Twelve': A Few Preliminary Considerations," in *Forming Prophetic Literature: Essays on Isaiah and the Twelve in Honor of J. D. W. Watts*, ed. James W. Watts and Paul R. House (Sheffield: Sheffield Academic Press, 1996), 125–56.

2. An example of this approach can be found in James Nogalski, *Literary Precursors to the Book of the Twelve* (Berlin: Walter de Gruyter, 1993), 2–20.

3. For a more thorough discussion of the manuscript evidence concerning the internal order of the Book of the Twelve, see Marvin A. Sweeney, *The Twelve Prophets* (Collegeville, MN: Liturgical Press, 2000), 1:xvi–xix.

4. James Nogalski, *The Book of the Twelve: Hosea–Jonah* (Macon, GA: Smyth & Helwys, 2011), 3–4.

5. Sweeney, *Twelve Prophets*, 1:28–31.

6. Ibid., xxxi.

7. Ibid., xxxv.

8. Ibid., xxxvi.

9. Nogalski, *Hosea–Jonah*, 5–6. Also see Nogalski's earlier development of this idea in *Literary Precursors*, 278–80.

10. Nogalski, *Literary Precursors*, 238–57.

11. Nogalski, *Hosea–Jonah*, 12–13.

12. This "reverse action" of metaphors has been given significant attention by Gerlinde Baumann, building on the general work on metaphors by Paul Ricoeur. See Baumann, *Love and Violence: Marriage as Metaphor for the Relationship between YHWH and Israel in the Prophetic Books* (Collegeville, MN: Liturgical Press, 2003), 27–37.

13. Julia M. O'Brien, *Challenging Prophetic Metaphor: Theology and Ideology in the Prophets* (Louisville, KY: Westminster John Knox Press, 2009), 49–61.

14. Here I depart from the NRSV's "This is what the Lord God showed me." My more literal rendering demonstrates the similarity between this phrase and the common introduction to a prophetic oracle: "Thus says YHWH. . . ."
15. This story is filled with historical subtexts and perhaps deliberate irony. The first king of northern Israel was Jeroboam I, who established Bethel as the central worship site for the northern kingdom by placing golden bulls there (1 Kings 12). The king who appears in the story in Amos 7:10–17 is often called Jeroboam II, who came nearly two centuries after the first Jeroboam. Jeroboam II was not the last king of Israel, but he reigned for 42 years, and the five kings who reigned after him produced a total of only 14 years, so he was the last king of great consequence. Prophetic figures are involved in both the establishment and destruction of Bethel. For more discussion of this, see Jerome T. Walsh, *1 Kings*, Berit Olam (Collegeville, MN: Liturgical Press, 1996), 189–90, 373–74.
16. Phyllis Trible, *Rhetorical Criticism: Context, Method, and the Book of Jonah* (Minneapolis: Fortress Press, 1994), 216–23.
17. For more on the role that the story of Micah plays in saving Jeremiah from a death sentence, see Mark McEntire, "A Prophetic Chorus of Others: Helping Jeremiah Survive in Jeremiah 26," *Review & Expositor* (2004): 303–5.
18. The NRSV produces a fifth use by adding the prophet's name, "Zechariah said . . ." (1:7), but this further use of the name is not in the Hebrew text (nor in KJV, etc.).
19. For more on these points of revision and addition, see David L. Petersen, *The Prophetic Literature: An Introduction* (Louisville, KY: Westminster John Knox Press, 2002), 178–79.
20. Numbers for verses and chapters are frequently different in versions of Hosea. Hence 13:16 in English Bibles equals 14:1 in the Hebrew, where it is in the book's final chapter.
21. Joel is moved to a later position in the Greek version of the Book of the Twelve, but its placement in the fourth spot, after Micah, still provides a primarily eighth-century context.
22. Aloysius Fitzgerald, *The Lord of the East Wind* (Washington, DC: Catholic Biblical Association of America, 2002), 1–5.
23. Ibid., 110.
24. Sweeney, *Twelve Prophets*, 1:xxx–xxxi, 273–74.
25. This would appear to be the position of Francis I. Andersen and David Noel Freedman in the outline of their commentary. See their *Amos: A New Translation with Introduction and Commentary* (New York: Doubleday, 1989), xxviii. There is some tension, however, between this outline and the commentary itself, where Andersen and Freedman make more of a division between Amos 2 and 3 (206).
26. For a presentation of this position, see Nogalski, *Hosea–Jonah*, 285–86; or Shalom M. Paul, *Amos: A Commentary on the Book of Amos* (Minneapolis: Fortress Press, 1991), 76–77.
27. Andersen and Freedman use this difference as the basis for calling Amos 1–4 "The Book of Doom" and Amos 5–6 "The Book of Woes." For explanations of these, see their *Amos*, 206–18, 461.
28. See the demonstrations of this in Jack M. Sasson, *Jonah: A New Translation with Introduction and Commentary* (New York: Doubleday, 1995), 317–18.
29. Ibid., 307–17.

30. See the discussion in William McKane, *Micah: Introduction and Commentary* (London: T&T Clark, 2000), 7–8.
31. See the discussion of signs of this process in Francis I. Andersen and David Noel Freedman, *Micah: A New Translation with Introduction and Commentary* (New Haven: Yale University Press, 2006), 27–29.
32. Julia M. O'Brien notes the use of Isa. 10 and 52 in Nah. 1:9–14. See her *Nahum* (London: Sheffield Academic Press, 2002), 14–15.
33. This is one of many places in the prophetic literature where the English Bibles' system of numbering chapters and verses is different from the Hebrew text, which most of them translate. The English verse labeled Nah. 1:15 is 2:1 in the Hebrew.
34. See the more extensive discussion of this in O'Brien, *Nahum*, 95–103.
35. Ibid., 97.

Chapter 4: The Scroll of Isaiah Continued: Response to the Babylonian Crisis

1. On this point, see Rainer Albertz, *Israel in Exile: The History and Literature of the Sixth Century B.C.E.* (Atlanta: Society of Biblical Literature, 2003), 190–91.
2. For a more thorough discussion of this, see Brevard Childs, *Isaiah: A Commentary* (Louisville, KY: Westminster John Knox Press, 2000), 127.
3. See the background on this in Joseph Blenkinsopp, *Isaiah 1–39: A New Translation with Commentary* (New Haven: Yale University Press, 2000), 288.
4. James L. Kugel, *Traditions of the Bible: A Guide to the Bible as It Was at the Start of the Common Era* (Cambridge, MA: Harvard University Press, 1998), 301–2.
5. George W. E. Nickelsburg, *1 Enoch: A Commentary on the Book of 1 Enoch*, vol. 1, on chaps. 1–36, 81–108 (Minneapolis: Fortress Press, 2001), 165.
6. See the discussion in Elaine Pagels, *The Origin of Satan* (New York: Random House, 1995), 47–49.
7. Chapter 2 of this book (above) discusses questions created by parallel accounts in 2 Kings 18–20 and Isaiah 36–39 more fully.
8. There is some difficulty with the translation of this term. The Hebrew word actually sounds like "sack," but "sackcloth" has no meaning for English readers. Characters typically put on this kind of garment after removing their normal clothes at a time of distress. It can be an act of repentance, as in Jonah 3:6, but it can also be for mourning a death, as in Gen. 37:34.
9. The word used here in Isa. 37:7 is ambiguous. It is a noun derived from the verb used right before it for "hear." Literally, he would "hear a heard thing." Some English versions minimize potential redundancy by rendering this word as "report" or "rumor."
10. On the connections between Isaiah 34–35 and 40–55, see John Goldingay and David Payne, *Isaiah 40–55: A Critical and Exegetical Commentary* (New York: T&T Clark, 2007), 1:5.
11. See ibid., 2:152–55; and Joseph Blenkinsopp, *Isaiah 40–55: A New Translation with Commentary* (New Haven: Yale University Press, 2002), 298–99.
12. "Coastlands" will typically not appear in English Bibles this many times. The form in Isa. 42:4 and 49:1 is plural in Hebrew. The singular form is usually translated as "coast" and the plural form as just "coastland."
13. Mary E. Mills, *Alterity, Pain, and Suffering in Isaiah, Jeremiah, and Ezekiel* (New York: T&T Clark, 2007), 60.
14. Goldingay and Payne, *Isaiah 40–55*, 1:30–37.

15. Hyun Chun Paul Kim, *Ambiguity, Tension, and Multiplicity in Deutero-Isaiah* (New York: Peter Lang, 2003), 208–16.

16. A third occurrence of "Cyrus" in the NRSV at Isa. 45:13 is the translation of a third-person masculine-singular pronoun in Hebrew. Apparently the committee thought that readers might be confused about the antecedent to this pronoun, with twelve verses lying between them, not an unreasonable assumption.

17. For more on this possible conflict and the differing political views found within the prophetic literature, see Robert R. Wilson, "The Persian Period and the Shaping of the Prophetic Literature," in *Focusing Biblical Studies: The Crucial Nature of the Persian and Hellenistic Periods; Essays in Honor of Douglas A. Knight*, ed. Jon L. Berquist and Alice Hunt (New York: T&T Clark, 2012), 119–20.

18. For more detail on this, see Blenkinsopp, *Isaiah 40–55*, 304–5.

19. Ibid., 319. Blenkinsopp also emphasizes the lack of shame that typically goes along with being the victim of abuse and the lack of a resulting request that this shame be removed by God.

20. For a discussion of these possibilities and the difficulties of precise identifications, see Christopher R. Seitz, "The Book of Isaiah 40–66: Introduction, Commentary, and Reflections," in *The New Interpreter's Bible*, ed. Leander Keck et al. (Nashville: Abingdon Press, 2001), 6:436–39.

21. For a presentation of the use of marriage imagery throughout Isa. 40–55, see Gerlinde Baumann, *Love and Violence: Marriage as Metaphor for the Relationship between YHWH and Israel in the Prophetic Books* (Collegeville, MN: Liturgical Press, 2003), 180–86.

22. This is my own translation of Isa. 55:6–9.

Chapter 5: The Scroll of Jeremiah: Introduction and Response to the Babylonian Crisis

1. For more explanation of this, see Martin Abegg Jr. et al., *The Dead Sea Scrolls Bible: The World's Oldest Bible Translated for the First Time into English* (New York: HarperOne, 1999), 382–83.

2. A good example of this joint process can be found in Carolyn J. Sharp, *Prophecy and Ideology in Jeremiah: Struggles for Authority in the Deutero-Jeremianic Prose* (London: T&T Clark, 2003).

3. This is not a complete list of the many superscriptions in the book. The book of Jeremiah strains the boundaries of the definition of this type of literary unit, which has elements in common with prophetic introductory formulas and chronological notes.

4. The Hebrew word is the same here in Jer. 18:7 as in 1:10, but the NRSV inexplicably changes it to "break down."

5. The Hebrew word translated as "destroy" here and in Jer. 1:10 and 31:28 is used many times in the book of Jeremiah, but only these three times in this sense. The English word "destroy" also appears many additional times in the book of Jeremiah as the translation of other Hebrew words.

6. The Hebrew word is the same as in Jer. 1:10, but the NRSV translates it as "break down." Compare with note 4. This means that it has rendered two different roots from the list in 1:10 as "break down" later in the book. This is a good example of a place where the choices of English translators can hide the literary texture of the Hebrew book.

7. Mark E. Biddle, *Polyphony and Symphony in Prophetic Literature: Rereading Jeremiah 7–20* (Macon, GA: Mercer University Press, 1996), 65–66.

8. Ibid., 40–44. Perhaps the most significant characterization of "daughter Jerusalem" is in the little book of Lamentations, which is often connected to the book of Jeremiah, including its placement immediately following the book of Jeremiah in the Christian Old Testament. This connection will be discussed more extensively later in this chapter.

9. Based on such observations, Leslie C. Allen has labeled Jer. 30–33 an "interim conclusion" and 34–45 a "new beginning." See *Jeremiah: A Commentary* (Louisville, KY: Westminster John Knox Press, 2008), 12–14. Allen has further argued that the Masoretic version of the book has "pushed positive material into the limelight" in its presentation of the Jeremiah tradition (14).

10. Kathleen M. O'Connor, *Jeremiah: Pain and Promise* (Minneapolis: Fortress Press, 2011), 29–30.

11. Ibid., 30.

12. I owe my introduction to this idea to conversations with my teacher Page H. Kelley, who used to refer to "the basket of potsherds."

13. This was the central premise of the influential work of Ernest W. Nicholson, that particularly the prose layer of Jeremiah was developed by exilic preachers, adapting the words of Jeremiah to the situation of their audience in Babylon. See his *Preaching to the Exiles: A Study of the Prose Tradition in Jeremiah* (Oxford: Blackwell, 1970), 135–38. Jack R. Lundbom has been even more specific in assigning one of the versions of the book of Jeremiah, the one corresponding to the Masoretic Text, to the character named Seraiah identified in 51:59–61, who wrote it in Babylon. See his *Jeremiah 1–20: A New Translation with Commentary* (New York: Doubleday, 1999), 100.

14. For more detail on this period and its relation to Jeremiah, see Lundbom, *Jeremiah 1–20*, 109–12.

15. For more discussion of some of the connections, see Christopher R. Seitz, "The Book of Isaiah 40–66," in *The New Interpreter's Bible*, ed. Leander Keck et al. (Nashville: Abingdon Press, 2001), 6:436–39.

16. It is certainly appropriate to notice a theological connection to Job here, and many interpreters have. The books of Jeremiah and Job likely come from two very different directions or sources, but they appear to be converging at least on this question.

17. This seems to be the primary conclusion of Louis Stulman on the suffering of Jeremiah. See his *Jeremiah* (Nashville: Abingdon Press, 2005), 15–16. Stulman refers to this as the development of a "moral symmetry" in the Confessions of Jeremiah.

18. Walter Brueggemann has given careful attention to how the language of the book of Jeremiah functions to present such a complex picture. In his words, "The rhetoric is open, teasing, and elusive, for it means to draw Israel into the very presence of divine anger, and divine helplessness." See his work *The Theology of the Book of Jeremiah* (Cambridge: Cambridge University Press, 2007), 98.

19. See the discussion of this aspect of the two halves of the book of Jeremiah in Patrick D. Miller, "The Book of Jeremiah," in *The New Interpreter's Bible*, ed. Leander E. Keck et al. (Nashville: Abingdon Press, 2001), 6:562.

20. For a full narrative analysis of this story, see Mark McEntire, "A Prophetic Chorus of Others: Helping Jeremiah Survive in Jeremiah 26," *Review & Expositor* 101 (2004): 301–14.

21. For more on the nature and meaning of this confrontation, see Stulman, *Jeremiah*, 247–49.

22. On the later desire to know more about the prophets, particularly their deaths, see chap. 12 of this book.
23. For more discussion of this sense of correspondence, see O'Connor, *Jeremiah: Pain and Promise*, 74–79. O'Connor refers to this phenomenon as "Judah's fate in Jeremiah's body."
24. This was the famous, or infamous, phrase of John Bright in his influential commentary. See his *Jeremiah: Introduction, Translation, and Notes* (Garden City, NY: Doubleday, 1964), lvi.
25. For such a demonstration, see Sharp, *Prophecy and Ideology in Jeremiah*, 100.
26. O'Connor, *Jeremiah: Pain and Promise*, 127–28. O'Connor argues that the "chaotic structure" of the book is a witness to its message, which challenges readers with "the task of making sense of the confusion." While this view has significant strengths, there is always the danger that the reader will betray the text by forcing too much "sense" onto it. In some cases it may be more appropriate to live with and embrace the confusion.
27. O'Connor, *Jeremiah: Pain and Promise*, 54–55. See also Julia O'Brien's connection of this passage in Jeremiah with the divine-warrior image and the practice of rape as an act of subjugation and humiliation in war, in her work *Challenging Prophetic Metaphor* (Louisville, KY: Westminster John Knox Press, 2008), 109–10.
28. O'Connor, *Jeremiah: Pain and Promise*, 55–56.
29. See the discussion of these texts and the idea of a Deuteronomistic editorial layer in Patrick D. Miller, "Book of Jeremiah," 565.
30. This is among the reasons that many scholars now consider the order of the book in the Greek version to be older (ibid.)
31. The former command may make some connection to the Nazirite vow look possible, but traditions about the Nazirites vary in the Old Testament. In the legal description in Num. 6, the Nazirite vow is presented as temporary and voluntary. Any adult Israelites may choose to separate themselves from the community for a restricted time, in which they consume no product of the vine (not just wine, but also grapes or raisins), do not cut their hair, and do not contact a corpse. The two examples of Nazirites, Samson and Samuel, do not fit this legal tradition well. In both of these cases it is a lifelong vow made by their parents that includes not drinking wine or cutting the hair. The Rechabite tradition of living in tents is similar to the Nazirite sense of separation, but the apparent assumption that all the descendants within this family automatically live by these special rules that extend beyond Torah is different from anything found in the Nazirite tradition.
32. For more on the complexity of this idea and how the situation is worked out in the text of Jeremiah, see Terrence E. Fretheim, *Jeremiah* (Macon, GA: Smyth & Helwys, 2002), 494–97.
33. On the "impossibility" of Jeremiah's task and the artistic vision it offers in response to it, see O'Connor, *Jeremiah: Pain and Promise*, 136–37.

Chapter 6: The Scroll of Ezekiel:
Introduction and Response to the Babylonian Crisis

1. For an example of this kind of argument, see Moshe Greenberg, *Ezekiel 1–20: A New Translation with Introduction and Commentary* (Garden City, NY: Doubleday, 1983), 12–15.
2. For an example of this type of position, see Walther Zimmerli, *Ezekiel* (Philadelphia: Fortress Press, 1979), 1:16–21.

3. For a more extensive review of this scholarship, see Margaret S. Odell, *Ezekiel* (Macon, GA: Smyth & Helwys, 2005), 2–5.

4. For a report on this activity, see ibid., 76–77.

5. See Ingrid E. Lilly, *Two Books of Ezekiel: Papyrus 967 and the Masoretic Text as Variant Literary Editions* (Leiden: E. J. Brill, 2012).

6. For a complete list of the location of these, the deciphering of the dates, and a discussion of their significance, see Greenberg, *Ezekiel 1–20*, 8–11.

7. See, e.g., the work of Tyler D. Mayfield, *Literary Structure and Settings in Ezekiel* (Tübingen: Mohr-Siebeck, 2012), 86–90.

8. From 29:17–18, Greenberg takes this date, 571, the latest recorded in the book, as the approximate date of the final edition of Ezekiel, in part because other predictions made by Ezekiel did not come to pass but are not revised or corrected. See *Ezekiel 1–20*, 15.

9. For a discussion and evaluation of these possibilities, see William Brownlee, *Ezekiel 1–19* (Waco: Word, 1991), xxiii–xxxiii.

10. Walther Eichrodt, *Ezekiel: A Commentary*, trans. Cosslett Quin (Philadelphia: Westminster Press, 1970), 7–11.

11. In a few cases, Jesus' use of the phrase "Son of Man" may relate to its appearance in Dan. 7:13, but most often it seems like a deliberately vague title. There has been an enormous amount of scholarly debate on the issue that need not concern us here. It is important to recognize, however, that no New Testament writer mentions Ezekiel by name, and the Gospels never quote Ezekiel. There may be a reference to Ezek. 37:27 in 2 Cor. 6:16–17, and Rev. 4 borrows imagery from Ezekiel's visions. Ezekiel has the sparsest presence in the New Testament of any of the prophetic scrolls.

12. August Klostermann, "Ezechiel: Ein Beitrag zu besserer Würdigung seiner Person und seiner Schrift," *Theologische Studien und Kritiken* 50 (1877): 424–31.

13. Edwin C. Broome, "Ezekiel's Abnormal Personality," *Journal of Biblical Literature* 65 (1946): 277–92. See a more thorough description of this episode in David J. Halperin, *Seeking Ezekiel: Text and Psychology* (University Park, PA: Pennsylvania State University Press, 1993), 11–30.

14. Halperin, *Seeking Ezekiel*, 215.

15. For more thorough attention to Ezek. 1–3 as the call narrative of the prophet, see Paul M. Joyce, *Ezekiel: A Commentary* (London: T&T Clark, 2007), 76–83. Because of its connection to this commissioning, Joyce even refers to the vision in Ezek. 1 as the "inaugural vision" of Ezekiel.

16. The muteness of Ezekiel may be connected to his eating of the scroll in 3:3, and to a movement away from spoken prophetic word to written prophetic literature, but 3:1 and 3:26 still refer to speaking. On this possibility, see Ellen F. Davis, *Swallowing the Scroll: Textuality and the Dynamic of Discourse in Ezekiel's Prophecy* (Sheffield: Almond Press, 1989), 47–58.

17. The command in the first, second, fourth, and fifth acts (here in Ezek. 4–5) uses the verb "take," making them look like the command that YHWH gives Hosea in Hos. 1:2, except that the object there is a wife. On this type of introduction to symbolic actions, see Nancy R. Bowen, *Ezekiel* (Nashville: Abingdon Press, 2010), 19–21.

18. On this point, and even the possibility of reading it both ways, see Katheryn Pfisterer Darr, "The Book of Ezekiel: Introduction, Commentary, and Reflections," in *The New Interpreter's Bible*, ed. Leander E. Keck et al. (Nashville: Abingdon Press, 2001), 6:1148–49.

19. For a more extensive discussion of this issue, see Bowen, *Ezekiel*, 23–25.

20. Kelvin G. Friebel has offered a plausible scenario for the actual performance of these acts, at a certain time and place each day, rather than continuously. See his work *Jeremiah's and Ezekiel's Sign-Acts: Rhetorical Nonverbal Communication* (Sheffield: Sheffield Academic Press, 1999), 222–26. Such an explanation requires numerous assumptions not present in the text, however, and further emphasizes the disconnect between textual presentation and any actual performance.

21. For an approach to these audience interactions that takes them more literally as responses of actual observers of Ezekiel's behavior and what that might indicate about the nature of his actions as nonverbal communication, see ibid., 461–67.

22. For more on the connections between Ezek. 6 and 35, see Joyce, *Ezekiel*, 90, 202.

23. On this possibility see Ronald E. Clements, *Ezekiel* (Louisville, KY: Westminster John Knox Press, 1996), 26.

24. For a more thorough discussion of divination and issues surrounding it, see F. Scott Spencer, "Divination," in *The New Interpreter's Dictionary of the Bible*, ed. Katherine Doob Sakenfeld et al. (Nashville: Abingdon Press, 2009), 2:143–45.

25. For more on these differences in imagery and their significance, see Odell, *Ezekiel*, 182.

26. The very similar story of Lot and his daughters in Gen. 19:30–38 makes this reading all the more likely. It appears to be a kind of "ethnic joke" that Israel told about its enemies, the Canaanites, Moabites, and Ammonites.

27. This term seems to have been coined by Athalya Brenner and used in various places. See "Pornoprophetics Revisited: Some Additional Reflections," *Journal for the Study of the Old Testament* 70 (1996): 63–86.

28. On this possibility, see Odell, *Ezekiel*, 180–82.

29. This proverb is also quoted in Jer. 31:29–30, within the Book of Consolation, which will receive attention in chapter 9 of this book.

30. For more discussion on this point, see Odell, *Ezekiel*, 323–25.

31. Part of this revision includes YHWH's giving over Egypt into the hands of the Babylonians, which also does not happen. For more detail on these events and the apparent frustration they created for Ezekiel, see Darr, "Book of Ezekiel," 1409–11.

32. See further discussion of these issues in Odell, *Ezekiel*, 357–60.

33. See the discussion of this issue in James Robson, *Word and Spirit in Ezekiel* (New York: T&T Clark, 2006), 99–105. Robson's interest is in the connection between the spirit and the proclamation of the word of YHWH.

34. See Dale F. Launderville, *Spirit and Reason: The Embodied Character of Ezekiel's Symbolic Thinking* (Waco: Baylor University Press, 2007), 9–10. These three texts are central to the argument of Dale F. Launderville that Ezekiel becomes a symbolic figure and that he and the Israelites are invited by YHWH to "enter into and embody symbolically" a "visionary reality" (15). Launderville's thesis is built upon reading Ezekiel in comparison to Mesopotamian and pre-Socratic Greek literature.

Chapter 7: The Scroll of the Twelve Continued: Response to the Babylonian Crisis

1. For a thorough review of the various positions on date and composition history of Obadiah, see Paul R. Rabbe, *Obadiah: A New Translation with Introduction and Commentary* (New York: Doubleday, 1996), 14–18.

2. For a complete list of these verbal overlaps, see ibid., 22–31.

3. These difficulties receive extensive treatment in Francis I. Andersen, *Habakkuk: A New Translation with Introduction and Commentary* (New York: Doubleday, 2001), 198–224.

4. For a discussion of these alternatives, see James Nogalski, *The Book of the Twelve: Micah–Malachi* (Macon, GA: Smyth & Helwys, 2011), 666–69.

5. For a more complete presentation of these views, see Theodore Hiebert, "The Book of Habakkuk: Introduction, Commentary, and Reflections," in *The New Interpreter's Bible*, ed. Leander E. Keck et al. (Nashville: Abingdon Press, 1996), 7:652–53. This final chapter is also conspicuously absent in some other versions of the book. For more on this, see Marvin A. Sweeney, *The Twelve Prophets* (Collegeville, MN: Liturgical Press, 2000), 2:457–58.

6. For the conclusions of a thorough argument that Hab. 3 represents an ancient hymn of triumph, see Theodore Hiebert, *God of My Victory: The Ancient Hymn in Habakkuk 3* (Atlanta: Scholars Press, 1986), 124–28.

7. For more detail on these elements and their literary function, see Sweeney, *Twelve Prophets*, 482–87.

8. See the discussion of this problem and the two differing positions in Marvin A. Sweeney, *Zephaniah: A Commentary* (Minneapolis: Fortress Press, 2003), 1–2.

9. See the arguments for this in Nogalski, *Micah–Malachi*, 697–99.

10. "Uneducated" renders the Greek text in *A New English Translation of the Septuagint*, ed. Albert Pietersma and Benjamin G. Wright (New York: Oxford University Press, 2007), 811. For more on the differences between the Hebrew and Greek versions of Zephaniah and the implications of these differences, see Sweeney, *Zephaniah*, 3.

11. See the discussion of this reversal in Nogalski, *Micah–Malachi*, 713.

12. For a more thorough discussion of this idea, see Adele Berlin, *Zephaniah: A New Translation with Introduction and Commentary* (New York: Doubleday, 1996), 120–24.

13. David Tuesday Adamo has argued for the translation of "Cush" as "Africa" and "Cushites" as "Africans." See Adamo, "The Images of Cush in the Old Testament: Reflections of African Hermeneutics," in *Interpreting the Old Testament in Africa: Papers from the International Symposium on Africa and the Old Testament in Nairobi, October 1999*, ed. Mary Getui, Knut Holter, and Victor Zinkuratire (New York: Peter Lang, 2001), 65–74.

14. On the various ways of understanding the nature of this insertion, see William McKane, *The Book of Micah: Introduction and Commentary* (Edinburgh: T&T Clark, 1998), 134–43.

15. The Hebrew text has only a third-person pronoun in Hab. 1:15, with no clear antecedent. The subject in the three previous verses has been God, thus providing a problematic antecedent. It is more likely that this is a continuation of the action of the Babylonians from 1:5–11, so the NRSV inserts a common noun here, "the enemy," that points back to that text more clearly. The New American Standard Version inserts "the Chaldeans" in order to be perfectly clear.

16. For more on this point, see McKane, *Micah*, 11–12.

Chapter 8: The Scroll of Isaiah Continued Again: Response to the Restoration Crisis

1. For an example of this, see J. Alec Motyer, *The Prophecy of Isaiah: An Introduction and Commentary* (Downers Grove, IL: InterVarsity Press, 1993), 25–30.

2. Sometimes this position is too dependent on the false claim that, because there is not complete agreement among interpreters who seek to divide the text based

upon stages of development, such division is an illegitimate way of reading. For an example of this kind of claim, see Christopher R. Seitz, "Isaiah 40–66: Introduction, Commentary, and Reflections," in *The New Interpreter's Bible*, ed. Leander E. Keck et al. (Nashville: Abingdon Press, 2001), 6:312–16.

3. The most thorough and complex proposal of this type has come from Odil Hannes Steck. While the entirety of Steck's proposal has not been widely accepted, some portions have, perhaps most significantly that most of the current Isa. 60–62 is the original core around which the remainder of 56–66 grew. See "Autor und/oder Redaktor in Jesaja 56–66," in *Writing and Reading the Scroll of Isaiah: Studies of an Interpretive Tradition*, ed. Craig C. Broyles and Craig A. Evans (Leiden: E. J. Brill, 1997), 1:219–62.

4. For a more detailed discussion of these stages, see Jacob Stromberg, *Isaiah after Exile: The Author of Third Isaiah as the Reader and Redactor of the Book* (Oxford: Oxford University Press, 2011), 11–27.

5. See, e.g., John Oswalt, *The Book of Isaiah, Chapters 1–39* (Grand Rapids: Wm. B. Eerdmans Publishing Co., 1986), 23–28, 441–43.

6. For a more detailed discussion of these attempts, see J. Todd Hibbard, *Intertextuality in Isaiah 24–27* (Tübingen: Mohr Siebeck, 2006), 32–34.

7. See the discussion in Joseph Blenkinsopp, *Isaiah 1–39: A New Translation with Introduction and Commentary* (New York: Doubleday, 2000), 346–48.

8. For more on this shift, see Joseph Blenkinsopp, *Isaiah 56–66: A New Translation with Introduction and Commentary* (New York: Doubleday, 2003), 29–30.

9. The plural word "servants" appears five times in Isaiah 36–37, but in all of these cases it refers to servants of the kings Hezekiah and Sennacherib, during the conflict between Judah and Assyria.

10. On this point, see Christopher R. Seitz, "Isaiah 40–66," 316–18.

11. This idea was highly developed in the work of Paul D. Hanson. While many of the details of Hanson's reconstruction of this work have been successfully challenged, the general idea of conflict within the Second Temple community has survived. See his work *The Dawn of Apocalyptic*, rev. ed. (Philadelphia: Fortress Press, 1979), 32–46.

12. Peter D. Miscall, *Isaiah* (Sheffield: JSOT Press, 1993), 33.

13. For more on this understanding, see Edgar W. Conrad, *Reading Isaiah* (Minneapolis: Fortress Press, 1991), 122–30. Conrad links this theme of failed leadership not only with Isa. 65–66 but also with 28–33 as he argues that the final version of the scroll of Isaiah was shaped to address an oppressed group in postexilic Judah amid an internal conflict.

14. Ibid., 87–91.

15. On this point, see James D. Tabor, "Martyr, Martyrdom," in *The Anchor Bible Dictionary*, ed. David Noel Freedman (New York: Doubleday, 1992), 4:575–76.

16. For a more thorough discussion of the narrative patterns in martyrdom stories of this period, see Jonathan A. Goldstein, *II Maccabees: A New Translation with Introduction and Commentary* (Garden City, NY: Doubleday, 1983), 282–317.

Chapter 9: The Scroll of Jeremiah Continued: Response to the Restoration Crisis

1. See an extensive list of this in Louis Stulman, *Jeremiah* (Nashville: Abingdon Press, 2005), 260–61.

2. On the difficulties of translating this parable and understanding its metaphor, see Bob Becking, *Between Fear and Freedom: Essays on the Interpretation of Jeremiah 30–31* (Leiden: E. J. Brill, 2004), 229–33.

3. Ibid., 241–43.
4. Ibid., 263–69.
5. See the discussion of these difficulties in Andrew G. Shead, *The Open Book and the Sealed Book: Jeremiah 32 in Its Hebrew and Greek Recensions* (Sheffield: Sheffield Academic Press, 2002), 26–31.
6. For a more thorough discussion of the uses of the ideas presented in Jer. 1:10, and the ways these may represent the views of differing parties in Judah, see Carolyn J. Sharp, *Prophecy and Ideology in Jeremiah: Struggles for Authority in the Deutero-Jeremianic Prose* (London: T&T Clark, 2003), 86–91.
7. For a more detailed reading of this text as a vision report, see Robin J. R. Plant, *Good Figs, Bad Figs: Judicial Differentiation in the Book of Jeremiah* (London: T&T Clark, 2008), 77–80.
8. For more on the theoretical underpinnings of a postcolonial reading of Jeremiah, see Steed Vernyl Davidson, *Empire and Exile: Postcolonial Readings of the Book of Jeremiah* (New York: T&T Clark, 2011), 39–54.
9. This book is sometimes called 1 Baruch because of the existence of three other books (*2, 3,* and *4 Baruch*) that have his name attached to them. The book of Baruch, or 1 Baruch, has six chapters in some printed editions; others separate chap. 6 as the Epistle of Jeremiah. This text is introduced as a letter from Jeremiah to the exiles in Babylon but is completely different in character from the letter in Jer. 29.
10. Baruch's name does not actually appear in Bar. 1:8, but a third-person masculine-singular pronoun that seems to refer to him does. Because this pronoun is so far from any possible antecedent, some translations, like the NRSV, insert the proper name of Baruch here.
11. For a more thorough discussion of the Baruch figure and the literature that surrounds it, see J. Edward Wright, "Baruch Writings," in *Encyclopedia of the Bible and Its Reception* (Berlin: Walter de Gruyter, 2011), 3:571–75.
12. Perhaps the best articulation of this view is in Sharp, *Prophecy and Ideology in Jeremiah*, 157–69.
13. For a more fully developed theology of exile in the Old Testament, see Daniel Smith-Christopher, *A Biblical Theology of Exile* (Minneapolis: Fortress Press, 2002), 30–48. On historical and archaeological grounds, it is possible to argue that the group left behind in Judah was much larger while the significance of those taken captive to Babylon is exaggerated. For this position, see Hans Barstad, *The Myth of the Empty Land: A Study in the History and Archaeology of Judah during the "Exilic" Period* (Oslo: Scandinavian University Press, 1996).
14. Louis Stulman has labeled Jeremiah an "archetypal figure who stands between two worlds," one that is dying and one that will be rebuilt. See Stulman, *Order amid Chaos: Jeremiah as Symbolic Tapestry* (Sheffield: Sheffield Academic Press, 1998), 158–66.
15. Terrence Fretheim, *Jeremiah* (Macon, GA: Smyth & Helwys, 2002), 577–78.

Chapter 10: The Scroll of Ezekiel Continued:
Response to the Restoration Crisis

1. See the development of this idea, based on the linking of Ezek. 32:17–32 and 33:1–20, in Marvin A. Sweeney, *Reading the Hebrew Bible after the Shoah: Engaging Holocaust Theology* (Minneapolis: Fortress Press, 2008), 138–42.
2. On the way larger stories function from behind the stories being told in the Old Testament, see Gregory Mobley, *The Return of the Chaos Monsters: And Other*

Backstories of the Bible (Grand Rapids: Wm. B. Eerdmans Publishing Co., 2012), 1–15.

3. Sweeney has divided Ezek. 33:21–39:29 into seven specific oracles that function to purify the land of Israel, preparing for the vision of the new temple in chaps. 40–48. See his *Reading the Hebrew Bible*, 139–42.

4. On the connection between Ezek. 4:14 and Lev. 22:8, see Michael A. Lyons, *From Law to Prophecy: Ezekiel's Use of the Holiness Code* (New York: T&T Clark, 2009), 144–45.

5. For a more detailed description of the use of elements from Gen. 1–2 in Ezek. 37:1–14, see Mark McEntire, *The Blood of Abel: The Violent Plot in the Hebrew Bible* (Macon, GA: Mercer University Press, 1999), 143–44.

6. For a well-developed summary of this scholarship, see Paul E. Fitzpatrick, *The Disarmament of God* (Washington, DC: Catholic Biblical Association of America, 2004), 23–46.

7. A Gog appears in 1 Chr. 5:4, but he is merely one of Reuben's grandsons, with no apparent relation to the figure in Ezekiel. A person named Magog appears in the genealogies in Gen. 10:2 and 1 Chr. 1:5 as a son of Japheth, thus a grandson of Noah. Again, there is no apparent connection to the place name that appears twice in in Ezek. 38–39 as the land of Gog. The popular fascination with Gog and Magog is also fueled by the reference to them in the New Testament book of Revelation (20:8), which frequently borrows from the book of Ezekiel.

8. See the discussion of the "combat myth" in relation to Ezekiel in Fitzpatrick, *The Disarmament of God*, 103–12.

9. Ibid., 133–65.

10. Ibid., 194–98.

11. For more on this understanding, see Jon Douglas Levenson, *Theology of the Program of Restoration of Ezekiel 40–48* (Missoula, MT: Scholars Press, 1976), 14–16.

12. Texts appearing earlier in the Bible, such as the creation story in Gen. 1 and Noah's ark in Gen. 6, may also be subtle reflections of the temple space. See Joseph Blenkinsopp, "The Structure of P," *Catholic Biblical Quarterly* 38 (1976): 275–76.

13. On the deficiencies of reading Ezek. 40–48 as a "blueprint" and the challenges of finding better ways to read it, see Kalinda Rose Stevenson, *The Vision of Transformation: The Territorial Rhetoric of Ezekiel 40–48* (Atlanta: Scholars Press, 1996), 3–7.

14. For a helpful summary of different positions and a thorough argument for a unified final form from the Restoration period, built around earlier materials, see Steven Shawn Tuell, *The Law of the Temple in Ezekiel 40–48* (Atlanta: Scholars Press, 1992), 2–17, 74–77.

15. On the significance of the title "Law of the Temple" for this section, see ibid., 42–46.

16. For a more thorough discussion of this conflict and how Ezekiel treats it, including the relationship to Isa. 56:1–8, see Steven Shawn Tuell, *Ezekiel* (Peabody, MA: Hendrickson, 2009), 306–14.

17. Tuell, *Law of the Temple*, 62–63.

18. On this understanding, see Walther Zimmerli, *Ezekiel* (Philadelphia: Fortress Press, 1979), 1:106–7.

19. This is the position of Zimmerli. See ibid., 236.

20. Walther Zimmerli, *Ezekiel* (Philadelphia: Fortress Press, 1983), 2:348.

21. Ibid., 526–27.
22. For a fuller expression of this conclusion, see Dale F. Launderville, *Spirit and Reason: The Embodied Character of Ezekiel's Symbolic Thinking* (Waco: Baylor University Press, 2007), 280–88. Launderville goes to the extent of reading Ezek. 22 as an expression of the exile as a sacrifice that purifies Israel from the corruption of its idolatry.

Chapter 11: The Scroll of the Twelve Continued Again: Response to the Restoration Crisis

1. See the discussion of these conflicts in Daniel L. Smith, *The Religion of the Landless: The Social Context of the Babylonian Exile* (Bloomington, IN: Meyer-Stone Books, 1989), 179–97.
2. There is some disagreement about the division of the book of Haggai. The outline here uses the four dates to establish four prophetic events and counts those as four oracles. Some interpreters further divide some of these events into separate oracles and count as many as six. For an example of the latter, see Tim Meadowcraft, *Haggai* (Sheffield: Sheffield Phoenix Press, 2006), 108–9.
3. The dates provided in Haggai all use the reign of Darius, king of Persia, as their benchmark.
4. For a detailed discussion of how the plot of the book of Haggai and its use of differing introductory formulas develop this sequence and set up the third oracle, see Mark McEntire, "Haggai—Bringing God into the Picture," *Review & Expositor* 97 (2000): 69–78.
5. See the discussion and resolution of this issue in David L. Petersen, *Haggai and Zechariah 1–8* (Philadelphia: Westminster Press, 1984), 70–85. Interpreters who differ on this point sometimes match this text closely with the conflict in Ezra 4 and identify the second group as northerners whose ethnic heritage has become mixed, and they attempt to locate the origins of the "Samaritan schism" in these texts.
6. See Carol L. Meyers and Eric M. Meyers, *Haggai and Zechariah 1–8* (Garden City, NY: Doubleday, 1987), 91–93.
7. See this explanation in Marvin A. Sweeney, *Form and Intertextuality in Prophetic and Apocalyptic Literature* (Tübingen: Mohr Siebeck, 2005), 227–29.
8. On the similarities and differences between Zachariah's visions of a restored Jerusalem and temple with those of Ezek. 40–48, see Petersen, *Haggai and Zechariah 1–8*, 116–20.
9. For a more detailed description of these connections, see Michael R. Stead, *The Intertextuality of Zechariah 1–8* (New York: T&T Clark, 2009), 130–32.
10. For more on the role of a new king in Zechariah and the contrast with Isaiah's understanding, see ibid., 230–34.
11. Paul Redditt has argued that Haggai and Zech. 1–8 are the core of pro-monarchic sentiment in the Book of the Twelve, and that other pro-monarchy texts like Mic. 4:1–5:8 and Amos 9:11–15 are later redactional units to those books drawn from traditions in Haggai and Zechariah. See Redditt, "The King in Haggai–Zechariah 1–8 and the Book of the Twelve," in *Tradition in Transition: Haggai and Zechariah 1–8 in the Trajectory of Hebrew Theology*, ed. Mark Boda and Michael Floyd (New York: T&T Clark, 2008), 56–82.
12. On these issues, see further Ben C. Ollenburger, "The Book of Zechariah: Introduction, Commentary, and Reflections," in *The New Interpreter's Bible*, ed. Leander E. Keck et al. (Nashville: Abingdon Press, 1994), 7:740–41.

13. On the general use of this term and the specifics of its use in Zechariah, see Carol L. Meyers and Eric M. Meyers, *Zechariah 9–14: A New Translation with Introduction and Commentary* (New York: Doubleday, 1993), 195–96.
14. Ibid., 250–51.
15. Perhaps the most extensive effort to find coherence in the use of the shepherd image in Zech. 9–14 is found in the work of Anthony R. Petterson, *Behold Your King: The Hope for the House of David in the Book of Zechariah* (New York: T&T Clark, 2009), 149–212. Petterson has argued that the image is used to explain "the past history, present experience, and future expectations concerning the house of David" (210). This complex task has led to diverse uses of the shepherd image and hence makes each individual text difficult to interpret.
16. On this point, see Julia M. O'Brien, *Priest and Levite in Malachi* (Atlanta: Scholars Press, 1990), 120–25.
17. For more on these similarities, see Jack M. Sasson, *Jonah: A New Translation with Introduction and Commentary* (New York: Doubleday, 1990), 344–45.
18. Ibid., 342.

Chapter 12: Hearing the Scrolls Together

1. The term "intertextuality" was first used by Julia Kristeva, a philosopher and literary theorist. Though its original appearance is difficult to identify, the ideas behind it are present in *Desire in Language: A Semiotic Approach to Literature and Art* (New York: Columbia University Press, 1980). Similar ideas were emerging at about the same time in the work of Jonathan Culler, as in *The Pursuit of Signs: Semiotics, Literature, Deconstruction* (New York: Cornell University Press, 1983), 100–118.
2. Richard L. Schultz uses the term "verbal parallels" to describe such occasions. For a thorough discussion of scholarship on this phenomena and discussion of the major methodological issues, see *The Search for Quotation: Verbal Parallels in the Prophets* (Sheffield: Sheffield Academic Press, 1999), 18–61.
3. Other occurrences are in Num. 14:18; Neh. 9:17, 31; Pss. 86:15; 103:8; 145:8.
4. The appearances in Joel and Jonah have the most in common and have sparked significant debate about the direction of literary dependence between those two books. For a summary of the arguments and a new thesis about the priority of Jonah, see Joseph Ryan Kelly, "Joel, Jonah, and the YHWH Creed: Determining the Trajectory of Literary Influence," *Journal of Biblical Literature* 132 (2013): 805–26.
5. Michael Fishbane, *Biblical Interpretation in Ancient Israel* (Oxford: Clarendon Press, 1985), 337. Fishbane's monumental work has helped to clarify the notion of intertextuality for studies of the Hebrew Scriptures by extending the idea of scribal/exegetical activity back into the actual production of the biblical books. In doing this, he was able to categorize the ways that biblical writers made use of earlier traditions. The most important of these for the prophetic literature are the "aggadic exegesis" of pentateuchal traditions within the prophetic literature, a means by which the prophetic scrolls joined each other in a conversation about these earlier traditions (292–379), and the "mantological exegesis" of dreams, visions, and oracles (447–505).
6. On the many reasons to avoid developing precise trajectories of tradition, depending on the chronological relationships of various texts and biblical books, see ibid., 525–27.

7. Schultz has argued for a multifunctional approach to prophetic quotation that makes use of diachronic and synchronic factors. See *Search for Quotation*, 222–39.

8. For a more detailed discussion of all of these occurrences, see H. G. M. Williamson, "Prophetesses in the Hebrew Bible," in *Prophecy and Prophets in Ancient Israel: Proceedings of the Oxford Old Testament Seminar*, ed. John Day (New York: T&T Clark, 2010), 65–80.

9. See Neil Asher Silberman and Israel Finkelstein, *The Bible Unearthed: Archaeology's New Vision and the Origin of Its Sacred Texts* (New York: Touchstone, 2012), 169–250.

10. See Robert R. Wilson, *Prophecy and Society in Ancient Israel* (Philadelphia: Fortress Press, 1980), 135–294; and Norman K. Gottwald, *The Hebrew Bible in Its Social World and Ours* (Atlanta: Society of Biblical Literature, 1993), 117.

11. Fishbane, *Biblical Interpretation in Ancient Israel*, 335–40.

12. For more detail on these texts and the use of "return," see Jason T. LeCureux, *The Thematic Unity of the Book of the Twelve* (Sheffield: Sheffield Phoenix Press, 2012), 172–204.

13. For a more complete discussion of the "debate" between these views and how they are represented in parallel texts of Isaiah and Micah, see Marvin A. Sweeney, *Form and Intertextuality in Prophetic and Apocalyptic Literature* (Tübingen: Mohr Siebeck, 2005), 210–21.

14. Material outside the canon of the Protestant Old Testament, such as Sirach and the Wisdom of Solomon, and among the writings labeled Pseudepigrapha, such as *1 Enoch* and *Jubilees*, may offer additional information that can help to answer this question. Careful scholarly attention to these texts is in relative infancy and may generate helpful proposals in the future. See, e.g., the work presented in Gabriele Boccaccini and Giovanni Ibba, eds., *Enoch and the Mosaic Torah: The Evidence of Jubilees* (Grand Rapids: Wm. B. Eerdmans Publishing Co., 2009).

15. Four of these seven (Nathan, Ahijah, Elijah, and Elisha) are well-known characters in the Former Prophets. Two others, Azariah and Zechariah ben Jehoiada, are known only from 2 Chr. 15 and 24:20–22, respectively. The account of "Joed" corresponds to the strange story of the "man of God" in 1 Kings 13. On the complex traditions relating to this character's name, see Charles Cutler Torrey, *The Lives of the Prophets: Greek Text and Translation* (Philadelphia: Society of Biblical Literature, 1946), 46.

16. David Satran, *Biblical Prophets in Byzantine Palestine: Reassessing the Lives of the Prophets* (Leiden: E. J. Brill, 1995), 2. As Satran has aptly noted, "There can be few phenomena more fascinating, or frustrating, than the intersection and potential inseparability of early Jewish and Christian literatures."

17. Ibid., 62–63. Satran's important "reassessment" of the *Lives of the Prophets* fits within the general trend of calling into question older assumptions about Jewish origins of much of the material generally assigned to the Old Testament Pseudepigrapha. He places the final form of this work in the late third or early fourth century CE and considers it a work of early Byzantine Christianity.

18. See the general discussion of this problem in George W. E. Nickelsburg, *Jewish Literature between the Bible and the Mishnah*, 2nd ed. (Minneapolis: Fortress Press, 2005), 301. Nickelsburg does not include the *Lives of the Prophets* in this discussion of "Texts of Disputed Provenance," nor anywhere else in his volume. This could be because he considers it either clearly Christian in provenance, post-Mishnaic in date or, likely, both.

19. See, e.g., Anna Maria Schwemer, *Studien zu den frühjüdischen Prophetenlegenden Vitae prophetarum*, vol. 1 (Tübingen : J. C. B. Mohr, 1995), 55–70. In this two-volume work on *Lives of the Prophets*, Schwemer argues for a first-century Jewish original that was expanded by Christians at a later date. Most notably, she contends that the account of Isaiah's death in *Lives* precedes the expanded story in *Martyrdom and Ascension of Isaiah*. The brevity of the reports in *Lives* and lack of attention to martyrdom, along with great interest in the geography of their burial sites, all reflect first-century Palestinian interests.

20. M. De Jonge, *Pseudepigrapha of the Old Testament as Part of Christian Literature: The Case of the Testaments of the Twelve Patriarchs and the Greek Life of Adam and Eve* (Leiden: E. J. Brill, 2003), 45–47.

21. An expanded version is found in the work known as *Paralipomena Ieremiou* (*4 Baruch*).

22. Again, the assessment of Satran is on point: "This is hardly the stuff of full-fledged martyrology." See *Biblical Prophets in Byzantine Palestine*, 52–53. Satran's primary conclusion here is that only two of the death accounts, Isaiah and Zechariah ben Jehoiada, are demonstrably connected to pre-Christian traditions. My own reading of the death accounts in the *Lives of the Prophets* is consistent with Satran's.

Index of Scripture

Index of Modern Authors

Index of Subjects

CPSIA information can be obtained at www.ICGtesting.com
Printed in the USA
LVOW11s2038281215

468156LV00004B/4/P